C000084555

The Logic of Connective Action

The Logic of Connective Action explains the rise of a personalized, digitally networked politics in which diverse individuals address the common problems of our times, such as economic fairness and climate change. Rich case studies from the United States, the United Kingdom, and Germany illustrate a theoretical framework for understanding how large-scale connective action is coordinated using inclusive discourses such as "We Are the 99%" that travel easily through social media. In many of these mobilizations, communication operates as an organizational process that may replace or supplement familiar forms of collective action based on organizational resource mobilization, leadership, and collective action framing. In some cases, connective action emerges from crowds that shun leaders, as when Occupy protesters created media networks to channel resources and create loose ties among dispersed physical groups. In other cases, conventional political organizations deploy personalized communication logics involving social media to enable large-scale engagement with a variety of political causes. *The Logic of Connective Action* shows how power is organized in communication-based networks and what political outcomes may result.

W. Lance Bennett is Ruddick C. Lawrence Professor of Communication and Professor of Political Science at the University of Washington, Seattle, where he is also Director of the Center for Communication and Civic Engagement (www.engagedcitizen.org). His research and writing address how communication processes and technologies can enhance citizen engagement with politics and social life. Bennett has received the Ithiel de Sola Pool Lectureship and the Murray Edelman Distinguished Career Award from the American Political Science Association; a Doctor of Philosophy, *honoris causa*, from Uppsala University; the Olof Palme Visiting Professorship in Sweden; and the National Communication Association Distinguished Scholar career award.

Alexandra Segerberg is a Research Fellow in the Department of Political Science at Stockholm University and Associate Editor of the ECPR Press, the publishing imprint of the European Consortium for Political Research. Her research centers on philosophical, political, and empirical theories of collective action.

Cambridge Studies in Contentious Politics

Editors

Mark Beissinger   *Princeton University*
Jack A. Goldstone   *George Mason University*
Michael Hanagan   *Vassar College*
Doug McAdam   *Stanford University and Center for Advanced Study in the Behavioral Sciences*
Sarah A. Soule   *Stanford University*
Suzanne Staggenborg   *University of Pittsburgh*
Sidney Tarrow   *Cornell University*
Charles Tilly (d. 2008)   *Columbia University*
Elisabeth J. Wood   *Yale University*
Deborah Yashar   *Princeton University*

Titles in the Series

Ronald Aminzade et al., *Silence and Voice in the Study of Contentious Politics*
Javier Auyero, *Routine Politics and Violence in Argentina: The Gray Zone of State Power*
W. Lance Bennett and Alexandra Segerberg, *The Logic of Connective Action: Digital Media and the Personalization of Contentious Politics*
Clifford Bob, *The Marketing of Rebellion: Insurgents, Media, and International Activism*
Charles Brockett, *Political Movements and Violence in Central America*
Valerie Bunce and Sharon Wolchik, *Defeating Authoritarian Leaders in Postcommunist Countries*
Christian Davenport, *Media Bias, Perspective, and State Repression*
Gerald F. Davis, Doug McAdam, W. Richard Scott, and Mayer N. Zald, *Social Movements and Organization Theory*
Donatella della Porta, *Clandestine Political Violence*
Todd A. Eisenstadt, *Politics, Identity, and Mexico's Indigenous Rights Movements*
Daniel Q. Gillion, *The Political Power of Protest: Minority Activism and Shifts in Public Policy*
Jack A. Goldstone, editor, *States, Parties, and Social Movements*
Tamara Kay, *NAFTA and the Politics of Labor Transnationalism*
Joseph Luders, *The Civil Rights Movement and the Logic of Social Change*

Continued after the Index

The Logic of Connective Action

Digital Media and the Personalization of Contentious Politics

W. LANCE BENNETT

University of Washington, Seattle

ALEXANDRA SEGERBERG

Stockholm University

CAMBRIDGE
UNIVERSITY PRESS

CAMBRIDGE
UNIVERSITY PRESS

32 Avenue of the Americas, New York, NY 10013-2473, USA

Cambridge University Press is part of the University of Cambridge.

It furthers the University's mission by disseminating knowledge in the pursuit of education, learning, and research at the highest international levels of excellence.

www.cambridge.org
Information on this title: www.cambridge.org/9781107642720

© W. Lance Bennett and Alexandra Segerberg 2013

This publication is in copyright. Subject to statutory exception and to the provisions of relevant collective licensing agreements, no reproduction of any part may take place without the written permission of Cambridge University Press.

First published 2013

A catalog record for this publication is available from the British Library.

Library of Congress Cataloging in Publication Data
Bennett, W. Lance.
The logic of connective action : digital media and the personalization of contentious politics /
W. Lance Bennett, University of Washington, Seattle, Alexandra Segerberg, Stockholm University.
    pages cm. – (Cambridge studies in contentious politics)
Includes bibliographical references and index.
ISBN 978-1-107-02574-5 (hardback) – ISBN 978-1-107-64272-0 (pbk.)
1. Communication in politics.   2. Social media.   I. Title.
JA85.B463   2013
320.01′4–dc23   2012050927

ISBN 978-1-107-02574-5 Hardback
ISBN 978-1-107-64272-0 Paperback

Cambridge University Press has no responsibility for the persistence or accuracy of URLs for external or third-party Internet websites referred to in this publication and does not guarantee that any content on such websites is, or will remain, accurate or appropriate.

Contents

List of Tables and Figures   *page* viii

Acknowledgments   xi

    Introduction   I

1   The Logic of Connective Action   19

2   Personalized Communication in Protest Networks   55

3   Digital Media and the Organization of Connective Action   87

4   How Organizationally Enabled Networks Engage Publics   114

5   Networks, Power, and Political Outcomes   148

6   Conclusion: When Logics Collide   194

Bibliography   217

Index   235

List of Tables and Figures

Tables

3.1 Breakdown of Tweets Containing Links Sent on Day of Protest,
by Media Levels *page* 103
3.2 Tweets in #cop15 by Date and Type of Use 109
3.3 Tweets in #cop15 by Link Type over Time 110
4.1 A Comparison of Four Categories of Public Engagement in UK
National-Level Environment and Fair Trade Networks 140
4.2 Engagement Levels in UK Fair Trade Networks Comparing
National-Level and EU-Level Networks (with and without
Overlapping Organizations) 141
4.3 Engagement Levels in German Fair Trade Networks Comparing
National-Level and EU-Level Networks (without Overlapping
Organizations) 142
5.1 Analysis of Network Power, Direct Public Engagement, and
Press Coverage in UK Economic Justice Network Campaigns 174
5.2 Occupy Network Platforms (September 2011–September 2012) 182

Figures

1.1 Defining elements of connective and collective action networks 47
2.1 Put People First coalition homepage, April 2009 65
2.2 G20 Meltdown coalition homepage, April 2009 66
2.3 Relative occurrences of interactive technology features
inventoried in seven related G20 and climate summit protest
sites, 2009 69
2.4 Number of technological engagement affordances used by three
coalitions in the London G20 March–April 2009 protests 70
2.5 Artist-blogger legofesto re-creates the death of a bystander at
London G20 protests 72

2.6 Core solidarity network of the G20 Meltdown coalition, with
     nodes sized by relative number of inlinks that organizations
     received from the network   79
2.7 Core solidarity network of the Put People First coalition, with
     nodes sized by relative number of inlinks that organizations
     received from the network   80
3.1 Posts in #cop15 over time (November 28, 2009–February 22,
     2010)   108
4.1 UK national-level fair trade and development network showing
     dense co-linking among organizations   133
4.2 EU-level fair trade and development network in the United
     Kingdom, showing a hierarchical or "star" structure with little
     co-linking among organizations   134
4.3 Four dimensions of public engagement measured by component
     indicators across organizations in issue networks   138
5.1 Two ideal-type network power curves   159
5.2 Network of networks organization model showing intersecting
     network threads stitching different networks together   162
5.3 The semantic network in UK mainstream news media and blogs
     surrounding the Robin Hood Tax during December 2011   170
5.4 Sources associated with inequality discourse in U.S. media,
     December 2011   190

Acknowledgments

This book has benefited from the efforts of many people. Several colleagues reviewed the project at different stages and challenged our thinking in significant ways. We offer special thanks to three scholars who shared crucial and most helpful comments on large parts of the manuscript: Sidney Tarrow, who contributed generous and patient readings as we worked through the thicket of conceptual issues involved in addressing different fields and paradigms; Bruce Bimber, who was an invaluable source of discerning comments, farsighted perspective, and encouragement along the way; and Andrew Chadwick, who pushed us in important ways on several topics, including the fundamental question of power.

We are also grateful to several colleagues for excellent comments on particular aspects of the project: Eva Anduiza, Alan Borning, Bob Boynton, Christian Christensen, Camilo Cristancho, Donatella della Porta, Mario Diani, Nils Gustafsson, Phil Howard, Muzammil Hussain, Steve Livingston, Michele Micheletti, Stefania Milan, Lorenzo Mosca, Rasmus Kleis Nielsen, Christopher Parker, Howard Rheingold, Kristina Riegert, and Alexa Robertson. In addition, we wish to thank two people for steadfastly encouraging the entire project from early on: Brian Loader, who has always struck just the right balance between cutting criticism and good laughs, and philosopher of action Frederick Stoutland, who provided important encouragement at the very beginning of this project but sadly passed away as it was heading into the final stretch.

As we note throughout the book, several of our studies have benefited from the data analysis heroics of an invaluable team of research assistants. Michael Barthel created our voluminous databases and helped us steer through a maze of methods, analyses, and manuscripts over several years. Nathan Johnson, Henrike Knappe, Curd Knüpfer, and Robert Richards contributed valuable effort and ideas. Several people arduously helped us gather and code data, while making our meetings all the more interesting. Among them were Sheetal Agarwal, Anna Bohm, Marianne Goldin, Allison Rank, Sofia Tahko, and Binh Vong.

Working with various technologies also presented challenges. Richard Rogers of Govcom.org at the University of Amsterdam was extremely kind about answering our many questions about the Issue Crawler, and Per Lindh and Kristofer Månsson of Silobreaker Stockholm were equally long-suffering in explaining the ins and outs of Silobreaker.

At a later stage in the process, several people at Cambridge University Press made a big difference for the development of this book. In particular, we are grateful to our Cambridge editor, Lew Bateman, for handling our many questions and steering this project to a successful conclusion. The manuscript also benefited greatly from the rigorous and sympathetic copyediting of Mary Becker. We feel privileged to have had such terrific support.

In a different vein, we are tremendously grateful for the support of the funding agencies and research institutions that have made this work possible. Some of the early ideas about networks, political engagement, and public spheres emerged during the time that Lance Bennett spent as a senior Fellow at the Kolleg-Forschergruppe "The Transformative Power of Europe" at the Freie Universität Berlin. The collegiality of the entire group of Fellows and staff was much appreciated, and the environment created by Thomas Risse and Tanja Börzel is hard to match. Funding for developing and deploying the civic technologies described in Chapter 6 was provided by the National Science Foundation under grant IIS-0966929.

Above all, the work in and on this book owes much to the generous support of the Swedish Research Council. It builds on two SRC-funded project grants to Alexandra Segerberg: "Mobs, Swarms and Networks: Collective Action Theory in a Digital Age" (grant 435-2007-1123) and "Digital Media and Civil Society Networks: National and Transnational Publics" (grant 421-2010-2303). In addition, we are thankful for the time and resources provided by the Olof Palme Guest Professorship awarded to Lance Bennett in 2010 (grant 429-2009-7994) and grateful to Michele Micheletti for helping to make this possible. Each of these grants provided precious time for the two of us to think, collaborate, and write, and valuable opportunities for us to discuss our work with colleagues in Seattle, Sweden, and other parts of Europe. We warmly thank the Department of Political Science at Stockholm University for its support, for hosting the Professorship, and for providing such a rich research environment in which to develop the project. We also thank the Center for Communication and Civic Engagement at the University of Washington, Seattle, for hosting the first SRC grant.

The Departments of Political Science and Communication at the University of Washington have been generous in their support, particularly in sponsoring the Center for Communication and Civic Engagement (www.engagedcitizen .org). The CCCE provided the creative space where this project was hatched, and it housed the research teams that helped put our ideas to the empirical test. We are grateful to department chairs Peter May and David Domke for fostering creative research cultures.

We also gratefully acknowledge the permission to draw on and reprint articles developed with the support of the SRC grants and previously published in Taylor & Francis journals.

Finally, we dedicate this book to our families – from the very bottom of our hearts. To Sabine and Andreas, who have sustained us, inspired us, and suffered us throughout the long years of toil and trouble across transatlantic time zones. To Oliver, who has had to put up with so many political scientists for so very long; and to Hedda, who has lived with this project her entire life.

Introduction

This book is about the organization of contentious political action in the digital age. Much contemporary activism still resembles the familiar protest politics of old, with people joining groups, forging collective identities, and employing a broad spectrum of political strategies from street demonstrations and civil disobedience to election campaigning, litigation, and lobbying. In the case of such traditional political action, access to digital media generally makes it easier and less costly for organizations to communicate with members and supporters. In a number of recent protests, however, digital media have shared the work of mobilizing and organizing action and, in some cases, have done more of it than did formal organizations. This shift in the underpinnings of contentious action is associated with the rise of more highly individualized publics. Such publics consist of a large number of people who experience a common problem or issue and seek common solutions, which may make them seem ripe to join traditional protest movements. In contrast with people who join conventional movements, however, these individualized publics are not inclined (or able) to join formal political organizations and prefer not to adopt definitions of their problems that require trading off personal beliefs for more restrictive group identifications. Despite the importance of communication processes and technologies in their organization, these mobilizations can be relatively stable, persistent, and effective. Indeed, they are commonly referred to as movements, as in "the Occupy Wall Street movement." We seek to understand patterns of participation and organization in these types of collective action and to complement current thinking on how movements can be organized.

A number of factors contribute to the personalization of large-scale political action, particularly changes commonly associated with economic globalization in the post-industrial democracies of Europe and North America. Dramatic changes affected many societies, both north and south, over a period dating roughly from the 1970s and punctuated, if not bounded, by the economic crisis of the early 21st century. This time of transformation witnessed the fraying of modern social, economic, and political structures, buffered differently, of course, in different societies. One fairly common result was a shift in political identifications of younger generations away from the broad group and institutional affiliations of unions, parties, churches, social class, established movement organizations, and the press – all of which had shaped the heart of 20th-century democratic politics. Those structures were weakened in different ways by globalization's emphasis on market deregulation and greater personal responsibility. While such programs were presented to voters with variations on the promise of "free markets, free people," economic inequality grew in most post-industrial democracies, and many ordinary people experienced their condition in terms of low mobility, increased risk, and reduced political choice. Reflecting these subjective experiences, opinion polls in many countries over several decades reveal declining popular confidence in parties, government, and business.

While there continued to be both more radical and more formally organized challenges to these developments, a growing number of concerned citizens found pathways to engagement through simple, everyday discourses anchored in lifestyles and shared with social networks. Rallying around cries of "Real Democracy, Now!" as the master frame that emerged from *los indignados* in Spain in 2011 or "We Are the 99%" in the Occupy protests in the United States later the same year, large-scale networked action spread through simple discourses that enabled easy personal associations to travel rapidly over social networks, both on- and offline. In some cases that we analyzed, non-governmental organizations (NGOs), churches, labor unions, and social movement organizations were involved, while in other cases such formal organizations were pushed to the periphery by crowd dynamics. What is surprising is that in both the organizationally enabled and crowd-enabled varieties, these easily personalized paths to engagement often developed into large and persistent organizations. This organizational process was made possible by access to everyday communication devices such as mobile phones and computers that connect people through common digital media platforms such as email, SMS, Twitter, YouTube, and hundreds of other technologies.

This book explores what we call digitally networked *connective action* that uses broadly inclusive, easily personalized action frames as a basis for technology-assisted networking. We seek to understand how connective action is organized and how various forms – from relatively more crowd-enabled to more organizationally enabled – differ in terms of political power and capacity to shape outcomes. We also examine how varieties of connective action compare with conventionally organized collective action that builds on strong leadership, brokered coalitions among formal organizations, and action frames that draw on ideology or group (class, race, gender, nationality) identity. In some cases old-style activists and NGOs can also be found in the connective mix, and it is important to understand the role they play in mobilizing (and, sometimes, demobilizing) larger public involvement. However, our primary focus is on sorting out what characterizes the different types of connective action and how they differ from each other. The cases that help define and challenge our theoretical formulations are drawn from the contemporary economic and environmental crises, which have produced an interesting array of contentious political mobilization, spanning the spectrum of network organization types that we seek to compare and critically evaluate in this book.

The first chapter of the book identifies two types of large-scale connective action networks, both of which differ from forms of collectively framed, organizationally brokered collective action that are already well understood in the study of contentious politics. The following chapters concentrate in more detail on the similarities and differences between the two connective types. Chapters 2–4 analyze cases of large-scale direct citizen participation in connective action networks, comparing those networks across issues (economic and environmental), action categories (demonstrations, issue advocacy networks, and campaigns), and political contexts (national and transnational). In Chapter 5 we look at how power is organized in the different types of connective action and how those power signatures relate to political outcomes. We use this power analysis to compare the effect of an organizationally enabled "Robin Hood Tax" campaign for a tax on speculative financial transactions in the United Kingdom with the impact of the crowd-enabled Occupy protests on public discourse about inequality in the United States.

In addition to summarizing this journey, the concluding chapter considers the conflicts that may occur within connective networks when they clash with more conventional collective action orientations from other groups and activists. The chapter also examines how different forms of networked activism negotiate transitions over time and in response to different external opportunities and threats. For example, what happens after Occupiers are evicted from their camps, particularly when those who remain committed to regrouping are split by very different conceptions of the ideal way to organize action? In addressing these fascinating questions about mobilization and political organization, we draw on our high-level analytical models that distinguish among different organizational forms in complex mobilizations in order to sort through ethnographic accounts of the tensions within those mobilizations. We also reflect on how custom technologies with organizational capacities far greater than Facebook, Twitter, and typical website configurations might better harmonize the divergent action logics that often clash in large-scale mobilizations.

The issues that run through the empirical cases in the book are two of the central concerns of our time: (a) economic justice, or fairness, in the ways economies work, particularly in the context of the global financial crisis that rocked many nations in the first years of the 21st century; and (b) the prospects and possible remedies for global climate change, a problem perceived by many citizens as threatening the quality of life on the planet, both north and south. These two issues are often linked by concerned citizens who worry that economic growth imperatives mean burning more fossil fuels, which contributes to global warming, and that policy makers in many nations sacrifice attention to climate change in order to introduce quick fixes to economies in crisis. The following pages of this introduction develop the basis for focusing on these issues and explain why they provide good cases for exploring our theoretical framework.

Connective Action and Global Crises

The political times spanning our research and writing have been both turbulent and fascinating. The global financial crisis that erupted in 2008 has been dubbed the "great recession," though for many the conditions better resembled a depression. Millions lost their homes and their jobs, and collapsing banks and financial firms extracted large bailouts at public expense, all leading to the slow-motion train wreck termed the "sovereign debt crisis" that ultimately threatened the viability of the European Union. Behind these headlining events, the climate crisis also reached critical mass due, in part, to the volume of carbon burned over the years of unprecedented global economic growth that preceded the collapse. Extreme weather in the form of heat waves, droughts, floods, melting ice caps, and rising sea levels, along with severe food shortages, gave this period an added degree of historic drama.

As these events unfolded, millions of people around the world joined in protest politics, including *los indignados* in Spain, the Tea Party and Occupy in the United States, and the largest environmental demonstrations on record in many nations. The protests were marked by citizens taking to the streets and squares in great numbers, often with boundaries blurring between seasoned activists and concerned citizens. The spaces were both physical, with encampments in and marches through cities, and virtual, as in the Livestream video coverage and Twitter feeds that linked-in bystander publics who, in turn, added their own voices using repertoires of online engagement techniques. The creative range of protests occurring both nationally and transnationally, and the prominence of dual economic and environment crises that were linked in many events, all provided rich material for developing, challenging, and comparing models of different forms of collective action.

The decade leading up to the financial crisis had already witnessed thousands of protest events, large and small, jumping across locations and causes, and targeting town councils, national leaders, international organizations and summits, and corporate brands. Activists using digital media to help mobilize this family of multi-issue, multi-arena, multi-target, shape-shifting protests can be traced at least as far back as the "Battle of Seattle," in which an unlikely band of "Teamsters and turtles" shut down the World Trade Organization meetings in 1999. Though they differed in size, composition, and levels of coherence and violence, these "global justice" protests bore a family resemblance in terms of the diffusion of action repertoires, campaign models, communication practices, and evolving moral and political discourses. They shared an ethos of diversity and inclusiveness, often enabling large and diverse mobilizations to overcome ideological and strategic differences to address an array of issues, including economic injustice and unfair trade practices in the global south, climate and environmental degradation worldwide, unsustainable energy and resource management, war and human rights, the predations of banking and finance, and all of these in a single event.

At the top of the long list of interrelated global issues is a cluster of economic and environmental concerns regarding the rise of inequality, unsustainable economic growth, and climate change. The organization and impact of national and transnational economic justice and climate change advocacy networks provided the initial focus of research for this book. However, we soon began thinking and theorizing about the uprisings that occurred in Iceland, Tunisia, Egypt, Spain, the United States, and elsewhere, as they presented interesting variations on large-scale organization using digital media. Although we could not cover all of these cases empirically, we have included analyses from the Occupy protests in the United States since they touched directly on our broad theme of economic justice issues. In addition, the added focus on the United States broadened the comparative scope of the book. However, we are not trying to retell the story of the global justice movement that is intertwined with some of our cases. Many other scholars have already addressed the historical origins of the movement, as well as the patterns of mobilization and mechanisms for individual involvement in global justice politics, and we build on their work in this book.

Ours is a story about organizational processes in complex (multi-arena, multi-issue) citizen mobilizations that often engage people in very personal ways: as consumers, animal and nature lovers, Facebook friends, Twitter followers, and self-styled global citizens who often prefer more direct ways of acting politically than voting or becoming formal members of organizations. More specifically, our story is about the forms of digitally networked action that we call connective action, which result from large-scale personalized and digitally mediated political engagement.

Throughout the book, we develop three themes that serve as touchstones for our investigation into connective action: (a) understanding the personalization of politics and what it means for political mobilization, (b) understanding communication as integral to political participation and organization, and (c) developing and grounding the different logics underlying the organization of collective versus connective action. In the following discussions, we briefly preview each of these themes and then conclude with a more detailed overview of the book.

Personalized, Digitally Mediated Political Engagement

A recurring theme in the book concerns the phenomenon of personalized politics and why personalization pairs so naturally with digital media. The kind of personalization of politics we are interested in has to do with citizens seeking more flexible association with causes, ideas, and political organizations. It is ironic that the very globalization processes that have become targets of so much political activism have also created the social conditions and global communication technologies largely responsible for expanding the available forms of that activism. Various globalization-related changes have resulted in the separation of many (particularly younger) individuals from the integrative structures of modern society, such as class identification, church, party, union, and traditional family and career models. Those more *individuated* citizens continue to experience common interests and political concerns (hence the impetus to join in action with others). However, their decoupling from the institutions of social and political aggregation has led to the adoption of more personalized brands of politics organized around individual lifestyles and social networks.

It is not so surprising that many forms of highly individualized political action embrace the DIY (Do It Yourself) spirit, as when people across nations take direct consumer actions to buy products such as fair trade or rainforest-certified coffee, knowing that the aggregation of small personal actions helps promote various social, economic, or environmental justice values. What is often taken for granted in accounts of personalized politics is the way in which these individualized acts are mirrored, modeled, scaled, and coordinated across digital media networks that have become part of the social structure of the individuated society. Indeed, one of the things that may keep the "politics of the personal" from disintegrating into chaotic or narcissistic gestures is that personal political stories can be shared and shaped as they travel over very large social networks in which technology of various sorts becomes part of the organization process. Because of this, it becomes important to understand what happens when citizens engage in collective action through digital media and social networks. This involves understanding the workings of these two interesting forces – the personalization of causes and the corresponding inclination to use scalable digital media to aggregate individual actions.

There is, of course, a great deal of content, and a large volume of noise, flowing through these networks. Content is an important part of the organization process, and our analyses look at the fit between media and the symbols, signs, slogans, rallying calls, targeted messages, resource links, videos, images, and multi-media creations shared over connective action networks. Just as social movement scholars have earlier examined the importance of collective action frames, we focus on personal (as in easy-to-personalize) action frames. Sometimes those frames are created by organizations offering easy personal access to events or actions being promoted by organizationally enabled networks. Sometimes these personal action frames emerge directly from crowds, and, in some cases, they "go viral" and become embraced as the common frame for action. In many ways, the U.S. Occupy protests in 2011 displayed personalized content in the extreme.

The noisy diversity of issues and problems arising from Occupy protesters was met by calls from the press to settle on a common demand, reflecting the journalistic logic that stories should be written around simple issue frames such as "tax the rich" that can be played against their targets for reactions. In response to such calls for reducing personal anger to a collective statement, the protesters turned the critics on their heads and adopted the slogan "What is our one demand?" – often followed by a statement that there are so many problems that they cannot be reduced to a single demand. This rejoinder circulated widely with the aid of Adbusters, the Vancouver-based "culture jamming" organization that was also instrumental in issuing an initial call to Occupy Wall Street. Adbusters produced an advertising-like graphic with the now-iconic image of a ballerina dancing on the head of the Wall Street bull. In response to this opening of a "What is my demand?" discourse space, people populated social media by issuing myriad personal demands: "change," "general strike," "get money out of government," "end war," "end American imperialism," "end health profiteering," "end poverty," "end joblessness," "end corporate censorship," "end police intimidation," "end wealth inequality," "end capital punishment," "Robin Hood Tax," "end fossil fuels," "living wage," "fix education," "stop home evictions," and "stop greed, free weed," to name just a few.

The multiple themes of the Occupy protests and other connective action formations are far more troublesome for the "one-to-many" logic of mass media than for the "many-to-many" logic of digital media technologies, given their ability to filter and reconfigure noisy communication. And sometimes these densely layered networks of digital media can distill broad personal action frames that accommodate diverse individual paths to engagement. Out of the many reasons Occupy protesters offered for their discontent, a broadly inclusive theme eventually emerged from the crowd and connected with the mass media and other social networks well beyond the protest population itself. The enduring slogan of the Occupy protests was "We Are the 99%." As we recount in Chapter 5, this theme was launched on Tumblr, a microblogging service, and quickly attracted a rich and diverse response from people who wrote their personal stories about life in the 99%. People typically shared their personal stories by holding them in front of a cell phone or desktop camera, in personal signatures ranging from longhand to refrigerator magnets, and posting the results in page after page of Tumbler entries. The statements were as varied as the people posting them. One teenage girl held a sheet of paper with these lines printed in marker: "I have type 1 diabetes. How can I afford COLLEGE when I may not be able to afford my INSULIN? I am the 99%.... occupywallst.org." People were still posting their stories and photos with many others commenting and tweeting about them more than a year after the Occupy protests emerged in 2011. More important, the overarching protest frame of the 1% versus the 99% traveled out across many digital media platforms and quickly spread through the mainstream press, igniting a long-deferred national and international discussion about the growth of inequality during the era of economic globalization.

Some observers dismiss this personalized shift as shallow and unlikely to make an impact on the serious struggles over power and policy. Our empirical analyses show, however, that personal action frames that emerge from connective networks often satisfy mass media demands for a simple angle and make it possible to intensify networking within various organizationally enabled or crowd-enabled organizations. Media coverage in different cases and in different countries was often better for connective action protests and issue campaigns than is typically associated with mobilizations under more confrontational collective action frames. Beyond offering empirical comparisons of how different kinds of networked organization operate, we do not take sides in the controversy over which organizational forms are superior. Instead, we try to understand different forms of personalized connective action on their own terms, with an eye to the factors that shape their scale, speed, flexibility, and impact, as well as the factors that lead them to fracture and fall apart.

Communication and the Organization of Connective Action

The second theme concerns the role of communication in contentious action. Communication has many faces, and scholars of contentious politics have focused on its role in information seeking and identity, persuasion, opinion, and the public sphere. Yet in the episodes described here, communication is often much more than a means of exchanging information and forming impressions, or an instrument for sending updates and instructions to followers. Communication routines can, under some conditions, create patterned relationships among people that lend organization and structure to many aspects of social life. As digital media become more prominent in contemporary contention, they too help to configure the protest space and the action that develops within it. Ultimately, technology-enabled networks may become dynamic organizations in their own right. At the core of this book is thus an idea about *communication as organization*.

The organizational capacity of communication is particularly evident in digitally networked action. In the span of a few years, technology developments have enabled people to establish various kinds of relationships across social, cultural, and geographical divides. Different technology platforms embed in each other and help people coordinate activities, establish relationships, and transfer information. Because these information and communication technologies undergird communicative actions with code that can be modified for unintended uses, people and organizations deploying these technologies may finetune the levels of automation and the mechanisms for sharing access or filtering inputs. The wide varieties of implementations of these technologies, meanwhile, allow even those with few resources to aggregate huge volumes of traffic across multiple platforms, each of which perform different sorts of organizational work. For example, we discuss the capacity of Twitter as a traffic direction and resource allocation system in Chapters 3 and 5. Twitter may well soon be replaced by something new, but in our cases it routinely emerges as the most highly used technology because of its unique meta-networking properties. This means that Twitter, among other things, enables people in the midst of crowded protests, as well as bystanders from afar, to coordinate resource flows through directed signals and links to various resource platforms inserted in those brief 140 character bursts. The point of the analyses is not Twitter or any other type of technology as such, but what people do with what the technology "affords" them and the structure this can create.

The kinds of network routines and resource flows evident in our case studies invite us to look squarely at how communication organizes action and what kinds of organization can result from different kinds of communication. Large-scale action networks are assemblages of individuals, formal organizations, and technologies in interaction. In some cases, formal organizations network deliberately to carry the brunt of the organizational burden for the network as a whole; in others, the burden shifts to technology-infused crowd networks with few conventional organizations. Tracing the organizational qualities of discursive and technological networking mechanisms in various cases allows us to explore the qualities of the different organizational forms.

We employ a variety of methods to examine the many forms of networks enabled by both organizations and individuals using different sorts of technology. For example, the simple process of mapping the hyperlinks among organizations involved in protest coordination, issue advocacy, or running campaigns can reveal a good deal about who is in, who is out, who is most commonly recognized by others, and who is sharing the work of linking other organizations into a network. The ways in which these link patterns change over time (as we describe in Chapters 2, 4, and 5) may reveal the coherence, stability, and strategic adjustments going on within the network. Drilling deeper into these networks makes it possible to examine how the patterns of interaction among various organizations, individuals, and technologies develop action networks that may respond to short-term events as well as long-term changes in issues, policies, and political opportunities. We also develop measures of how technologies deployed in both organizationally enabled and crowd-enabled networks actually engage people: What kinds of personal engagement do different technologies afford? Beyond analyzing (and empirically comparing) different network patterns of "affordances" that may engage individuals in different kinds of action, we also examine the power signatures of entire networks, based on whether we can locate organizational coalition backbones from which most engagement flows or whether power is more highly dispersed across layered networks of networks. We are also mindful throughout of the importance of media sites as models or repertoire archives for future action. Even when events or campaigns come to an end, their traces often remain behind online or in archives as testaments to what actually happened according to those who participated and as resources for future activists to consult or incorporate.

In summing up these properties of networked action, the book explores how even seemingly disjointed crowd-enabled connective action networks may achieve coherent organizational form in the sense that they develop capacities for (a) resource allocation and provision, (b) responsiveness to short-term external events such as police actions or the success or failure of protest actions, and (c) long-term adaptive responses such as resource seeking in the long tails of dying or transitioning networks. Using these three minimal defining conditions of organization, we explore how differently organized networks coordinate or conflict with one another in different political contexts, revealing a good deal about the outcomes of different protest actions. The quest to understand how these and other aspects of digitally networked action work becomes a navigating light of the book.

Three Models of Action in the Spectrum of Contentious Politics

The third theme at the core of this work builds on the topics of personalization and communication-as-organization and develops a framework showing the different organizational logics that may underlie different mobilizations. First, we acknowledge and then depart from the well-known "logic of collective action" that has long been associated with the study of collective action, with its many challengers and variants over the years. We focus most of our analysis on a second logic, the *logic of connective action*, which gives this book its name. In order to make progress in understanding digitally networked action, it is important not to conflate the two logics of action. Different assumptions about the underlying logic of why people participate at the individual level and how they associate at the collective level point to different dynamics at work in large-scale networks. Identifying the different action logics at work in particular situations helps explain how digital media play different roles in different types of organization. What is more, not only are networks of collective and connective action in their pure forms different from each other, but there are characteristic differences between the two types of connective networks that we examined as well. This led us to develop a typology of three ideal types of large-scale action networks relevant to contemporary contentious action.

We became interested in applying our framework to analyses of economic justice and climate change networks for several reasons: they have attracted large-scale citizen action on two of the most pressing issue agendas of our time; they have introduced various forms of contention into different comparative political contexts, locally, nationally, and transnationally; and their organizational boundaries shift as campaigns and other protest activities converge or diverge along issue and policy lines. Our initial focus was on coalitions of formal organizations and the different ways they defined and engaged their publics. In some cases, we noticed that organizations (and their surrounding network partners) regarded followers primarily as members for whom the organizations provided leadership aimed at building collective identifications and common ways of defining issues and acting in concert. In contrast to such well-known patterns of collective action, other organizations and their networks (including many large, well-known NGOs) soft-pedaled demands for formal membership, as well as collective issue and action framing. Instead, they focused on enabling large-scale individual engagement in often highly personalized terms. In some cases, organizations and networks even shifted from one mode to another depending on the calculus of issues, political opportunities, and the strategic value assigned to different forms of public engagement.

This contrast between what we call *organizationally brokered* (emphasis on strong coalitions and collective framing of issues and actions) and *organizationally enabled* (emphasis on loosely tied coalitions and personalized framing of issues and actions) forms of organization also corresponded to sharp differences in how organizations and their larger issue networks use digital media. Organizations that heavily manage the branding of issues and the engagement of followers tend to use digital media in rather limited ways, such as setting up Facebook groups as news sites for one-to-many postings from the organizations that offer little opportunity for interaction, or sending out action alerts on email lists or Twitter. By contrast, organizations forming issue networks that enable concerned citizens to personalize their involvement with issues are more likely to deploy creative forms of interactive and social media that enable individuals to join action networks and share their engagement along their social networks, all on their own terms.

For example, as we write these words, Oxfam has developed a partnership with the rock band Coldplay that invites fans to "become food rock stars" and help fix the broken world food system, starting with changing personal food habits and sharing stories, photos, and tweets on the Oxfam/Coldplay fan wall that followed the tour around the world. A fan named Flore tweeted, "I'm hungry for change: #lovefoodhateinjustice Supporting @oxfamontour with @Coldplay Oxfam.org/coldplay." Inserting traffic directions such as #, @, and the Oxfam/Coldplay URL enabled Flore to personally share her support across various social networks and to provide links back to the Oxfam resource and coordination site for those who may get Flore's message as it passes through its various communication channels. Such fine-grained personal engagement bypasses entry-level demands for membership or ideological commitments or for "correct" understandings of issues or actions. This Oxfam pathway to mediated engagement entails little more than finding a personal connection with the rather inclusive idea "lovefoodhateinjustice" and/or having some personal reason for being a fan of Coldplay.[1] One happens to connect with Oxfam and its issue agenda in the bargain. As with most of the organizationally enabled action forms, this example has a hybrid quality, mixing the idea of economic justice (which often comes with more stark collective framing) and highly personalized expressions of action, fandom, and traffic directing along one's social network.

Such relaxed, highly personalized terms of engagement are typically enabled and managed by digital media technologies of various sorts, from conventional social media, such as Facebook and Twitter, to custom-built (and often open-sourced) campaign or event coordination technology platforms that serve as stand-alone virtual organizations. Sites such as the Put People First campaign platform that helped mobilize 50,000 demonstrators in London in an early protest against the economic crisis in 2009 provided a rich interactive

---

[1] Flore describes herself on her Twitter account as "[p]assionate about sustainable solutions for urban & innovative environments, I am a global citizen enjoying New York City life."

environment for people to learn about issues, see what other people were doing about them, find actions to take at various levels, blog about their involvement, activate their own personal networks, and publicize the results of their involvement. The face of the site was not branded by the sponsoring organizations, nor were people cued about how to understand the economic crisis. Rather, the site engaged visitors personally by providing a message box for them to "Send your own message to the G20." In our scheme, such a model would be classified as one of "hybrid" organizationally enabled action. Such models enable individuals to personalize and share in the organization of protest actions with the help of digital media. In more organizationally brokered protest networks, by contrast, digital media serve less as organizational infrastructure than as a cost-saving means of sending messages and coordinating actions, as in hosting the obligatory Facebook group or Twitter feed.

To these two types of action organization, we soon added a third as we observed the crowd-organized/technology-enabled (which we have shortened to *crowd-enabled*) popular uprisings of 2009–2012 that cascaded around the world. These cases suggest a different part of the spectrum of digital media and the organization of collective action. First in this category came the Icelandic banking crisis of 2009–2011 with its fluid and rapidly organized networks (popularly termed the Anthill) that mobilized people to demonstrate in front of the homes of bankers and politicians as well as the parliament building, and eventually formed a popular assembly to press parliament for constitutional reforms.[2] Next, the Tunisian uprising overthrew an unpopular and repressive government. Then came the Tahrir Square protests in Egypt in 2011–2012, whose focus morphed quickly from anger against police corruption to demands that the regime itself must go. Starting with a now-famous Facebook site as the most visible public organization, legions armed with mobile phones employed Twitter as a mechanism for engaging broader publics in Egypt and around the world through tens of millions of tweets connecting networks of activists, journalists, and interested publics. The next protests in this diffusion series returned to the financial crisis, as the *indignados* in Spain and Occupy Wall Street in the United States drew millions of ordinary citizens into the mix. These events expanded our thinking about digital media and large-scale individualized engagement even further to encompass the question of how loosely organized crowds of commonly concerned citizens can employ a mix of personal media and face-to-face gatherings to create coherent structure and process that is far less dependent on formal organizations than the other two types we identify (even though there may be plenty of organizers and organizations also involved).

In sum, we identify three ideal types of action involving digital media in contemporary contentious politics. One of these types spans the oft-explored spectrum of traditional collective action, and we classify the other two as

---

[2] We are indebted to Icelandic journalist Baldvin Bergsson for sharing eyewitness accounts and the digital affordances at a workshop at Stockholm University in 2010.

different types of what we propose to call *connective action*. The following analytical categories, and forms of connective action in particular, frame our studies throughout the rest of the book:

- *Organizationally brokered* collective action: coalitions of heavily brokered relations among organizations seeking a common collective action framing. The focus is on resource-intensive mobilization and formalized (leadership-based, professionally organized) relations with followers, with the aim of cultivating commonly defined emotional commitments to the cause. Digital media are used primarily to reduce communication and coordination costs, but they do not fundamentally change the logic of participation or the organization of action.
- *Organizationally enabled* connective action: loosely tied networks of organizations sponsoring multiple actions and causes around a general set of issues in which followers are invited to personalize their engagement (more or less) on their own terms. Digital media and personal action frames become integral network-building mechanisms that enable individuals to contribute in important ways to how and with whom to participate, changing the locus of agency and individual leverage in the organization process.
- *Crowd-enabled* connective action: dense, fine-grained networks of individuals in which digital media platforms are the most visible and integrative organizational mechanisms. The actions of face-to-face activists gain scale and publicity through these intersecting media networks, with various degrees of political tension, filtering, viral discourse, and focused action resulting from the densely networked processes. The centrality of media platforms as organizational hubs, along with the roles of individuals in activating their own social networks, results in dynamic organizations in which crowds (with various degrees of cohesion) allocate resources, respond to external events, and display transitional changes over time.

These three types are abstracted composites of qualities that simplify more complex realities. Such neatly bounded packages of traits are unlikely to occur in pristine forms in society. However, our types enable us to theorize about, measure, and parse the empirical patterns, differences, tensions, and changes in complex protest spaces.

The studies in this book thus reflect a rich array of cases that crossed national boundaries, reflected multiple issue agendas, and, most important for our purposes, displayed strikingly different organizational forms. With reference to our three ideal types of action organization, we examine the relative presence and prominence of different organizational forms in complex contentious action and show how they incorporate various communication mechanisms into the organizational process. We also examine how these different types of organization play into or against each other and how they may be more or less effective in shaping political outcomes under different political conditions. For example, the interplay of particular forms of action with political opportunity structures and other conditions can help explain why some events or campaigns gain supporters, why some receive favorable media attention or official recognition, and even why some succeed in getting ideas translated into policy. By contrast, we can also show why other campaigns or protest events developed in more chaotic or less popular or politically effective ways.

None of the types of digitally networked action are inherently superior to the others. Like other forms of contention, connective action networks can have adaptive or maladaptive relationships to broad contextual factors such as political opportunities, institutional arrangements, and the surrounding ecology of protest. We are attentive in our analyses to various contextual and opportunity factors, such as how a global economic crisis triggered public and elite attention to issues of economic inequality; how the electoral success of the Green Party and the political pressures on other parties in Germany made institutions open to formal consideration of climate change issues; and how the movement of G20 summit conferences across different cities and nations attracted differently organized protest networks, often with competing coordination challenges and strategic concerns, and meeting different levels of police reactions.

Sorting out the combinations and capacities of different kinds of protest organization interacting with these contextual factors may help resolve some of the debates over the relative values of engagement enabled by social media versus more conventional face-to-face organizing and resource mobilization. Our analyses suggest that greater restraint is in order for those who outright dismiss digitally mediated engagement as mere "clicktivism" or "slacktivism," referring to the problem of people gaining political satisfaction from online action with meager effect. Likewise, they also indicate where equally inflated optimism about "Twitter Revolutions" might be tamped down. Instead we hope to stimulate more useful discussions about different forms of political organization, different means of projecting power, and different ways of thinking about outcomes.

The Organization of the Book

We selected a broad array of cases within the general domain of economic justice and climate change protest networks, which we sampled to assess the organizational dynamics of (a) different kinds of political configurations (public demonstrations, issue or policy campaigns, and "backbone" issue advocacy networks), (b) the operation of different political forms in different political contexts, and (c) their operation at different levels, in both national settings (primarily the United States, Britain, and Germany) and transnational settings (primarily the European Union).

Some of our cases involve protests displaying more conventional social movement politics, as when *brokered* coalitions of groups march under common banners and rally around classic collective action frames such as "Eat the Bankers!" Other cases involve more loosely linked networks of organizations constituted by dense digital media mechanisms that *enable* individuals to participate in coordinated actions (more or less) on their own terms by personalizing their actions (e.g., by telling their own stories about why they support the Robin Hood Tax). Finally, some of our observed networks are organized by large numbers (sometimes millions) of individuals appropriating a mix of commercial and custom digital media and using various kinds of hardware, from phones to computers, not just to communicate with each other, but also to create an organizational order (e.g., routines, divisions of labor, allocation of resources, gatekeeping, and policing) in the crowd. As we have explained, three organizational types become the seeds for the typology that organizes the book.

Throughout our analyses our narrative is driven by key questions about how connective action networks work. These questions unfold as we investigate the various cases in Chapters 2–5 that add depth to the model and contribute to the broad themes of personalization and political organization. These questions include:

- How are connective action networks organized?
- What sustains them?
- When are they politically effective?
- What are the trade-offs among our three ideal types of action networks in terms of commitment, sustainability, flexibility, scale, and speed of mobilization?

Our analyses draw on these and related questions to examine the power dynamics that accompany different patterns of network organization. For example, we explore whether or not NGOs that focus on enabling more personalized and loosely tied mediated networks maintain the coherence of their political agendas. We also look at whether crowd-enabled protests can produce agendas and what the outcomes of these crowdsourced agendas are. Again, in asking these questions, we do not suggest normative positions. Instead, we seek to critically assess how digitally networked action, and in particular the two forms of connective action, work.

Our analyses document and assess varieties of digital media use and public engagement in different kinds of contention. Through these studies, we hope to develop a model and set of empirical methods that are applicable to other issues and forms of contention as well. Our various studies identify, inventory, and compare (e.g., through coding and categorizing) both the forms of public discourse (e.g., personal vs. collective action frames) and the forms of digital media (e.g., from one-way newsletters and email, to interactive platforms for co-producing protest planning) that are deployed across protest events, campaigns, and issue networks operating in different national and transnational political settings. The methods we have developed in this project enable us to observe the composition, growth, activity patterns, stability, and public engagement potential of different activist networks.

We have selected a variety of cases across the spectrum of contentious political movements that involve digital media in different roles. This variety enables comparisons among issues, political arenas, opportunity structures, and different kinds of media deployments. All of the cases relate to the politics of economic justice and climate change. Adopting an empirical focus on two of the most visible issue clusters of our time offers us the advantage of being able to study a broad array of events and issue networks in a variety of national and transnational political contexts, while holding the underlying substantive focus relatively constant. At the same time, we can compare two different and important issues on the contemporary political scene. Here is how we plan to do it.

The Chapter Outline

Chapter 1 focuses on the logics of collective and connective action and what these mean for the study of digitally networked action. It outlines the basis and the organizational logics of ideal types that, taken together, span a spectrum of organizational forms of contemporary large-scale contention. The roles and interrelations of organizations differ significantly from one type to another, and so do the ways in which media engage individuals in opportunities to participate. Digital media are, of course, ubiquitous in today's world, and they are involved one way or another in most political mobilization. *But how they are involved matters.* Are they merely helping individuals receive traditional political information such as news feeds from the press or updates from advocacy organizations? Or are they enabling people to commit to an action and recommend it to others by sharing their personal participation stories, photos, or videos, and do they connect large populations across time and space as individuals make fine-grained networked decisions about filtering ideas, taking up roles, linking others in, and coordinating actions? Since digital media play distinctive roles in organizing personal engagement in the types of contention we have termed *organizationally enabled* and *crowd enabled*, we refer to both of these as types of *connective action* to distinguish them from collective action networks. The chapter argues that both connective action and collective action deserve to be approached on their own terms.

Chapter 2 turns to personalized communication – the extent to which protest organizers enable different degrees of flexibility in affiliation, issue definition, and expression among participants. Here we examine the challenges facing protest organizers regarding how to produce protests with the classic properties of unity and large numbers when potential supporters may expect flexible relations with causes and organizations. The empirical focus is two different mobilizations in the protests targeting the G20 London Summit in the spring of 2009, one a case of organizationally enabled connective action and the other a case of organizationally brokered collective action.

At the end of Chapter 2, we steer away from further contrasting connective with collective action in order to concentrate on the variations between the two connective types. Chapter 3 develops the theme of network organization and digital networking mechanisms, and examines protests around the United

Nations climate conference in Copenhagen that took place in the winter of 2009. We contrast the organizational characteristics of Twitter streams used in the organizationally enabled networks in the London climate protest (which included several of the same organizations from the earlier economic justice demonstrations discussed in Chapter 2) with a slice of the even larger protests that occurred in Copenhagen at the climate summit itself, showing how demonstrators operating outside of more conventional organizations used Twitter as part of a crowd-enabled formation that also attracted virtual participants around the world.

A recurring question about large-scale connective action is whether it is sustainable. The next two chapters shift attention from focused, time-bound demonstration events to longer-term action of various kinds. Chapter 4 focuses on the organization of underlying economic justice and environment issue networks in different national and transnational contexts. Here we compare organizationally enabled connective action networks in the United Kingdom and Germany during the same time periods (early 2010) to see how national political contexts and opportunity structures may affect issue-based connective action formations. We also compare national networks with parallel issue networks operating at the European level as national members of the EU civil society platforms created by Brussels to establish civil society representation.

Another recurring question is whether connective action achieves anything. Chapter 5 considers how to locate the workings of power in different kinds of networks in order to assess their outcomes and the conditions under which power is wielded more or less effectively. We identify the differing "power signatures" of network organizations in terms of the concentration or dispersion of recognition and influence, and again compare two types of connective action networks. One is the long-running organizationally enabled British economic justice campaign for a Robin Hood Tax on speculative financial transactions, which displays the relatively more centralized characteristics of an organizationally enabled network. The other is the relatively more dispersed crowd-enabled U.S. Occupy protest "network of networks," which moved the emergent discourse on inequality into the mainstream media in 2011–2012. These two very different ways of organizing connective action also display very different power signatures. The chapter highlights the complex nature of network power and the ways it interacts with political context. Contrary to conventional expectations about the relationship between power in networks and political capacity, both networks in this case turn out to have similar outcomes as measured by media and elite uptake of economic inequality discourses, although an edge may be given to the Robin Hood Tax network for helping to move policy decisions onto government agendas.

The book focuses primarily on empirical cases of connective action that are "successful" in various ways in order to explore how connective action works when it does work and to understand the differences between the two main types. However, it is also important to examine "failures" in order to provide a more complete understanding of the organizational processes and their limits. As a step in this direction, the concluding chapter addresses problems that emerge in the complex action ecologies from which we draw our cases throughout the book. As we emphasize, many instances of large-scale contention involve elements of both connective and collective action, whether this comes in the form of transitioning between phases in the evolution of contention or simply reflects overlaps between different kinds of networks operating in the same arenas. The potential for friction among different models of network organization leads to a number of interesting problems, two of which preview our discussion in the conclusion.

The first problem concerns transition. The same technologies that enable the rapid rise of crowd-enabled networks may also limit their capacity to transform as the context changes. We explore how crowd-enabled networks might become more enduring or stable by noting the limits inherent in the kinds of commercial, off-the-shelf digital technologies often employed in such networks, and discuss the potential of next-generation technologies in this context. The other problem concerns the overlap and potential clash of different organizational logics operating in different networks within the same political arena. In some cases, groups may anticipate clashes resulting from different models of protest organization and partition the protest space between them (as our cases in Chapter 2 exemplify). In other cases, significant overlap emerges inside a single protest space and results in deep and sometimes chaotic conflicts. One conflict that we explore in the conclusion arises from the fundamentally different philosophies among protesters and organizations over the uses of technology and what this can mean for networks of connective action. We offer a look at the decline of the Occupy protests as partly a story of the resistance among some activists to adopting innovative technologies to create virtual assembly spaces after police actions displaced them from physical spaces. The "blurred boundaries" between activists and bystander publics in protests from Tahrir Square to Zuccotti Park turns out to be an interesting part of the story when we begin to understand which actors used what kinds of technologies in what ways.

Our analyses cannot answer all of the questions about everything going on in the vast universe of contention swirling beyond the bounds of our cases: from Internet pirates to the Tea Party and from neo-Nazis to al-Qaeda. Nevertheless, by casting a broad net and using a variety of methods, we contribute to a framework for understanding some of the most compelling democratic stories of our time, as millions of people across the planet utilize basic communication technologies to share simple, personally engaging ideas and press for change.

The Logic of Connective Action

With the world economy in crisis, the heads of the 20 leading economies held a series of meetings beginning in the fall of 2008 to coordinate financial rescue policies. Wherever the G20 leaders met, whether in Washington, London, St. Andrews, Pittsburgh, Toronto, or Seoul, they were greeted by protests. London was the scene of nearly a week of coordinated events scheduled on different days to accommodate activists of various political stripes. The largest of these demonstrations was sponsored by a number of prominent NGOs, including Oxfam, Friends of the Earth, Save the Children, and World Vision. This loose coalition launched a campaign called "Put People First" (PPF), promoting public mobilization against the social and environmental harms they felt would result from "business as usual" solutions to the financial crisis. The website for the campaign carried the simple statement:

Even before the banking collapse, the world suffered poverty, inequality and the threat of climate chaos. The world has followed a financial model that has created an economy fuelled by ever-increasing debt, both financial and environmental. Our future depends on creating an economy based on fair distribution of wealth, decent jobs for all and a low carbon future. (Put People First 2009)

The centerpiece of this PPF campaign was a march of some 35,000 people through the streets of London a few days ahead of the G20 meeting, a march intended to give voice and show commitment to the campaign's simple theme. It drew together a large and diverse protest, fueled by participants sending personal messages about the crisis to broader publics and world leaders both in the streets and online. Despite (or perhaps because of) the absence of more confrontational collective grievances and demands, the PPF actions

An earlier version of this chapter was published as "The Logic of Connective Action: Digital Media and the Personalization of Contentious Politics," *Information Communication & Society*, 15, no. 5 (2012), pp. 739–768. Reprinted by permission of Taylor & Francis (www.tandfonline .com).

displayed impressive levels of what Tilly (2004, 2006) termed WUNC: *worthiness*, embodied by the endorsements of some 160 prominent civil society organizations and recognition of their demands by various prominent officials; *unity*, reflected in the orderliness of the event; *numbers* of participants, which made PPF the largest of a series of London G20 protests and the largest demonstration during the string of G20 meetings in different world locations; and *commitment*, reflected in the presence of delegations from some 20 different nations who joined local citizens in spending much of the day listening to speakers in Hyde Park or attending religious services sponsored by church-based development organizations.[1] The large volume of generally positive press coverage reflected all of these characteristics, while recognition from various heads of state accentuated the worthiness of the event.[2]

The protests continued. In 2010 the G20 issued a policy statement making it clear that debt reduction and austerity would be the centerpieces of a political program that could send shock waves through economies from the United States and the United Kingdom to Greece, Italy, and Spain, while pushing more decisive action on climate change onto the back burner. Public anger swept cities from Madison to Madrid, as citizens protested that their governments, no matter what their political stripe, offered no alternatives to the economic dictates of a so-called neo-liberal economic regime that seemed to operate from corporate and financial power centers beyond popular accountability and, some argued, even beyond the control of states.

In contrast to the clear imprints of organizational networks on the series of protests following from the London actions, other collective action triggered by the economic crisis emerged with far less involvement by conventional organizations. For example, in Spain *los indignados* (the indignant ones) mobilized in 2011 under the name "15M" for the date (May 15) of the mass protests in some 60 cities. One of the most remarkable aspects of this sustained protest organization was its success at keeping political parties, unions, and other powerful political organizations out. Indeed, they were targeted as part of the political problem. There were, of course, civil society organizations supporting 15M, but they generally stayed in the background to honor the personalized identity of the movement: the faces and voices of millions of ordinary people displaced by financial and political crises. The most visible organization consisted of the richly layered digital and interpersonal communication networks centering around the media hub of *¡Democracia real YA!*.[3] This network soon included links to more than 80 local Spanish city nodes and a number of international solidarity networks. On the one hand,

---

[1] Simultaneous protests were held in other European cities, with tens of thousands of demonstrators gathering in the streets of Berlin, Frankfurt, Vienna, Paris, and Rome.

[2] U.S. Vice President Joe Biden asked for patience from understandably upset citizens while leaders worked on solutions, and the British prime minister at the time, Gordon Brown, said: "[T]he action we want to take (at the G20) is designed to answer the questions that the protesters have today" (Vinocur and Barkin 2009).

[3] www.democraciarealya.es/.

¡Democracia real YA! seemed to be a website; on the other, it resembled a strongly supported and effective organization. It makes sense to think of the core organization of the *indignados* as both of these and more, revealing the hybrid nature of digitally mediated organization (Chadwick 2013).

Given its seemingly informal organization, the 15M mobilization surprised many observers by sustaining and even building strength over time, using a mix of online media and offline activities that included face-to-face organizing, encampments in city centers, and marches across the country. Throughout, the participants communicated a collective identity of being leaderless, signaling that labor unions, parties, and more radical movement groups should stay at the margins. A survey of 15M protesters by a team of Spanish researchers showed that the relationships between individuals and organizations differed in at least three ways from those in other, more conventional movement protests they studied, including a general strike, a regional protest, and a pro-life demonstration: (1) whereas strong majorities of participants in other protests recognized the involvement of key organizations with brick and mortar addresses, only 38 percent of *indignados* did so; (2) only 13 percent of the organizations cited by 15M participants offered any membership or affiliation possibilities, in contrast to large majorities who listed membership organizations as being important in the other demonstrations; and (3) the ages of organizations (such as parties and unions) listed in the comparison protests ranged from 10 to more than 40 years, while the organizations cited in association with 15M were, on average, less than 3 years old (Anduiza, Cristancho, and Sabucedo forthcoming). Despite, or perhaps because of, these interesting organizational differences, the ongoing series of 15M protests attracted participation from somewhere between 6 and 8 million people, a remarkable number in a nation of 40 million (rtve 2011).

Like PPF, the *indignados* achieved impressive levels of communication with outside publics, both directly, via images and messages spread virally across social networks, and indirectly, when anonymous Twitter streams and YouTube videos were taken up as mainstream press sources. Their actions became daily news fare in Spain and abroad, with the protesters receiving generally positive coverage of their personal messages in local and national news – again defying familiar observations about the difficulty of gaining positive news coverage for collective actions that spill outside the bounds of institutions and take to the streets (Gitlin 1980).[4] In addition to communicating concerns about jobs and the economy, the clear message was that people felt the democratic system had broken to the point that all parties and leaders were under the influence of banks and international financial powers. Despite avoiding

---

[4] Beyond the high volume of Spanish press coverage, the story of the *indignados* attracted world attention. *BBC World News* devoted no fewer than eight stories to this movement over the course of two months in 2011, including a feature on the march of one group across the country to Madrid, with many interviews and descriptions of encounters in the words of the protesters themselves.

association with familiar civil society organizations, lacking leaders, and displaying little conventional organization, *los indignados*, like PPF, achieved high levels of WUNC.

Two broad organizational patterns characterize such digitally enabled action networks. The first, as in the case of PPF, entails behind-the-scenes coordination by networks of established issue advocacy organizations that step back from branding the actions in terms of particular organizations, memberships, or conventional collective action frames. Instead, these organizations cast a broader public engagement net using interactive digital media and easy-to-personalize action themes, often deploying batteries of social technologies to help citizens spread the word over their personal networks. The second pattern, typified by the *indignados* and the Occupy protests in the United States, entails technology platforms playing the role of virtual political organizations to coordinate the actions of people operating in geographically scattered face-to-face settings, where important but otherwise potentially isolated decisions, plans, and actions take place. In this digital network mode, political demands and grievances are often shared in very personalized accounts that travel over social networking platforms, email lists, and online coordinating platforms. An example is the easily personalized action frame "We Are the 99%" that emerged from the U.S. Occupy protests following the rise of the *indignados* in 2011. The 99% meme[5] quickly traveled the world via personal stories and images shared on social networks such as Tumblr, Twitter, and Facebook.

There are important differences in these patterns of what we term *organizationally enabled* (e.g., the London PPF) and *crowd-enabled* (e.g., *los indignados*, Occupy) action, and we will explore them throughout the book. However, both forms of mobilization also share organizational logics involving technology-enabled, often highly personalized communication. It is important at the outset to briefly introduce the origins and appeal of personalized digitally mediated politics.

Origins of Personalized, Digitally Mediated Politics

An important backdrop to the different forms of protest described in this chapter is the process of structural fragmentation and individualization in many contemporary societies over the past several decades.[6] Toward the close of

---

[5] Memes are easily imitated, appropriated, and shared symbolic packets that cross social network boundaries more easily than other symbolic content that either may take greater cultural work (e.g., education or ritual enactment) to share or may explicitly serve to mark network boundaries. We discuss memes in more detail later on.

[6] Our theoretical focus in this discussion is primarily northern, post-industrial democracies. However, other countries may arrive at similar (particularly crowd-enabled) action formations through different processes, as when forces such as the policing and destruction of civil society structures in authoritarian regimes also result in social fragmentation and individuation. When those conditions combine with weak regime monitoring of digital communication networks and uses of technologies, as happened in Tunisia and Egypt, similar mass mobilizations may occur via very different historical paths.

the 20th century most national political and business leaders, including many labor and social democratic parties on the left, were caught up in a wave of belief in, and advocacy of policies favoring, free markets, the deregulation of industries and financial sectors, and the downsizing and privatization of public goods and services. This updating of classical liberal thought (hence the name *neo-liberalism*) was accompanied by an emerging public discourse that upheld consumerism as a defining element of individual freedom and means of enhancing people's lives. These and related pressures of economic globalization from roughly the 1970s through the end of the preceding century produced dramatic shifts in social organization and political orientations in what we now term the post-industrial democracies, resulting in engagement with politics increasingly as an expression of personal hopes, lifestyle values, and the promise of individual opportunity that further eroded group memberships and loyalties to parties and political institutions, particularly among younger citizens. Surveys of most post-industrial societies show that the largest groups of voters under 30 are now either apolitical or independent, a trend that does not seem to give way to party loyalty later in life (Dalton and Wattenberg 2002; Berglund et al. 2006; Dassonneville, Hooghe, and Vanhoutte 2012).

Underlying this pattern are deep changes in the typical (particularly younger) individual's sense of location and identity in society. These changes affect how people view the world and participate in politics. People may still experience a shared set of concerns: riskier careers, less social support, the dangers of climate change, excessive business influence on government, questionable corporate and political behavior that triggered the economic collapse, and so on. However, a growing number of citizens are less likely to see conventional political organizations as avenues for engaging with these and other issues (Micheletti 2003). They want a personal path to engagement – a politics by other, more self-expressive and self-satisfying means (Giddens 1991; Inglehart 1997). These trends track rather closely with the transformation of societies as the so-called neo-liberal consensus swept through think tanks, governments, social and economic policies, and world trading systems with its mantra of "free markets, free people" (Beck and Beck-Gernsheim 2002).

Under these circumstances, electoral politics increasingly resemble consumer marketing and branding of voters, and middle voters need to be resold every election. As a result, the costs of conventional politics have soared in nations such as the United States, where election spending has grown nearly exponentially as parties and candidates spend more on communication strategies to send more messages to a relatively small number of hard-to-reach voters who in turn confess sensory overload and general disdain for the political process. While conventional politics is in a state of drift, the world of issue politics aimed at mobilizing people around things they care about personally is exploding with the growth of issue advocacy NGOs, volunteer associations, and online communities. However, it is not always clear how to involve people effectively in these causes, even though they may have common concerns or problems. The conventional models for aggregating support and mobilizing participation stemming from the modern society that dominated much of the 20th century were predicated on joining groups, adopting identifications, and marching under common banners. Citizens coming of age in the current era tend to seek personally expressive modes of action about problems they share with others. The trouble is that those others are less likely than they were in past eras to be assembled via connections to party, union, church, or club. Rather, they are more often joined through social networks, friend circles, trusted recommendations, media sharing (photos, videos, mashups), and technologies that match demographic and lifestyle qualities so that political partners and activities align across loosely tied, opt-in/opt-out networks.

These DIY politics – particularly when enabled by technology platforms of various sorts – often produce large mobilizations of concerned citizens, as happened on a single day (January 18, 2012) while the U.S. Congress was considering two pieces of Internet piracy legislation sponsored by the entertainment industry. Millions of individuals awoke to find that Wikipedia had gone dark and offered its users a brief education on the possible infringements of freedoms stemming from the legislation. The darkened website invited users to "IMAGINE A WORLD WITHOUT FREE KNOWLEDGE" and encouraged them to "make your voice heard," by providing links to Facebook, Google groups, and Twitter. Google covered its colorful logo with a black censored bar and gave visitors direct links for sending personal messages to members of Congress. By conservative estimates, more than 7,000 websites participated in the protest (some estimates were far higher). Wikipedia claimed that more than 160 million people saw its invitation to protest, and Google alone claimed that more than 7 million individuals signed the petition it sent to Congress. This largest online protest in history crashed the congressional servers and, at least for the time being, forced withdrawal of the legislation.[7] Other actions that day included denial of service attacks by hacker networks such as Anonymous on the websites of CBS and other "legacy" media corporations.

The point of this story is that personalized politics need not be scattered, disorganized, or ineffective, and yet it does tend to work differently than conventionally organized political action. To be sure, the multi-faceted processes of individualization are articulated differently in different societies, but they generally include the propensity to develop flexible political identifications based on personal lifestyles (Giddens 1991; Inglehart 1997; Bennett 1998; Bauman 2000; Beck and Beck-Gernsheim 2002), with implications for collective action (Melucci 1989; McDonald 2002; Micheletti 2003; della Porta 2005) and organizational participation (Putnam 2000; Bimber et al. 2012). The nominal issues championed by these politics may resemble older movement or party concerns in terms of topics (environment, rights, women's equality, and fair trade), but the ideas and mechanisms for organizing action become more personalized than in cases where action is organized on the basis of social group identity,

---

[7] For documentation on these protests see en.wikipedia.org/wiki/Protests_against_SOPA_and_ PIPA and en.wikipedia.org/wiki/Stop_Online_Piracy_Act. We have adopted the more conservative estimates from the latter article.

membership, or ideology. A large number of people may still join in action, but the identification is derived more through inclusive and diverse large-scale personal expression than through group or ideological affiliation.

The rise of similar actions in decidedly undemocratic contexts suggests that there are different paths to social fragmentation, individuation, and, ultimately, the personalization of politics. When enabled by various communication technologies, the resulting digitally networked actions in post-industrial democracies bear some remarkable similarities to action formations in repressive regimes, such as those witnessed during the Arab Spring (Howard and Hussain 2011). In both contexts, large numbers of similarly disaffected individuals seized upon opportunities to organize collectively through access to various technologies, with digital networks feeding in and out of intense face-to-face interactions in squares, encampments, mosques, and general assembly meetings. This suggests a set of mechanisms through which similar forms of contention may diffuse across time and (very different) places. Beissinger (2007) refers to these replications of protest routines as "modular."

Compared with more conventional protests, which have identifiable membership organizations leading the way under common banners and collective identity frames while brokering any differences that may arise, these more personalized, digitally mediated collective action formations often:

- scale up more quickly;
- produce large and sometimes record-breaking mobilizations;
- display unusual flexibility in tracking moving political targets and bridging different issues (e.g., economy and environment); and
- build up adaptive protest repertoires, share open-source software development, and embrace an ethos of inclusiveness.

Another interesting feature of these digitally mediated mobilizations is that because of the densely layered, sometimes viral nature of the communication that flows from them, large publics may attend to them directly (even joining in by sharing the communication with friends or taking other actions, pro and con), and this may occur without cueing from conventional media coverage. Indeed, in what may prove a reversal of journalistic convention, the news media are increasingly taking cues from social media originating in and around these crowded protests. Whether we look at PPF, the Arab Spring, the *indignados*, or Occupy, we note surprising success in the communication of simple political messages directly to outside publics using common digital technologies such as Facebook or Twitter, along with a rich array of custom media platforms, which we will discuss in Chapters 2 and 4. The buzz of the digital media crowd combined with the physical presence of activists in camps, marches, and other events often makes the news. And, as previously noted, digital media feed directly from activists, meaning that movement members may even be used as sources by conventional journalism organizations, whether because they are unable to get reporters into particular areas or because conventional journalistic methods cannot reproduce the dramatic immediacy and authenticity of media that emerge from the crowd.[8] As a result, these digitally mediated action networks may be accorded as high or even higher levels of WUNC than some of their more conventional social movement counterparts.

Getting Beyond "What's New?"

Despite the features mentioned so far, the rise of digitally networked activism (DNA) has been met with some understandable skepticism about what really is so very distinct about it, mixed with concerns about what it means for the political capacities of organized dissent. We take these challenges seriously but prefer to shift to a more modest question: What's different? It turns out that while some things are different, others remain much the same, and while some features of DNA seem surprisingly effective, others appear less so. Our goal is thus not to debate what is sweepingly new, but to compare, contrast, and explain some demonstrably different forms of contention. In particular, this book is aimed at understanding how these more personalized, digitally mediated varieties of collective action work. The book revolves around questions of how they are organized, what sustains them, and when they are politically effective.

This first chapter argues that convincingly addressing such questions requires recognizing that differing logics of action may underpin distinct kinds of collective action networks. In particular, there seem to be interesting differences between digitally networked, crowd-enabled action and more conventional organization-centered and -brokered collective action. Understanding these root differences is not helped by accounts that conflate different types of action or that use concepts developed for understanding one kind of mobilization to impose meaning on the other. While we recognize that our efforts to distinguish two broad forms of contemporary mobilization will strike some as making the differences overly stark, we offer our categorical distinctions only to cast light on pathways for better conceptual development. We also recognize (and show in our analyses) that we need to soften categorical differences when analyzing cases that contain hybrid organizational forms or chaotic mixtures that reflect different visions of ideal political organization brought into play by activists themselves.

---

[8] An early example of direct journalistic sourcing of crowd information followed the shooting death of protester Neda Agha-Soltan during public demonstrations protesting election corruption after the 2009 Iranian elections. Several videos were made of the incident using mobile phone cameras, and subsequent postings on YouTube were mashed up and reposted in different languages and viewed millions of times. The hashtag #neda quickly trended on Twitter, and the citizen-journalists' videos were aired on CNN and other networks. The anonymous citizen-journalists in the crowd were given the prestigious George W. Polk Award in 2009. Noting that this was the first time the prize had been given for anonymous reporting, the curator of the awards, John Darnton, said: "This award celebrates the fact that in today's world a brave bystander with a cellphone camera can use video-sharing and social networking sites to deliver the news" (Associated Press 2010).

Thus, it is with an eye toward the empirical uses of our model that we proceed in this chapter to identify two broad logics of action. The focus of the book is on the less familiar logic of *connective action* that highlights the role of communication as an organizing principle in personalized, digitally networked action. This focus invites attention to networks involving large-scale personal-level communication as organizational structures in their own right. Since much has already been written on the familiar means of organizing collective action using resource-intensive organizations to develop collective identifications with causes, we refer to these studies and underlying theories mainly to point out contrasts and complements to our connective action model. In contrast to the familiar idea of organizationally brokered collective framing of motives, problem definitions, and political demands, we point toward less conceptualized parts of the mobilization spectrum where we find large numbers of people who clearly share common threats, deprivations, and other concerns but who seek more personalized, individually expressive action frames that develop organizational structure when personal communication devices (e.g., phones or computers) are networked through shared media platforms (e.g., Facebook, Twitter, or custom tools built by activist-developers and enabling organizations).

Our goal is to trace the implications of how *personal action frames* combine with social technologies in the organization of digitally networked action. The key contribution of this chapter is a three-part typology of large-scale action networks contrasting more conventional types of collective action with the two modes of connective action already introduced (organizationally enabled and crowd enabled). This framework serves to differentiate between conventional collective and digitally networked (connective) action. More important, it helps sort out potential confusion about forms of connective action that involve familiar organizations such as Oxfam which may facilitate highly personalized engagement within loose networks, while at other times operate in other, perhaps more familiar modes such as brokering interest coalitions within policy processes. This framework enables us to address many questions and concerns about how personalized digital action networks work, which provide the focus for the remainder of the book.

Two Organizational Logics: Collective and Connective Action

As previously outlined, we propose that more fully understanding large-scale networks in contemporary contentious action involves distinguishing between at least two logics that may be in play: the familiar logic of collective action and the less familiar logic of connective action. The *logic of collective action* that has been perceived to typify the modern social order of hierarchical institutions and membership groups stresses the organizational dilemma of getting individuals to join in actions where personal participation costs may outweigh marginal gains, particularly when people can ride on the efforts of others for free. It often requires people to make more difficult choices and adopt particular social identities that may receive disapproval from others. The spread of such collective identifications requires various measures of education, pressure, or socialization, which in turn makes higher demands on formal organizations and resources such as money to pay rent for organization offices, to generate publicity, and to hire professional staff organizers (McAdam, McCarthy, and Zald 1996).

Digital media help reduce some of the costs of these processes, but they do not fundamentally change the action dynamics. In the model defined by the *logic of connective action*, however, digital media do change the dynamics of the action: these networks operate through the organizational processes of social media, and their logic does not require strong organizational control or the symbolic construction of a united "we." Such networks are becoming increasingly prominent in those parts of late modern societies in which formal organizations are losing their grip on individuals and group ties are being replaced by large-scale, fluid social networks (Castells 2000).[9] This said, the arguments in the following sections are not designed to categorize networks in terms of either/or, past/future, or good or bad alternatives. The one does not necessarily solve the problems of the other. The point is rather that the logic of connective action entails dynamics of its own and thus deserves analysis on its own analytical terms.

This is important because while movements characterized by the logic of collective action are clearly visible in contemporary society, they have been joined by other mobilizations that lack many of those defining characteristics. Efforts to push the latter mobilizations into the old categories diminish our ability to understand one of the most interesting developments of our times: the capacity of fragmented, individualized populations that are hard to reach and even harder to induce to share personally transforming collective identities to somehow find ways of mobilizing protest networks from Wall Street to Madrid to Cairo. Indeed, when people are individualized in their social orientations, and thus structurally or psychologically unavailable to modernist forms of political movement organization, resource mobilization becomes increasingly costly and has diminishing returns.[10] Approaching such populations with techniques designed to overcome free-riding or to help them develop common identities is

---

[9] As noted earlier, although we focus primarily on cases in late modern, post-industrial democracies, some of our theoretical propositions may also apply to other settings where authoritarian rule may result in individualized populations that fall outside of sanctioned civil society organization, yet may have direct or indirect access to communication technologies such as mobile phones.

[10] This principle applies equally to organizational dilemmas in conventional institutional politics such as elections. As noted previously, the electoral process in the United States, for example, has witnessed dramatic growth in the sums of money spent on communicating with a small number of increasingly individuated voters who appear responsive (if at all) to more personalized emotional messages, as they are less engaged by appeals to party, ideology, or other collective framing. In this communication environment, the marginal effects of such costly communication become small.

not necessarily the most successful or effective strategy for organizing collective action, as Bimber, Flanagin, and Stohl (2012) have demonstrated even in the case of mainstream interest organizations. Meanwhile, when people who seek more personalized paths to concerted action are familiar with practices of social networking in everyday life and when they have access to technologies from mobile phones to computers, they are already familiar with a different logic of organization: the logic of connective action. This logic enables personal framing of communication in ways that may not entail shifts in categorical thinking, emotional identification, or risk or cost calculation,[11] and yet individual actors can nonetheless join with others as connectivity is established, filtered, and coordinated in networks organized by both human and technological agents.

The Evolution of Different Forms of Protest Organization

Some observers marked a turning point in patterns of organization, communication, and issue diversity in contentious politics with the iconic union of "Teamsters and turtles" in the Battle of Seattle in 1999.[12] The World Trade Organization (WTO) meetings in Seattle were planned to showcase the emergence of the U.S. technology industry in a city that Boeing and Microsoft had put on the world map. The dignitaries present included U.S. President Bill Clinton, Microsoft CEO Bill Gates, and Boeing CEO Phil Condit (Condit and Gates were official co-hosts of the meeting), along with a host of world leaders and prominent bureaucrats. Their gathering was disrupted by what would soon become a familiar "global justice" mix of workers, students, environmentalists, religious groups, and anarchists, and a large number of concerned citizens, many of whom were organized around personal "affinity groups" such as workplaces, neighborhoods, church affiliations, lifestyles, schools, sexual orientations, or friendships (Gillham and Marx 2000). The number of people in the streets was estimated at 40,000–50,000, reflecting the broad participation of loose coalitions of hundreds of organizations and individuals that saw burly union members marching alongside environmental activists wearing turtle costumes. Foreshadowing the issue focus of the case studies in this book, these different factions came together around a broad consensus that the rising neo-liberal trade regime was a threat to democratic control of both national economies and the world environment.

---

[11] Risk and cost calculations are different when regimes police communication networks, but even then, technological workarounds have been developed to create various levels of anonymity and related choices regarding how to participate.

[12] There were earlier large-scale globalization protests dating as far back as the so-called International Monetary Fund riots in Lima in 1975, large demonstrations in 1985 at a Bonn G7 meeting, and demonstrations of 80,000 people in Berlin at the 1988 meetings of the World Bank and the IMF. However, the Seattle demonstrations signaled both a structural shift toward more inclusive protest organization and a more central role for communication technologies.

Studies of the Battle of Seattle and dozens of subsequent protest events show that they entailed plenty of old-fashioned meetings, issue brokering, and coalition building (Polletta 2002).[13] However, the emphasis on forging large-scale, broadly inclusive, loosely tied protest networks, with pragmatic roots in early protests such as Seattle, was quickly elevated to an organizational principle through the "open space" networks of the World Social Forum that first met in 2001. An ethos of inclusiveness and diversity quickly evolved, and activists began crowdsourcing broad frames for their "movement of movements" and shifted the focus of their discourse from the negative term "anti-globalization" to "global justice" and the common refrain "Another World Is Possible," themes that were also more positively relayed by the mainstream media.

Although some veteran activists tend to discount the value of networking via digital media as fostering lightweight relationships or favoring lesser levels of commitment than physical investment of time and risk (points to which we return in Chapter 6), it is interesting that proliferating digital media platforms and mobile applications have nonetheless followed and, in some ways defined, the trajectory of these modular (Beissinger 2007) economic justice and environmental protest networks up to the present day. As our cases in Chapters 2, 3, 4, and 5 indicate, the dense arrays of digital mechanisms form signatures that mark the styles of public engagement with issues; network organizational structures; and power distributions in campaigns, demonstrations, and issue networks. Indeed, the Seattle WTO protests gave birth to the activist media network Indymedia, which quickly became an early means of coordinating and sharing information from local to global networks. In the view of many activists, forming their own communication networks freed them from dependence on the mass media for reaching broader publics and defining their causes.

Since those beginnings, there has been increasingly sophisticated technology-enabled networking (Livingston and Asmolov 2010) that makes highly personalized, socially mediated communication processes fundamental structuring elements in the organization of many forms of connective action. Multiple organizational forms operating within such ecologies may be hard to categorize, not least because they may morph over time or context, displaying hybridity of various kinds (Chadwick 2007, 2013). In addition, protest and organizational work occurs both on- and offline via technologies of different capabilities, making the online–offline distinction relevant in some cases but more often not (Earl and Kimport 2011; Bimber et al. 2012; Chadwick 2013).

Alongside these seemingly different kinds of protest networks that rely less on brokered coalitions and collective identity framing, there is often a good deal of more conventional organizing work also going on. These more familiar

---

[13] One study showing the loosely knit and often fractious network building of WTO activists was directed by Lance Bennett and Margaret Levi. The *WTO History Project* contains, among other resources, an oral history archive of interviews with more than 80 organizers and rank-and-file participants. See depts.washington.edu/wtohist/.

forms of social movements and contentious politics are not by any means all of the same form. They extend over many different kinds of phenomena (Melucci 1996; McAdam, Tarrow, and Tilly 2001; Tarrow 2011), and discussions of new forms of collective action reflect political ecologies and opportunity structures that are increasingly complex (Chesters and Welsh 2006). Given these emerging distinctions between connective and collective action and the prospects of different organizational forms within each of these broad categories, the critical question is: How do we sort out what organizational processes contribute which qualities to collective and connective action networks? How do we identify the borders between fundamentally different types of action formations: that is, what are the differences between collective and connective action, and where are the hybrid overlaps? A first step in sorting out some of the complexity is to distinguish between two logics of action that may be involved. The two logics are associated with distinct dynamics, and thus draw attention to different dimensions for analysis. It is important to separate them analytically, as the one is less familiar than the other, and this in turn constitutes an important stumbling block for the study of much contemporary political action that we term connective action.[14]

Defining the Logic of Collective Action

The more familiar of the two logics is the *logic of collective action*, which emphasizes the problem of getting individuals to contribute to a collective endeavor that typically involves seeking some sort of public good (e.g., democratic reforms). The classical formulation of this problem was articulated by Olson (1965), but the implications of his general logic have reached far beyond the original formulation. Olson's intriguing observation was that people cannot be expected to act together just because they have a common problem or goal. He held that in large groups in which individual contributions are less noticeable than they normally are in smaller groups, rational individuals will free-ride on the efforts of others: it is more cost efficient not to contribute if you can enjoy the good without contributing. Moreover, if not enough people join in creating the good, your efforts are wasted anyway. Either way, it is individually rational not to contribute, even if all agree that all would be better off if everyone did. This thinking fixes attention on the problematic dynamics attending the rational action of atomistic individuals and at the same time makes resource-rich organizations a central concern. Both solutions that Olson discerned – coercion and selective incentives – implied organizations with a substantial capacity to monitor, administer, and distribute such measures.

In this view, formal organizations with resources are essential to harnessing and coordinating individuals in common action. The early application of this

---

[14] Routledge and Cumbers (2009) make a similar point in discussing horizontal and vertical models as useful heuristics for organizational logics in global justice networks (cf. Robinson and Tormey 2005; Juris 2008).

logic to contentious collective action was exemplified in the most straightforward way by resource mobilization theory (RMT), in which social movement scholars explicitly adopted Olson's framing of the collective action problem and its organization-centered solution. Part of a broader group of thinkers who rejected the idea that social movements constituted irrational behavior based on social dysfunction, early RMT scholars accepted the problem of rational free-riders as a fundamental challenge and regarded organizations and their ability to mobilize resources as critical elements of social movement success. Classic formulations came from McCarthy and Zald (1973, 1977), who theorized the rise of external support and resources available to social movement organizations (SMOs) and focused attention on the professionalization of movement organizations and leaders in enabling more resource-intensive mobilization efforts.

The contemporary social movement field has moved well beyond the rational-choice orientation of such earlier work. Indeed, important traditions developed independently of, or by rejecting, all or parts of the resource mobilization perspective and by proposing that we pay more attention to the role of identity, culture, emotion, social networks, political process, and opportunity structures (Melucci 1989, 1996; Jasper 1997; McAdam, Tarrow, and Tilly 2001; cf. della Porta and Diani 2006). We do not suggest that these later approaches cling to rational-choice principles. We do, however, suggest that echoes of the modernist logic of collective action can still be found to play a background role even in work that is in other ways far removed from the rational-choice orientation of Olson's original argument.[15] This is apparent in assumptions about the importance of particular forms of organizational coordination and collective identity that underlie the attention given to organizations, resources, leaders, coalitions, brokering differences, and cultural or epistemic communities, as well as assumptions about the importance of formulating collective action frames and the bridging of differences among those frames. All of these issues become more marginal in analyzing connective action. Connective action networks may vary in terms of stability, scale, and coherence, but they are organized by different principles. Connective action networks are typically far more individualized and technologically organized sets of processes that result in action without the requirement of collective identity framing or the levels of organizational resources necessary to respond effectively to opportunities.

One of the most widely adopted approaches that moved social movement research away from its rational-choice roots and toward a more expansive

---

[15] We are not arguing that all contemporary analyses of collective action rely on resource mobilization explanations (although some do). Our point is that whether resource assumptions are in the foreground or background, many collective action analyses typically rely on a set of defining assumptions centered on the importance of some degree of formal organization and some degree of strong collective identity that establishes common bonds among participants. These elements become more marginal when one is thinking about the organization of connective action.

collective action logic is the analysis of collective action frames, which centers on the processes of negotiating common interpretations of collective identity linked to the contentious issues at hand (Snow et al. 1986; Snow and Benford 1988; Hunt, Benford, and Snow 1994, 2000). Such framing work may help to mobilize individuals and ultimately lower resource costs by maintaining individuals' emotional commitment to action. At the same time, the formulation of ideologically demanding, socially exclusive, or high-conflict collective frames also invites fractures, leading to an analytical focus on how organizations manage or fail to bridge these differences. Resolving these frame conflicts may require the mobilization of resources to bridge differences between groups that have different goals and ways of understanding their issues. Thus, while the evolution of different strands of social movement theory has moved it away from economic collective action models, many still tend to emphasize the importance of organizations that have strong ties to members and followers, and the resulting ways in which collective identities are forged and fractured among coalitions of those organizations and their networks.

Sustainable and effective collective action from the perspective of the broader logic of collective action typically requires varying levels of organizational resource mobilization deployed in organizing, providing leadership, developing common action frames, and employing brokerage to bridge organizational differences. The opening or closing of political opportunities affects this resource calculus (Tarrow 2011), but overall, large-scale action networks that reflect this collective action logic tend to be characterized in terms of the number of distinct groups networking to bring members and affiliated participants into the action and to keep them there. On the individual level, collective action logic emphasizes the role of social network relationships and connections as informal conditions for more centralized mobilization (e.g., in forming and spreading action frames, and forging common identifications and relations of solidarity and trust). At the organizational level, the strategic work of brokering and bridging coalitions between organizations with different standpoints and constituencies becomes central (cf. Diani forthcoming). Since the dynamics of action in networks characterized by this logic tends not to change significantly with digital media, this invites analysis primarily of how such technologies serve as tools to help actors do what they were already doing. However, we agree with a growing number of collective action scholars that media may play very different roles in different kinds of networks defined by different relationships at different network levels: between individuals and organizations, among organizations, and sometimes directly among individuals with media platforms serving as the primary organizational nodes (Earl and Kimport 2011; Bimber et al. 2012).

Defining the Logic of Connective Action

The *logic of connective action* foregrounds a different set of dynamics from the ones just outlined. At the core of this logic is the recognition of digital media as organizing agents. Several collective action scholars have explored how digital communication technology alters the parameters of Olson's original theory of collective action. Lupia and Sin (2003) show how Olson's core assumption about weak individual commitment in large groups (free-riding) may play out differently under conditions of radically reduced communication costs. Bimber, Flanagin, and Stohl (2005) in turn argue that public goods themselves may take on a new theoretical definition as erstwhile free-riders find it easier to become participants in political networks that diminish the boundaries between public and private – boundaries that are blurred in part by the simultaneous public–private boundary crossing of ubiquitous social media.

The most theoretically developed account of the contrasting economic logic underlying digitally mediated social networks is offered by Yochai Benkler in his aptly titled book *The Wealth of Networks* (2006). He proposes that participation in online networks can, under the right conditions, arise from self-motivation rather than external incentives, as personally expressive content is shared with, and recognized by, others who in turn repeat these networked sharing activities. Digital media scholars call this form of economic production "peer production" because it is based on voluntary cooperation among participants who contribute to a mutually valued project in order to produce a public good. That good or product would not be possible without the contribution of various skills or resources from different collaborators to create an openly accessible result, whether that result be a piece of software, a video, a file-sharing platform and the content contributed to it, or millions of people tweeting resources into protest crowds that may behave in surprising ways like organizations. The reward system for peer production is a mix of personal recognition for contributions to the network and the various goods or outcomes that result only from the sum of personally satisfying contributions. The objects of this kind of cooperative activity can, of course, range from the relatively trivial (e.g., FarmVille on Facebook) to the rather more impressive (Wikipedia and various other communities of knowledge development).

It is important to emphasize that the motivation for participation here is not altruism, which may easily arise also within market societies for various reasons, but a different economic logic in which the production of things (email links shared among friends, funny videos, software, websites, blogging communities, or protest coordination platforms) requires sharing, both as a division of labor and as a means of production. This applies to such examples as collaboratively understanding a computing or communication problem, writing a code to address it, and making it available to others. We also apply this perspective to more open-ended projects such as grappling with how to understand, engage with, and address political problems like environmental or economic crises. As we discuss later, it is important in this context to emphasize that connective action often leaves (digital) traces that help to configure the action space and the development of the networked organization within it, as when coordinating websites from old protests remain live online or in archived form to provide a historical record, memory narratives, and examples and models for future action to emulate or transcend.

This idea of a *sharing-based networked economic logic* points to the creation of fundamentally different technologies of association and social organization that enable this aspect of human action to be expressed, so the notion of technology-enabled association becomes important. While the communication potentials of digital networking surely do not determine particular modes of organization, they do enable forms of work and organization that may otherwise become difficult, cumbersome, or even impossible in hierarchical, organizationally bounded "silo society." Of course, much, and probably most, online communication does not work like this. The network principles of the Internet and the sharing capacities of interactive technologies enable peer production, but they do not determine it. Looking at most online newspapers, blogs, or political campaign sites makes it clear that the logic of the organization-centered, brick and mortar world is often reproduced online, with little change in organizational logic beyond possible efficiency gains (Bimber and Davis 2003; Foot and Schneider 2006).[16] Yet many socially mediated networks do operate with an alternative logic that also helps to explain why people labor collectively for free to create such things as open-source software, Wikipedia, WikiLeaks, and the Free and Open Source Software that powers many protest networks (Calderaro 2011), and to participate in the protests themselves.

When interpersonal networks are enabled by technology platforms of various designs that coordinate and scale the networks, the resulting action can resemble collective action, yet without the same role played by formal organizations or the need for exclusive, collective action framings. In place of content that is distributed and relationships that are brokered by hierarchical organizations, connective action networks involve co-production and co-distribution, revealing a different economic and psychological logic: peer production and sharing based on personalized expression. Personalized expression, as discussed later, is facilitated by more open, sometimes inclusive action framing (e.g., "We Are the 99%"), in contrast to the often exclusive, polarizing framing that occurs

[16] Whole areas of life online can be (and are) dominated by one economic logic or the other: witness the historic copyright battles between old media corporations and new media producers and consumers discussed by Lawrence Lessig in his organically crowdsourced book variously called *code*, *code 2.0*, *code 2.5* . . . , which has been developed collaboratively on a wiki with a community of co-producers (with Lessig getting the final edits) and can be downloaded legally: codev2.cc. (Also available under creative commons licensing is his more recent book, *Remix*: archive.org/details/Remix_219.) Nevertheless, to fully understand the different economic foundations of these ways of organizing relationships and affiliations, it is helpful to transcend stereotypical dichotomies such as found in the discourses on "private property vs. piracy" or in assumptions about what kind of people may choose one mode of organization or the other. On the latter point, it is interesting that the earliest example of a sharing, cooperative economy organized over a digital network can be attributed to the defense scientists who created the prototype Internet-like packet switching network ARPANET (Advanced Research Projects Agency Network) in the late 1960s to coordinate defense research projects. This pioneering scientific culture adopted a cooperative communication-based organizational form to better solve complex scientific problems. Fred Turner (2006) suggests that in many ways that scientific ethos mirrored a similar ethic of the contemporary counterculture that also understood the potential for technology to facilitate fundamentally different forms of social and economic organization.

in familiar collective action situations, demanding greater identification shifts from individuals (e.g., "Eat the Bankers"). For these theoretical reasons, we apply the term *connective action* to these digitally mediated networked modes of organization.

In this connective logic, taking public action or contributing to a common good becomes an act of personal expression and recognition or self-validation achieved by sharing ideas and actions in trusted relationships. Sometimes the people in these exchanges may be on opposite sides of the world, but they do not require a club, a party, or a shared ideological frame to make the connection. In place of the initial collective action problem of getting the individual to contribute, the starting point of connective action assumes contribution: the self-motivated (though not necessarily self-centered) sharing of already internalized or personalized ideas, plans, images, actions, and resources with networks of others. This "sharing" may take place on networking sites such as Facebook or via more public media such as Twitter and YouTube through, for example, comments and retweets, potentially building connections as it goes.[17]

Action networks characterized by a connective logic do not scale up automatically. The empirical questions we address later in the book include:

- When, why, and how do connective action networks scale up?
- Why do large-scale connective action networks emerge in some cases and not others?
- What power dynamics and political outcomes accompany these different patterns?
- What outcomes can we trace to different forms of connective protest organization?

Our observations suggest that personalized communication – the combination of easily disseminated personal action frames and personal digital communication technology enabling such communication – plays a key role in such processes. The next section develops this point and discusses how recognizing the central role of communication in networks in turn focuses analytical attention on the network as an organizational structure in itself.

Personal Action Frames and Social Media Networks

As we followed various world protests, we noted that they shared key features. In each case there was a dazzling array of personal action frames that spread through social media: the acts of sharing these personal calls to action and the social technologies through which they spread help explain both how events

---

[17] We are indebted to Bob Boynton for pointing out that this sharing occurs both in trusted friends networks such as Facebook and in more public exchange opportunities among strangers of the sort that occur on YouTube, Twitter, or blogs. Examining the dynamics and interrelationships among these different media networks and their intersections is an important direction for research.

are communicated to external audiences and how the action itself is organized. The personalized communication we observed was not defined by intimacy or as an overt expression of personal identity – indeed, some was anonymous. Instead, we identified two elements as particularly important in personalized communication and, by extension, in the development of large-scale connective action formations:

1. *Symbolic inclusiveness.* Large-scale connective mobilizations often involve political content in the form of easily personalized ideas such as "Put People First" in the London 2009 protests or "We Are the 99%" in the later Occupy protests. These frames require little in the way of persuasion, reason, or reframing to bridge differences in others' feelings about a common problem. *These personal action frames are inclusive of different personal reasons for contesting a situation that has to be changed.*

2. *Technological openness.* Most large-scale connective mobilizations are based on a variety of personal communication technologies that make it possible to share these inclusive themes. Whether through texts, tweets, social network sharing, or posting YouTube mashups via phone, computer or some other personal device, the communication process itself often involves further personalization through the spread of digital connections among friends, among trusted others, and beyond. Some sophisticated custom coordinating platforms begin to resemble organizations that exist more online than offline.

These two elements were present in each connective action case, even though the cases were intriguingly diverse in other ways.

The case of the Put People First protests (which we identify as organizationally enabled connective action) occupies an interesting middle part of the spectrum of collective to connective contentious action because so many conventional organizations were involved in the mobilization, from churches to social justice NGOs. Yet visitors to the sophisticated, stand-alone PPF coordinating platform (which served as an intriguing kind of organization in itself) were not asked to pledge allegiance to specific political demands on the organizational agendas of the protest sponsors. Instead, they were met with an impressive array of social technologies, enabling them to communicate in their own terms with each other and with various political targets. The centerpiece of the PPF site was a prominent text box under an image of a megaphone that invited the visitor to "Send your own message to the G20." Many of the messages to the G20 echoed the easy-to-personalize action frame of PPF, and they also revealed a broad range of personal thoughts about the crisis and possible solutions.

"Put People First" as a personal action frame was easy to shape and share with friends near and far. It became a powerful example of what students of viral communication refer to as a *meme*: a symbolic packet that travels easily across large and diverse populations because it is easy to imitate, adapt personally, and share broadly with others. Memes are network building and bridging units of social information transmission similar to genes in the biological sphere (Dawkins 1989). They travel by means of personal appropriation and then by imitation and personalized expression via social sharing in ways that help others appropriate, imitate, and share in turn (Shifman forthcoming). The simple PPF protest meme traveled interpersonally, echoing through newspapers, blogs, Facebook friend networks, Twitter streams, Flickr pages, and other sites on the Internet, leaving traces for years after the events.[18] Indeed, part of the meme traveled more than a year later to Toronto, where the leading civil society groups gave the name "People First" to their demonstrations. And many people in the large crowds in Seoul in the last G20 meeting of the series could be seen holding up red and white PPF signs in both English and Korean (Weller 2010).

The inclusiveness of personal action frames in crowd-enabled networks is captured nicely by the Occupy meme "We Are the 99%," which we discuss in more detail in Chapter 5. Another good example of inclusive discourses coordinated by crowds over technology platforms appeared in the website "15.10.11 united for #global change,"[19] created by anonymous activists to facilitate the series of global protests that developed alongside Occupy in 2011. Instead of the usual "Who are we?" section of the website, #globalchange asked, "Who are you?"

Sometimes these personal action frames travel far, as happened when crowds of *indignados* raised banners and chants of "Shhh . . . the Greeks are sleeping," a reference to the crushing debt crisis and severe austerity measures facing that country. This idea swiftly traveled to Greece, where members of Facebook networks agreed to set their alarm clocks at the same time in order to wake up and demonstrate. Banners in Athens proclaimed: "We've awakened! What time is it? Time for them to leave!" and "Shhh . . . the Italians are sleeping" and "Shhh . . . the French are sleeping."

Such efforts to send personalized protest themes across national and cultural boundaries met with various degrees of success, making for an important cautionary point: We want to stress that not all personal action frames travel equally well or equally far. The fact that these messages traveled more easily in Spain and Greece than in France or Italy is an interesting example that points to the need to study failures as well as successes. Just being easy to personalize (e.g., I am personally indignant about *x*, *y*, and *z*, and so I join with *los indignados*) does not ensure successful diffusion. Both political opportunities and conditions for social adoption may differ from situation to situation. For example, the limited success of the Italian action frames may reflect the existence of an already established popular antigovernment network centered on

---

[18] A Google search of "put people first g20" more than two years after the London events produced nearly 1.5 million hits, with most of them relevant to the events and issues of the protests well into 75 search pages.

[19] www.15october.net (accessed 19 October 2011).

comedian-activist Bepe Grillo. The French case may reflect the efforts of established groups on the left to lead incipient solidarity protests with the *indignados*, efforts that, ironically, became too heavy-handed in suggesting messages and action programs.

This means that personal action frames do not spread automatically. People must show each other how they can appropriate, shape, and share themes. In this interactive process of personalization and sharing, communication networks may become scaled up and stabilized through the digital technologies people use to share ideas and relationships with others. These technologies and their use patterns may remain in place as organizing mechanisms such that the communication processes come to represent important forms of organization in themselves. While the idea of memes helps us to focus on the transmission mechanisms involved, we will refer to the conceptual pairing of personal action frames and collective action frames to locate this discussion alongside the well-established social movement literature on framing (Snow and Benford 1988; Benford and Snow 2000).

In contrast to personal action frames, other calls to action more clearly require joining with established groups or ideologies. These more conventionally understood collective action frames are more likely to stop at the edges of communities and may require resources beyond communication technologies to bridge the gaps or align different collective frames (Snow and Benford 1988; Benford and Snow 2000). For example, another set of protests in London at the start of the financial crisis was organized by a coalition of more radical groups under the name G20 Meltdown. Instead of mobilizing the expression of large-scale personal concerns, they demanded ending the so-called neo-liberal economic policies of the G20, and some even called for an end to capitalism itself. Such demands typically come packaged with more high-cost calls to join in particular repertoires of a collective action. Whether those repertoires are violent or non-violent, they typically require the adoption of shared ideas and behaviors. These demonstrations drew on familiar anti-capitalist slogans and calls to "Storm the Banks" or "Eat the Rich" while staging dramatic marches behind "the four horsemen of the [economic] apocalypse" riding from the gates of old London to the Bank of England. These more radical London events drew smaller turnouts (some 5,000 turning out for the march on the Bank of England), higher levels of violence, and generally negative press coverage. While scoring high on commitment in terms of the personal costs of civil disobedience and displaying unity around anti-capitalist collective action frames, these demonstrations lacked the attributions of public worthiness (e.g., recognition from public officials, news coverage of its messages) and the large number of participants that gave PPF its higher levels of WUNC.

Collective action frames that place greater demands on individuals to share common identifications or political claims can also be regarded as memes, in the sense that slogans such as "Eat the Rich" have rich histories of social transmission. This particular iconic phrase may possibly date to Rousseau's quip "When the people shall have nothing more to eat, they will eat the rich." Such collective memes generally require more cultural work (ritual, socialization, artistic reproduction) to pass along networks through time, and of course, they are often not intended to be inclusive. The crazy course of the passage of "Eat the Rich" through the ages includes its appearance on T-shirts in the 1960s and in rock songs of that title by Aerosmith and Motörhead, just to scratch the surface of its history of travel through time and space, reflecting the sequence of cultural reproduction, appropriation, personal expression, and sharing.

Both personal and collective action frames can be highly emotionally compelling. However, as previously noted, as collective action frames become more exclusive and confrontational, more elaborate packaging and ritualized action may be required to reintroduce them into new contexts for a large number of followers. For example, the G20 Meltdown "Storm the Banks" march on the Bank of England involved an elaborate theatrical ritual with carnivalesque opportunities for creative expression as costumed demonstrators marched behind the four horsemen of the economic apocalypse. At the same time, the G20 Meltdown discourse was rather closed, requiring adopters to accept it for the confrontational call to action that it was. The Meltdown coalition had an online presence, but it did not offer easy means for participants to express themselves in their own voices, as we show more fully in our analysis in Chapter 2. This suggests that more demanding and exclusive collective action frames can also travel as memes, but more often they hit barriers at the intersections of social networks defined by established political organizations, ideologies, interests, class, gender, race, or ethnicity. Overcoming these barriers often requires resources beyond social technologies, if indeed the action frames are intended to cross those boundaries at all.

Where some forms of contention make it fairly clear whether the organizational work and primary relationship building are being done mainly online or offline, the frequently discussed online–offline distinction is decidedly not helpful most of the time when one is trying to understand the dynamics of connective action. While there may be some qualitative differences in relationships formed on- and offline, many of the most interesting dynamics in digitally mediated networks of contention may entail ties and frictions among people and organizations having both on- and offline relations. We thus seek to move the reader's attention beyond this distinction.

Moving Beyond Online versus Offline

As should be obvious, the differences we are sketching between personal and collective action frames are not related to whether the action and discourse are online or offline. There are, of course, many interesting cases of purely online activism that have impressive outcomes, and we can address them within our framework. We have been enlightened in this area by the work of Earl and Kimport (2011), among others, who demonstrate that many forms of contention could not be organized as effectively offline as online and that the results they achieve cannot be dismissed as mere "clicktivism." For the most part, however, the online–offline divide is itself misleading. Even when public attention is riveted on vast Twitter crowds or Facebook mobilizations, much of the action is embodied and enacted by people on the ground (Juris 2008; Routledge and Cumbers 2009). Moreover, social media do not play the same role in mobilizations such as Tahrir Square, Occupy, and the *indignados* that they do in mobilizations led by conventional political organizations that have discovered that social media can reduce the resource costs of public outreach and coordination. In Chapter 3 we contrast different roles of Twitter, for example, in two differently organized climate change protests. The question here is not whether a particular medium is being used, but how and in what context, by whom, and with what sort of control and conflict within organizations and broader user communities.

The main point here is that the same media may operate very differently in networks characterized by a connective or collective action logic. Even the same network organization type may develop differently depending on opportunity structures, ideological mixes of activists and organizations on the ground, presence of technology developers, and levels of state repression, among other factors. Despite these important variables, it is nonetheless possible to detect different organizational properties that involve different uses of the same digital media. Connective action networks are characterized not only by the spread of personal action frames but also by the prominence and layering of the communication networks that enable and facilitate the sharing of such frames.[20] They typically involve layers of communication technologies, many of which invoke "mundane" media that users take for granted (Kleis Nielsen 2011). These layers may include media forms ranging from websites, mobile phones, and flyers, as well as Facebook, YouTube, and Twitter and custom platforms that activists themselves create. The combination of personal action frames and personal communication technologies may result in complex and densely meshed networks of crosscutting relations, information, and action that have the capacity to scale up rapidly beyond the constraints of the brokered network. The transmission of personal expression across networks scales up, stabilizes, or becomes capable of targeted action depending on the kinds of social technology designed and appropriated by participants and the kinds of opportunities that may motivate anger or compassion among a large number of individuals. Thus, the Occupy Wall Street protests that spread in a month from New York to more than 80 countries and 900 cities around the world might not have succeeded without the inspiring models of the Arab Spring uprisings or the *indignados* protests in Spain, or the worsening economic conditions that provoked anger in an increasing number of displaced individuals.[21]

---

[20] *Layering* refers to networks emanating from different platforms that intersect and feed back into each other, sometimes evolving clear divisions of labor for different media, from SMS blasts to Twitter crowds.

[21] This convergence of human oppression, political opportunities, observing the examples of others, and finding available local tools of communication and organization may account

Personalized communication and the (occasionally) resulting connective action networks are intriguing political forms, since they enable individuals beset with similar problems and concerns to engage in collective action (more or less) on their own terms (i.e., using personal motives and issue definitions, and engaging in ways that suit the individual). This is not to say that individuals are thereby "empowered" in the sense that they can accomplish anything they desire or that they are equally placed in these processes. Many standard issues of social and political empowerment continue to operate, along with digital (and other) divides of access, skill, time, and economic resources. Moreover, many large-scale mobilizations have different forms of action organization, motivated by actors who hold different views about how to organize, how to communicate, and, ultimately, what to do. In this chapter we develop a framework that enables both researchers and practitioners to identify (a) which actors (b) use what organizational logic and (c) how the positions of these differently organized blocs in the larger protest ecology affect the coherence, stability, and impact of the action. This said, the emergence of flexible "weak tie" networks (Granovetter 1973) based in personal-level engagement through digital networking seems to have become important in enabling large-scale mobilizations to navigate complex and changing social and political landscapes. The intriguing question is: How does this work?

Communication Networks as Political Organization

The important point for the purposes of analyzing connective action is to understand the distinctive role that communication plays in these often densely interwoven networks of human actors, discourses, and technologies. Beyond sharing information and sending messages, the *organizing* properties of communication become prominent in connective action networks. Communication mechanisms establish relationships, activate attentive participants, channel various resources, and establish narratives and discourses.[22]

The organizational structure of people and social technology emerges more clearly if we draw on the actor-network theory of Latour (2005) in recognizing digital networking mechanisms (e.g., various social media and devices that run them) as potential network agents alongside human actors (i.e., individuals

---

for the diffusion of remarkably similar protest forms and repertoires discussed as "modular" political forms by Beissinger (2007).

[22] Although our thinking developed from a different direction, our focus on communication as organization overlaps with organization-theoretical approaches that view communication as constitutive of organization. (See among others Taylor and Van Every 2000; Putnam and Nicotera 2009; Blaschke, Schoeneborn, and Seidl 2012; see also Ashcraft, Kuhn, and Cooren 2009 and Cooren et al. 2011 for overviews of the different strands of research sharing this approach.) In particular, we share the basic assumptions that communication in various forms can have significant organizational properties and that non-human agents such as texts, sites, and digital mechanisms play an important role (Cooren 2000; 2004; Ashcraft, Kuhn, and Cooren 2009; Cooren et al. 2011).

and organizations). Latour referred to technologies as non-human "actants" in networks. This highlights how individuals interact with technology and how technology acts on individuals (including pushing information at them, spying on them, structuring action), which is in turn important for how people interact with each other on- and offline. Such digital mechanisms may include organizational connectors (e.g., web links), event coordination (e.g., protest calendars), information sharing (e.g., YouTube and Facebook), and multi-function networking platforms in which other networks become embedded (e.g., links in Twitter and Facebook posts), along with various capacities of the devices that run them. Also important are the traces that may remain behind on the Web to provide (often incomplete) memory records or action repertoires that might be passed on via different mechanisms associated with more conventional collective action such as rituals or formal documentation.

This means that connective action networks are replete with discursive net-working mechanisms (e.g., personal action frames) but also technological net-working mechanisms that structure action and relations in the networks. The presence or absence of digital mechanisms constrains and enables action in these often densely linked and navigable spaces. Different affordances invite different kinds of actions, sometimes in ways that go beyond what the designers envisaged.[23] At the same time, digital mechanisms at various levels help struc-ture relations among different actors, issues, and events, and calibrate relation-ships by establishing levels of transparency, privacy, security, and interpersonal trust (Elmer 2006; Foot and Schneider 2006; Braman 2006). Whether in auc-tions on eBay or protests in different cultural and social settings, the digital technologies through which connective networks are established and scaled are as such not value neutral in the way they enable action to be undertaken and organized and different kinds of communities to form.

Networking mechanisms play a role not just for the individual experience, but more broadly for the resulting connective action network. Many such networks are hybrid assemblages of different kinds of actors at different levels of the action that must be carefully traced (Chadwick 2013; cf. DeLanda 2006). As previously noted, these complex networks of people, organizations, and technologies may operate very differently under different conditions. In some cases, formal organizations carry the brunt of the organizational burden. In others, technology networks do.[24]

---

[23] Earl and Kimport (2011: 10) define an affordance as "the type of action or the characteristic of actions that a technology enables through its design." Even though affordances may go beyond what the designer intended, the design of technology significantly affects the properties of the network. Since humans design technologies and often give them specific value-driven discourse and decision-making capacities, the category boundaries between people and software may be blurring to the point that even laws are changing in terms of how we define rights, ownership, property, and agency (Braman 2002).

[24] Speaking of technology as a network agent or technology-enabled action networks should not be understood to imply that technology is *the* agent of social and political change (cf. Latour 2005: 70–74).

All of this means that recognizing the logic of connective action at the core of digitally networked action invites attention to networks in a particular way. Although there has been a recent surge of interest in networks in the context of contentious politics, in part due to the ideal of networked action associated with the global justice movement (Castells 2000, 2012; Bennett 2003, 2005; della Porta, Massimilano, and Mosca 2006; Juris 2008; Routledge and Cumbers 2009; Pleyers 2010), networks have always been a part of society, helping people navigate life within groups or between groups. The role of both strong and weak social ties in specifically contentious collective action has long been recognized (Tilly 1978; Snow, Zurcher, and Ekland-Olson 1980; Melucci 1989; Gould 1991, 1993; McAdam and Paulsen 1993; Diani 1995; Mische 2008; cf. Diani and McAdam 2003; Diani 2004; della Porta and Diani 2006; Tarrow 2011). Nevertheless, attention has been paid above all to networks as conditions for action, and in particular to the link between strong ties and recruitment to high-risk, high-cost participation such as in the civil rights movement or terrorist action (McAdam 1986, 1988a, 1988b; della Porta 1988; Chong 1991). In other cases, the focus on networks directed attention to inter-organizational alliances (Gerhards and Rucht 1992; Diani 1995; van Dyke and McCammon 2010). The connective networks that are becoming noticeable in late modern society, however, are multi-layered complexes of weak and strong ties – some with organizations in their midst, some with few formal organizations – that have organizationally interesting qualities in their own right (Castells 1996, 2000; cf. Monge and Contractor 2003). To understand the import of such networks, we need to think in terms beyond individual recruitment or brokered coalitions.

Communication technologies play into the dynamics of connective action in ways that shift focus from networks as conditions or pathways to participation to networks as organizational units. Mario Diani has stressed that social movement and civil society networks are important not only as precursors of collective action but also as organizational structures that transcend the elemental units of organizations and individuals (Diani 2003, forthcoming). This is, if anything, particularly striking in the case of digitally networked action. With the recombinant nature of the DNA that emerges through this logic, web spheres and their offline extensions go beyond communication systems to become flexible organizations in themselves, often enabling coordinated adjustments and rapid action aimed at shifting political targets, even crossing geographic and temporal boundaries in the process. Where classic starting points in the analysis of collective action typically highlight the relationships between individuals, or between individuals and organizations, this perspective moves across levels of action to think about individuals, organizations, and networks in one broad framework. Expanding our perspective to include technologies helps shed light on the formation of fluid organizational assemblages in which agency becomes shared or distributed across individuals and organizations as networks reconfigure in response to changing issues and events. Networking mechanisms embedded in the layers of networks become particularly important from this perspective, as they help calibrate the dynamics of the action.

We look more closely at digital networking mechanisms in Chapter 3, showing how in some cases crowds can use densely layered communication processes to attain some of the features of loosely bounded organizations, including (a) the mobilization and distribution of resources, (b) sensible responses to short-term external events, and (c) longer-term changes in internal coordination and adaptation (with various degrees of success and longevity). This understanding of communication-as-organization in technology-enabled networks illuminates both the organization of economic justice demonstrations analyzed in Chapter 2 and the issue advocacy networks on fair trade and climate change analyzed in Chapter 4.

Up to this point, the chapter has argued that collective and connective logics are distinct logics of action involving differences in (a) how individual identification processes are engaged by (b) different symbolic and discourse categories, (c) resulting in different choice processes and (d) different roles for communication mechanisms as means of coordinating the resulting actions. In reality, collective action and connective action often co-occur in various formations within the same action ecology. Nevertheless, it is possible to discern three ideal types of large-scale action networks with relevance to contemporary contentious politics. One is characterized primarily by collective action logic, but the other two are variations on connective action that are, among other things, distinguished by the role of formal organizations in facilitating personalized engagement. As previously noted, conventional organizations play a less central role than social technologies in relatively *crowd-enabled* networks such as those of the *indignados* of Spain, the Arab Spring, and Occupy. In contrast to these more technology-assisted networks, we also observe hybrid *organizationally enabled* networks (such as PPF) where conventional organizations operate in the background of protest and issue advocacy networks to enable large-scale personalized engagement. This hybrid form of organizationally enabled connective action sits in the mid-range of our continuum, with more familiar types of *organizationally brokered* collective action filling out the spectrum. The following section presents the details of this three-part typology. It also suggests that co-existence, layering, and movement across the types become an important part of the story.

A Typology of Connective and Collective Action Networks

We draw upon the two logics of action (and the hybrid organizationally enabled form that reveals a tension between them) to develop a three-part typology of large-scale action networks that feature prominently in contemporary contentious politics. One type represents the brokered organizational networks characterized by the logic of collective action, but the other two represent the significant variations on networks characterized primarily by the logic of connective action, which constitute our focus for the remainder of this book.

All three models may explain differences between and dynamics within large-scale action networks in event-centered contention, such as protests and sequences of protests, as in the examples we have already discussed. They may also apply to more stable issue advocacy networks that engage people in everyday life practices that support causes outside of protest events such as campaigns. The typology is intended as a broad generalization to help us understand different dynamics. None of the types are exhaustive social movement models. Thus, this is not an attempt to capture, much less resolve, the many differences among those who study social movements. We simply want to highlight the rise of two forms of digitally networked connective action that differ from some common assumptions about collective action in social movements and, in particular, that rely on mediated networks for substantial aspects of their organization. Figure 1.1 presents an overview of the two connective action network types and contrasts their organizational properties with more familiar collective action network organizational characteristics.

Organizationally Brokered Collective Action

The ideal collective action type on the right side of the figure describes large-scale action networks that depend on brokering organizations to carry the burden of facilitating cooperation and bridging differences when possible. As the anti-capitalist direct action groups in the G20 London Summit protests exemplified, such organizations tend to promote more exclusive collective action frames that require frame bridging if they are to grow. As discussed further in Chapter 2, these organizationally brokered networks may use digital media and social technologies primarily as means of mobilizing and managing participation and coordinating goals rather than inviting personalized interpretations of problems and action. In addition to a number of classic social movement accounts (e.g., McAdam 1986), several of the NGO networks discussed by Keck and Sikkink (1998) are in accord with this type (Bennett 2005).

Crowd-Enabled Connective Action

At the other extreme from organizationally brokered collective action, we identify connective action networks that are organized by the crowd largely without central or "lead" organizational actors, as shown on the left in Figure 1.1. Our cases of Twitter streams used by global climate change protests in Chapter 3 and the emergence of a discourse on economic inequality from Occupy networks in Chapter 5 suggest different ways in which technologies become prominent organizational agents, and personal action frames overshadow collective action frames as the transmission units across social networks. A lot of face-to-face organizing work may go on in these cases, and daily agendas and decisions are often significantly shaped offline. However, the networks are primarily technology-enabled and subject to notable reconfiguring as sub-networks shift

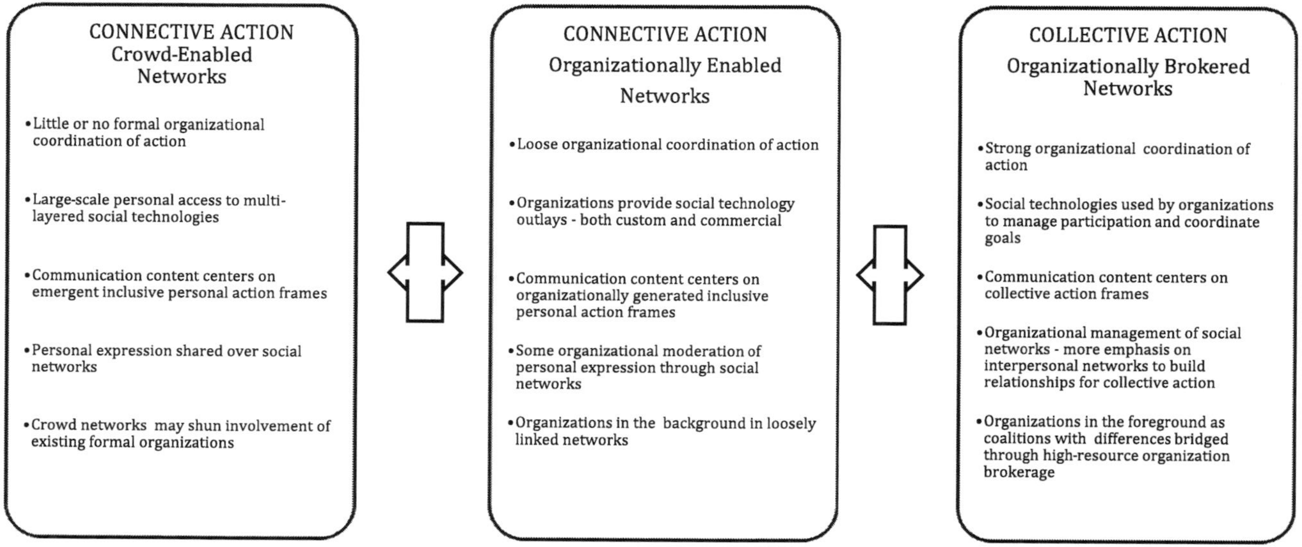

CONNECTIVE ACTION
Crowd-Enabled Networks

- Little or no formal organizational coordination of action

- Large-scale personal access to multi-layered social technologies

- Communication content centers on emergent inclusive personal action frames

- Personal expression shared over social networks

- Crowd networks may shun involvement of existing formal organizations

CONNECTIVE ACTION
Organizationally Enabled Networks

- Loose organizational coordination of action

- Organizations provide social technology outlays - both custom and commercial

- Communication content centers on organizationally generated inclusive personal action frames

- Some organizational moderation of personal expression through social networks

- Organizations in the background in loosely linked networks

COLLECTIVE ACTION
Organizationally Brokered Networks

- Strong organizational coordination of action

- Social technologies used by organizations to manage participation and coordinate goals

- Communication content centers on collective action frames

- Organizational management of social networks - more emphasis on interpersonal networks to build relationships for collective action

- Organizations in the foreground as coalitions with differences bridged through high-resource organization brokerage

FIGURE 1.1. Defining elements of connective and collective action networks.

47

their activities and the crowd responds to external events such as police raids on camps or positive recognition from politicians and celebrities.

We use the term *crowd-enabled* to put the focus on the (networked) structures that emerge from the local interactions of numerous individual actors but that become connected across time and space via various, often densely layered technology networks (cf. Bonabeau, Dorigo, and Theraulaz 1999: 6; Castells 2000). This choice of terminology is intended to balance human agency, technology, and the ongoing interplay of power dynamics and organizational change. It also seeks to avoid confusion with the self-organization of purely spontaneous emergent patterns and with the more purposefully intentional kind of self-organization that has been studied in bounded groups seeking a common goal (e.g., Ostrom 1990; Mueller 2010).

Organizationally Enabled (Hybrid) Connective Action

As shown in Figure 1.1, and discussed in the introduction and earlier in this chapter, perhaps the most intriguing organizational type in our scheme is the organizationally enabled (hybrid) connective action network type that lies between the organizationally brokered and the crowd-enabled types. The role of personalized action framing and digital media networking distinguishes these networks from more conventional collective action networks that may involve similar or even the same organizations operating in different political contexts. An important task for our empirical analyses is to show how organizations in these networks behave differently than *even the same organizations* might behave when they join in more conventionally organized interest lobbying or movement networks. As our cases in Chapter 4 show, these organizationally enabled networks may be centered around prominent, resource-rich NGOs of the sort that may also appear in some more classic movement configurations (cf. Diani forthcoming). However, the key to the organizationally enabled network action repertoire is that constituent organizations adopt the signature mode of personalizing the engagement of publics. In particular, this means deploying discourses and interactive media that offer greater choice over how people may engage. This personalization leads to necessarily relaxed relations with other organizations in the network due to mutual requirements to put harder-edged demands and issue frames in the background. We show in Chapter 4 that these loosely organized issue networks often deploy impressive and broadly shared batteries of digital mechanisms for personalizing the ways individuals may engage with the issues and causes that matter to the network actors.

Animating the Typology: Overlaps and Dynamics in Network Forms

The real world is, of course, far messier than this three-type model. The model is intended to help put the spotlight on broad differences, general tendencies, and dynamic tensions in forms of mobilization. In reality, the three forms of network organization interact and overlap, and various tensions may arise when they come into conflict. In some cases, we see action formations corresponding to our three types side by side in the same action space. The G20 London protests offered a rare case in which organizationally enabled and more conventional collective action were neatly separated on different days. More often, the different forms layer and overlap, and sometimes we see organizational changes over time. Such variations on different organizational forms offer intriguing opportunities for further analyses aimed at explaining whether mobilizations achieve various goals and attain different levels of WUNC.

For example, crowds often have interesting kinds of relationships with more formal organizations both on their peripheries and in their midst. One common pattern involves conventional political organizations deliberately being forced out, being relegated to background roles, or otherwise being marginalized by the crowd. This is exemplified by the ways in which the *indignados* actively discouraged visible participation or claims to leadership by formal organizations such as unions (which would otherwise be at the head of many economic justice protests in Spain). Similar policing by the crowd occurred during the Tahrir Square uprisings in Egypt in 2011, as many members of the crowd sought to avoid co-optation of the movement by the Muslim Brotherhood (the largest and best-organized civil society network that survived the repression of the Mubarak regime). However, efforts to transform the movement into some sort of Tahrir 2.0 organization that could compete in the elections that the protests effectively triggered proved less successful. The ironic result was that the Brotherhood became the main beneficiary of the 2012 elections, suggesting the importance of tensions that play out between crowds and more conventionally organized political networks as opportunity structures shift.

The idea of crowds transforming their organizational structures in response to opportunities and other external conditions is developed further in Chapter 3 as we observe organizational resource-seeking behavior in a Twitter stream that became part of the larger protest ecology at the UN Climate Change Conference in Copenhagen in 2009 (COP15). We observed an increase in links to particular kinds of outside organizations inserted in tweets of the #cop15 hashtag that emerged during the Copenhagen protests. The shifting link patterns occurred as the stream tailed off over the course of the next year. These increasing links to organizations (many of them digital media organizations such as climate blogs) helped stabilize and sustain the #cop15 Twitter stream until its eventual "handoff" to a successor #cop16 hashtag that spiked during the next UN climate conference.

Another kind of dynamic that may occur in crowd-enabled connective action involves the tensions between local face-to-face groups and the larger network of bystanders and distant local groups that may have different agendas and values. There may be various organizational presences operating in the shadow of larger crowds. In the case of Occupy in the United States, for example, the dispersed city assemblies and encampments represented nascent organizational nodes of the network, indicating that even these relatively informal networks developed some capacities of conventional organization in terms of resource mobilization and intentional network building without seeking to impose strong ideological brands or collective identities.[25] Thus, many of the general assemblies in the Occupy protests became resource centers, with regular attendance, division of labor, allocation of money and food, and coordination of actions. At the same time, the thick communication networks that swirled around these protest nodes greatly expanded the nature and impact of the larger network, making the whole organization greater or at least different than the sum of its parts. Moreover, as we discuss in Chapter 6, the surrounding technology networks invited loosely tied participation that was often in tension with the face-to-face ethos of the assemblies, where more committed protesters spent long hours with a dwindling number of peers debating how to expand participation without diluting the levels of commitment and action that they deemed core to their value scheme. Thus, even as parts of Occupy displayed concerted self-organization, the overall organization was defined primarily as a crowd-enabled movement. The strain between the different layers was part of its decline.

This said, emergent groups within a crowd differ in many ways from the organizational profiles that define the hybrid middle type, which involves formal organizational actors stepping back from projecting strong agendas, political brands, and collective identities in favor of using resources to deploy social technologies enabling loose public networks to form around personalized action themes. This pattern fit the PPF demonstrations discussed earlier (and again in Chapter 2), where some 160 civil society organizations – including major NGOs such as Oxfam, Tearfund, Catholic Relief, and the World Wildlife Fund – stepped back from their organizational brands to form a loose social network inviting publics to engage with each other and take action. They did this even as they negotiated with other organizations over things like which day would be reserved for which kind of protest. At the same time, the uses of personal action frames and digital technologies to share them become common defining elements of the two types of connective action.

The configurations of network ties, technology, and discourses of issue engagement in this middle – organizationally enabled – network type reflect the pressures that Bimber, Flanagin, and Stohl (2005, 2012) observe in interest organizations that are suffering from declining memberships and have had to develop looser, more entrepreneurial relations with followers. Just as particular organizations use social technologies to develop loose ties with followers, so do many organizations develop loose ties with other organizations to form vast online networks that share and bridge various causes. Although these networks differ in scale and complexity from the social networks that Granovetter (1973) observed, we associate his idea about the strength of weak ties in such networks with the elements of connective action: loose organizational linkages, technology deployments, and personal action frames. Chapter 4 traces

25 We thank a referee for *Information, Communication & Society* for highlighting this possibility as a subtype in the model.

the pattern of issue advocacy organizations that facilitate personalized protest networks in a number of economic justice and environment networks, charting protests, campaigns, and issue networks in the United Kingdom and Germany. In each case, we found (with theoretically interesting variations) campaigns, protest events, and everyday issue advocacy networks that displayed similar organizational signatures: (a) familiar NGOs and other civil society organizations joining loosely together to provide something of a networking backbone (b) for digital media networks personalizing the engagement of publics with contested political issues, yet with (c) remarkably few efforts to brand the issues around specific organizations, own the messages, impose collective framing, or otherwise control the understandings of individual participants. The organizations had their political agendas on offer, to be sure, and there were plenty of educational materials just a click away, but the face of an organizationally enabled networked organization entails social technologies enabling personal engagement through easy-to-share images and personal action frames.

The organizations that refrain from strongly branding their causes or policy agendas in this hybrid model do not give up their broader missions or agendas as name-brand public advocacy organizations. Instead, some organizations interested in mobilizing large and potentially WUNC-y publics in an age of social networking are learning to shift among different organizational repertoires, morphing from hierarchical, mission-driven NGOs in some settings to facilitators in loosely linked public engagement networks in others. As noted by Chadwick (2007, 2013), organizational hybridity makes it difficult to apply fixed categories to many organizations as they variously shift from being issue advocacy NGOs to policy think tanks, to SMOs running campaigns or protests, to multi-issue organizations, to networking hubs for connective action. In other words, depending on when, where, and how one observes an organization, it may appear to be an NGO, SMO, international NGO, transnational NGO, nongovernmental development organization, interest advocacy group, political networking hub, and so on.[26] Indeed, one of the advantages of seeing the different logics at play in the typology is to move away from fixed categorization schemes and to observe actually occurring combinations of different types of action within complex protest ecologies, as well as shifts in dominant types in response to events and opportunities over time.

In such varying ways, personalized connective action networks cross paths (sometimes with individual organizations morphing in the process) with more conventional collective action networks centered on SMOs, interest organizations, and brand-conscious NGOs. This intersection of organizational forms in practical contexts is one reason we argue for thinking about these networks as organizations. However, most formal, stand-alone organizations are centered (e.g., located in physical space), hierarchical, bounded by mission and territory,

---

[26] See also Bimber, Flanagin, and Stohl (2012) for an interesting discussion of why it is increasingly difficult to classify given organizations in particular categories.

and defined by relatively known and countable memberships (or in the case of political parties, known and reachable demographics). By contrast, many of today's issue and cause networks are relatively de-centered (constituted by multiple organizations and many direct and cyber activists), distributed, or flattened organizationally as a result of these multiple centers, relatively unbounded in the sense of crossing both geographical and issue borders, and dynamic in terms of the changing populations who may opt in and out of play as different engagement opportunities are presented (Bennett 2003, 2005). Understanding how connective action engages or fails to engage diverse populations under such conditions constitutes part of the analytical challenge ahead.

Compared with the vast number of theoretically grounded studies on social movement and advocacy and interest coalition organizing, there is relatively little theoretical work that helps explain the range of connective action formations running from relatively crowd-enabled to organization-enabled connective action networks. While there are many pathbreaking accounts of connective action (e.g., Castells 2000; Rheingold 2002), we are concerned that the organizational logic and underlying dynamic of such action is not yet well established. It is important to gain a clearer understanding of how such networks function and what organizing principles explain their growing prominence in contentious politics.

Conclusion

Digitally networked action is emerging during a historic shift in late modern democracies in which, most notably, younger citizens are moving away from parties, broad reform movements, and ideologies. Individuals are relating differently to organized politics, and many organizations are finding they must engage people differently. They are developing relationships to publics as affiliates rather than as members and offering them personal options for engaging and expressing themselves. Thus, they are giving them a greater choice as to the content they contribute and introducing micro-organizational resources in terms of personal networks, content creation, and technology development skills. Collective action based on exclusive collective identifications and strongly tied networks continues to play a role in this political landscape, but it has been joined by, interspersed with, and in some cases supplanted by personalized collective action formations in which digital media become integral organizational parts. Some of the resulting DNA networks turn out to be surprisingly nimble, demonstrating intriguing flexibility across various conditions, issues, and scale. Others, as we have seen, dissolve.

It has been tempting for some critics to dismiss participation in such networks as noise, particularly in reaction to sweeping proclamations by enthusiasts of the democratic and participatory power of digital media. Whether from digital enthusiasts or critics, hyperbole is unhelpful. Understanding the potential and effectiveness of connective and collective action formations – democratic or otherwise – requires careful analysis. At the same time, there is often considerably more going on in DNA than clicktivism or facile organizational outsourcing of social networking to various commercial sites. A key point of this argument is that fully explaining and understanding such action and contention requires more than just adjusting the classic social movement collective action schemes. Connective action has a logic of its own, and thus attendant dynamics of its own. It deserves analysis on its own terms.

The linchpins of connective action are the formative elements of sharing and co-production: the networking elements of personalization that make it possible for actions and content to be distributed widely across social networks. Communication technologies enable the growth and stabilization of network structures across these networks. Together, the technological agents that enable the constitutive role of sharing in these contexts displace the free-rider calculus and, with it, the dynamic that flows from it – most obviously, the logical centrality of the resource-rich organization. In its stead, connective action brings the action dynamics of recombinant networks into focus, a situation in which networks and communication become something more than mere preconditions and providers of information. What we observe in these networks are applications of communication technologies that contribute an organizational principle that is different from notions of collective action based on core assumptions about the role of resources, networks, and collective identity. We call this core structuring principle the logic of connective action. Analyzing connective action networks and their variation requires attention to networks as organizational units.

Developing ways to analyze connective action formations will give us more solid grounds for attending to some persistent questions about digitally networked action to do with its sustainability, impact, and power. As noted in the margins throughout this discussion, technology-enabled action presupposes power on several levels: there are the implications of digital divides, the ways in which code and affordances help shape action and user communities, and the vulnerabilities involved in depending on technology controlled by others. Beyond this, the following chapters, and particularly Chapter 5, explore further questions about the power in and power of large-scale connective networks taken as a whole.

We approach these issues through empirical cases without presuming that digitally networked action is necessarily successful. Just as traditional collective action efforts can fail to result in sustained or effective movements, there is nothing preordained about the results of digitally mediated networking processes. Even as the contours of political action may be shifting, it is imperative to develop means of thinking meaningfully about what sustainability and effectiveness in relation to connective action may mean and to gain a systematic understanding of how such action plays out in different contexts and conditions. Such understanding is essential if we are to attain a clear view of some of the most prominent forms of public engagement in the digital age.

In the next chapter, we address a set of core concerns about power in such networks by asking a question about political capacity: In what measurable ways is digitally networked action – that is, connective action – politically effective? Chapter 2 explores conventional measures of political capacity of collective action in democratic settings that focus on mobilization, agenda setting, and the ability to sustain engagement and effort over time. These continue to be important issues with respect to connective action as well. The chapter analyzes a rich series of protests that began in London and followed the meetings of the G20 around the world during the early days of the global economic crisis. We compare how activists and concerned citizens of many different political stripes seized the crisis as an opportunity to pressure elites and fellow citizens to rethink the assumptions and policies of the neo-liberal economic regime.

2

Personalized Communication in Protest Networks

As discussed in the introduction, activists have associated a host of issues with what they regard as the neo-liberal economic project of globalization. These issues include labor market inequities, both north and south; poor working conditions and lack of labor protections; unfair trade practices and their impacts on community sustainability and quality of life in the global south; and a collection of environmental effects, such as the acceleration of species extinction, food and water shortages, and global warming. For many activists these and other challenges add up to a growing precariousness of life (sometimes termed *precarity*) both for individuals and for humankind. Indeed, a common critique of the neo-liberal agenda is that risks of different sorts have been offloaded to individuals as states cut back public goods and services in favor of privatization programs, while businesses seek to reduce commitments to workers through technology innovations, outsourcing, hiring of temporary labor, and reductions in job security and benefits.

These political conditions present interesting dilemmas for organizing protest politics (Smith and Wiest 2012). First, government control over many of these issues has become problematic, meaning that political pressure must be targeted at diverse local, national, and transnational institutions, as well as at corporations using global business models to escape regulation. Second, both within nations and transnationally, political issues are interrelated in ways that cut across conventional social movement sectors: labor and human rights often occupy common agendas, and economic justice initiatives align with environmental causes. The organizational incentives for greater flexibility in defining issues, targets, and protest strategies are magnified by a third factor involving the growing separation of individuals in late modern societies from

An earlier version of this chapter was originally published as "Digital Media and the Personalization of Collective Action: Social Technology and the Organization of Protests against the Global Economic Crisis," *Information, Communication & Society*, 14, no. 6 (2011), pp. 770–799. Reprinted by permission of Taylor & Francis (www.tandfonline.com).

traditional bases of social solidarity, such as parties, churches, unions, and other mass organizations. This separation results in the individualization of risk and responsibility, which has been glorified in discourses of personal freedom by neo-liberals and condemned in terms of injustice and precarity by many activists. Whether regarded as good or bad, these very individuation processes also lead people to seek more personalized paths to political engagement, even when a large number of individuals recognize and have common problems. In this chapter we focus on how social individuation and related personalization of politics give rise to an interesting mix of challenges and opportunities for organizing collective political action.

The most familiar social protest formations associated with modern society have been – and, in many cases, still are – organized around single issues, such as peace, nuclear power, or group rights, and issues defined in terms of ideology or group identity, such as race, gender, religion, or ethnicity. Increasingly characteristic of late modern, individuated societies are personalized forms of contention that involve multiple causes and are engaged through personal lifestyles (Melucci 1989, 1996; Giddens 1991; Inglehart 1997; Bennett 1998; Touraine 2000; Beck and Beck-Gernsheim 2002; Micheletti 2003; della Porta 2005). The organization of political meanings around lifestyle elements (e.g., brands, leisure pursuits, jobs, traffic, health, or the interests of friends and social networks) results in the personalization of issues such as climate change (e.g., personal carbon footprints), labor standards (e.g., clothes choices), food production (e.g., fair trade consumer practices and slow food), and economic downturns (mortgage assistance and student loan relief). Seemingly disparate issues become related as they fit into crosscutting demographics and consumer lifestyles (Micheletti 2003).

The personalized action forms that often accompany this more flexible approach to issues raise questions among more traditional activists and observers about their political impact or effectiveness. At a theoretical level, questions have been raised about collective action dilemmas produced by individuals resisting formal organizational memberships and instead seeking more personal choices regarding how to act and how closely to align with organizational definitions of issues, causes, and standards of commitment (Bimber, Flanagin, and Stohl 2005, 2012; Flanagin, Stohl, and Bimber 2006). How to channel organizational resources efficiently to less manageable publics is a familiar problem that confronts election campaigns, issue advocacy and interest lobbying networks, and social movement coalitions.

As explained in Chapter 1, the growing demand for personalized relations with causes and organizations makes digital technologies increasingly central to the organization and conduct of collective action. Communication technologies aimed at personalizing engagement facilitate organizational communication and coordination at the same time as they enable flexibility in how, when, where, and with whom individuals may affiliate and act. Greater individual control over the terms of action creates the potential for more personalized identifications than may be characteristic of the collective framing commonly associated with organization-centered and leader-driven protests (McDonald

2002; della Porta 2005). It also creates the potential for personal networks to play a more prominent role in protests. While networks have long been recognized to be important in protest mobilization, as has the related capacity of "bridging" organizational- and personal-level networks to facilitate the diffusion of information and appeals (McAdam 1988b; Gould 1991, 1993; Diani 1995; Carrol and Ratner 1996; Diani and McAdam 2003; Mische 2003; Kavanaugh et al. 2005; della Porta and Mosca 2007), recent evidence suggests that digitally networked individuals with multiple affiliations, identities, and rich network connections are becoming increasingly central in large protests (Bennett, Breunig, and Givens 2008). Indeed, the widespread adoption of digital media may be shifting the burden of mobilization from organizations to individuals (Walgrave et al. 2011).

All of these trends suggest that the personalization of political action presents protest organizers with a set of fundamental challenges, chief among which concerns negotiating what they perceive as a trade-off between flexibility and effectiveness. For organizations trying to mobilize the type of participants who seek greater personalization in affiliation, definition, and expression, the associated demands of flexibility may challenge the standard models for achieving effective collective action (e.g., organizational coalitions based on shared political agendas expressed through ideological or solidarity-based collective action frames). The problem is that personalized communication would seem to be at odds with the emphasis on unity and alignment conventionally associated with the communication processes of effective collective action. The puzzle we address here is how large-scale and effective political action can be achieved under conditions of digitally enabled personalization. Put another way, our questions in this chapter concern the scale, sustainability, and outcomes of connective action.

Personalized politics may, of course, take different forms, some of which are relatively independent, while some assume large numbers of people acting in highly coordinated events. In some cases, personalized action may stem from self-absorbed or self-centered concerns (Dean 2010; Van Deth 2012). However, the forms that we examine in this book revolve around common problems and, at least for some, even stem from concerns for the political commons and the common good (Hands 2011). In this chapter, we examine different pathways to engaging in protests aimed at the same political targets and organized in response to a common political situation: the global financial crisis that struck many nations beginning in 2008–2009. In particular, we look at how a large number of people found more or less personalized ways to join in public displays of protest. We contrast these large-scale connective actions with collective actions organized by more conventional, ideologically focused groups.

Digital Networks: The DNA of Personalized Politics

The chapter analyzes how two different networks in the G20 London Summit protests in 2009 – one more "connective" and the other more "collective" – employed respectively more and less personalized communication strategies with their publics by inviting different degrees of flexibility in

affiliation, issue definition, and expression. These dimensions of personalization are observed both in terms of action framing and, perhaps more important,
in the uses of various types of digital media. In keeping with the definition in
the preceding chapter, we understand an organization's or coalition's public
communication to be personalized if it involves (a) *symbolic inclusiveness*, as
defined by the presence of cues and opportunities for customizing engagement
with issues and actions and the relative absence of cues (e.g., collective action
frames) that signal ideological and definitional unanimity; and (b) *technological openness*, as defined by the presence of digital media that permit interaction
and networking between individuals and organizations and directly between
individuals.

After analyzing how the London protest networks used digital media to
engage diverse individuals, we examine what such processes meant for the
political capacity of the respective coalitions. The chapter analyzes three questions about digital communication in protest organization, all of which address
the issue of whether mobilizing individualized publics may come at the cost
of undermining the conventional political capacity of the resulting action
networks. The questions revolve around the networks' capacity to engage
publics, set their agenda, and sustain their organizational network. In particular, we explore whether the coalition offering looser organizational affiliations with individuals (the organizationally enabled Put People First connective action network) displayed any notable loss of public engagement, policy
focus, or mass media impact. We also examine whether the organizationally brokered anti-capitalist coalition (in this respect a more conventional
collective action network) displayed any evident gain in network coherence,
dominance, and stability according to the measures introduced later in the
chapter.

Throughout this discussion, it is important to recognize that protest organizers have different views about the goals of protest as well as about using
communication technology for these purposes. Depending on the actors' goals,
conditions, and ideologies, various kinds of media present differing opportunities and limitations (Diani 2000; Stein 2009; Mattoni et al. 2010; Lievrouw
2011; Cammaerts 2012; Mattoni 2012). Just like individuals, organizations
have differing resources of skill, time, and money to dedicate to digital media.
Some may judge that face-to-face interaction is the best way to mobilize their
grass roots and, if their goal includes reaching wider publics, may or may
not judge mainstream media to be helpful in getting the message out. There
may be concerns about surveillance or about depending on media that others
control, leading to a reluctance to make use of existing technology or efforts
to develop custom technologies. Further, ideological resistance to commercial
media or preferences for certain kinds of mediated action may also influence
organizational decisions about technology use; there may be underlying media
preferences associated with different styles of activism. The analysis in this
chapter, however, does not delve into why the organizers of the G20 protests
communicated as they did. It focuses instead on what they did in their public

digital communication in order to spotlight concerns about personalization, connective action, and its political capacity.

Dilemmas of Personalized Communication in the Organization of Protest Networks

As previously noted, personalized communication involving inclusive action frames and open technologies entails greater opportunities for individuals to define issues in their own terms and to network with others through social media, thus distributing the organizational burden among participants who may look to NGOs and SMOs more as facilitators than as active directors or leaders of actions. As also noted, this typically entails relaxing the requirement for more unified public communication processes (e.g., collective action frames) often associated with efficacious collective action.

Concerns about trends toward personalized political action have been expressed by social movement scholars who theorize collective identity framing as crucial to the coherence of protest actions (Benford and Snow 2000; Tilly 2004; Tarrow 2011). At the same time, many observers also agree that protests in this era of relaxed individual affiliation have often been impressive in terms of speed of mobilization, scope of issues, and ability to focus public attention on these issues in the short term. The core issue here seems to be whether the very features of contemporary connective action protests that are so impressive are also the ones that may undermine conventional political capacity such as maintaining agenda focus and strong coalition relationships (Bennett 2003). Critics doubt that loose multi-issue networks that are easy to opt in and out of generate the commitment, coherence, and persistence of action required to produce political change (Diani 2000; Tilly 2004). Variations on these concerns have been expressed by organizational communication scholars who question the capacity of organizations that impose strong membership requirements to mobilize publics that confer legitimacy on their causes or, conversely, ask whether the pursuit of more independent-minded publics reduces the integrity of organization identity and mission (Bimber 2003; Bimber, Flanagin, and Stohl 2005).

Viewed from these perspectives, protest organizers face two potentially contradictory challenges. On the one hand, there is the task of engaging individualized citizens who spurn conventional membership for the pursuit of personalized political action. Since such citizens may be less receptive to unambiguous ideological or organization-centered collective action frames, the question becomes how to mobilize them. On the other hand, organizations continue to face the challenge of achieving conventional political goals, which requires maintaining political capacity in areas such as mobilization and agenda control. In the language of political action that has developed in modern democracies, the effectiveness of collective action has hung on what Charles Tilly described as the ability to display "WUNC": worthiness, unity, numbers, and commitment (Tilly 2004). It has also involved developing relations with the targets of protests and the ability to clearly communicate the claims being made. The capacity to develop and maintain WUNC and relations with targets, in turn, has depended on sustaining a certain level of formal and centralized organization (McAdam, Tarrow, and Tilly 2001; Tarrow 2011).

The pressing question when it comes to the organization of contentious collective action is how to develop WUNC and maintain focus on political targets while sharing communicative control with individuals and other organizations. Communicating with publics through personalized (i.e., interactive and social networked) digital media seemingly compounds the tension between the two challenges. Various technologies may facilitate flexible communication as previously described, but the interactivity of the digital and social media also threatens to compromise organizational control over communication and action (Foot and Schneider 2006; Gillan, Pickerill, and Webster 2008; Fenton and Barassi 2011).

The struggle to balance flexibility and control is often reflected in the organization's most public of faces, its website. Many organizations use their website strategically to present information about themselves, their cause, and proposed actions (della Porta and Mosca 2009; Stein 2009). Aside from posting information, they may provide signals about themselves and their cause by linking to other organizations and inviting individual connections with members of the public (e.g., joining a Facebook group). In a dynamic similar to "friending" others on social networking sites, the extent to which other actors publicly respond – for example, by linking back, becoming fans, and contributing content – becomes part of the organization's public profile (boyd and Heer 2006; Donath 2007; Kavada 2009). Like the producers of fictional trans-media narratives (Jenkins 2006), protest organizers may choose to offer various points of entry into the protest space that speak to different publics. The organization's actions both enable and constrain action in the contemporaneous protest space (Foot and Schneider 2006) and potentially establish "sedimentary" digital structures (Chadwick 2007), such as email lists that may be reactivated or redirected for future action (e.g., see the multiple uses of the follower lists from the Obama 2008 election campaign). As with fictional "fan edits," however, user contributions not only help constitute the organizational protest space but also expand it (e.g., through web links) and may end up diluting or contradicting the organization's messages about itself and its cause.

Three basic questions about the digital communication of organized protest thus emerge as central for assessing the general concern about whether looser organizational communication with publics undermines conventional political capacities associated with an organized protest:

- Does personalized communication undermine engagement strength (commitment and mobilization capacity)?
- Does personalized communication undermine agenda strength?
- Does personalized communication weaken organizational network strength?

The first question, about engagement strength, approaches the personalization of organizational communication from the perspective of participant mobilization in a protest. The ability to mobilize a large number of co-present participants has evolved as a central means for organizations to signal the commitment of their supporters to both the targets of the protest and the general public (Tilly 2004). Early social movement framing theory underlined the importance for the mobilization process of communicating clear frames and alignment between the organization and the supporters' interpretative frames (Snow et al. 1986; cf. Polletta 1998). Subsequent studies explored how various kinds of heterogeneity reduce the effects of particular frames (e.g., Druckman and Nelson 2003; Heaney and Rojas 2006). If organizations, by contrast, work to personalize communication about their proposed actions, does this complicate protest coordination to the extent that it makes turnout weak and unpredictable and more difficult to convey as a unified act of commitment?

The latter issue relates to the second question, which centers on another conventional measure of political capacity: the ability to communicate clear collective claims to the targets of a protest and the general public (agenda strength). While new media grant protest organizers crucial means of bypassing mass media (Bennett 2003, 2005), the ability to disseminate claims through mass media is still assumed to be central (Gamson 2004). The important issues here are, first, whether personalizing communication with participants leads organizations to compromise their articulated goals (e.g., by underspecifying them) and, next, whether personalized protest messages produce incoherent noise, which results in messages failing to travel well or at all in the mass media. Such problems were brilliantly illustrated during a segment of the popular U.S. political comedy program *The Daily Show*, which parodied the 2009 G20 Pittsburgh Summit protests as ineptly organized in terms of getting their message across. The mock reporter pointed to the success of the right-wing Tea Party movement and turned to a group of its activists to offer G20 protesters advice about "staying on message," developing relationships with major news channels, and organizing more coherent events (*Daily Show* 2009).

The third question has to do with the relations between protest organizations. The stakes involved in engaging individualized citizens are magnified when large coalitions must agree on messages, communication strategies, and social technology affordances. The challenges of personalized communication from this perspective invite attention to network strength, the character of a coalition's organizational network as measured by coordinated action in the protest space, both on- and offline. Network strength can be measured in part via linking patterns on organizational websites. Linking patterns are intentional signals about the public affiliation preferences of organizations. Since some organizations may link indiscriminately to others, we will adopt a tougher standard for assessing network inclusion, size, and coherence: co-link analysis, which admits an organization into a network only if it is linked to by at least two other organizations. Other measures of the strength and coherence of protest networks such as the relative equality of inlinking and outlinking among organizations will be introduced later.

The risk from this perspective is that communicative flexibility with individuals may undermine the coherence of the organizational network in terms of the relations of prestige and mutual recognition between actors in the protest space. For example, it can deflect affiliation or linking patterns away from resource-rich and influential organizations, because organizations become more entrepreneurial in their shopping for followers. Contrary to expectations, however, Bennett, Foot, and Xenos (2011) suggest that this is not always the case. Arguing that narratives and their distribution may constitute structuring elements of organizational solidarity networks, their study shows how conflict over competing (personalized consumer vs. collective economic justice) narratives was reflected in a fragmented network in the U.S. fair trade movement, while tolerance for multiple narratives was reflected in a more cohesive network in the UK counterpart. The associated question in the present context is whether the communication of personalized narrative opportunities pertaining to the economic crisis affects a coalition's relative dominance of the collective action space in a protest event. Variations in these questions about communication and the organization of networks may also be posed with respect to the dynamics of the networks over time (Monge and Contractor 2003; Diani 2004): Do similar network structures persist in protests over time; do they appear only in campaigns related to specific protest issues; and can they be traced in stable policy advocacy networks over time independent of protests and campaigns?

This chapter explores the tension lodged in the personalization of collective action from the perspective of these core questions about the organization and qualities of collective action. Our immediate case involves a related series of protests that attracted a diversity of organizations using very different mobilization communication strategies. The aim is to understand whether the personalization of communicative relations with followers affected organizational and coalition capacities in terms of engagement strength, agenda strength, and network strength. The protests in question occurred in London on the eve of the G20 summit in late March and early April 2009, marking the first in a series of protests at various world power meetings in response to the global financial and economic crises.

The case of the G20 London Summit protests is interesting in several ways. The protests involved very different organizational networks, all simultaneously seeking to mobilize publics to send messages to the G20 (and to larger publics) about how to address the world crisis. The case thus offers comparisons between connective action networks employing highly personalized communication and collective action networks pressing more conventional collective action frames on their followers. The uses of digital media both in linking among organizations and in communication with publics allowed us to observe how relatively more and less personalized media affected both coalition structures and the general qualities of collective action strength.

Protesting the Economic Crisis

The world's 20 leading economic nations, the G20, met in London on April 2, 2009, amid a global economic crisis. Their announced intention was to address the "greatest challenge to the world economy in modern times" through common actions to "restore confidence, growth, and jobs," "repair the financial system," and "build an inclusive, green and sustainable, recovery."[1] The London Summit attracted a complex protest ecology involving multiple actors with different protest agendas and tactics. Several protests were planned. An earlier meeting in Paris of more than 150 civil society groups from all over Europe, including union, student, faith-based, environment, and development groups, had resulted in an agreement to divide the protests into two days: March 28 was to be the day of general mobilization, and April 1 (dubbed "Financial Fool's Day") was to be the preferred day for direct action (Paris Declaration 2009). This division of the protest space into different days allocated to two large and different coalitions provided a perfect natural laboratory for implementing our research designs.

The March 28 London mobilization was organized by Put People First, a British civil society coalition of more than 160 development NGOs, trade unions, and environmental groups (e.g., Oxfam, the Catholic Overseas Development Agency, and Friends of the Earth). Their march for "Jobs, Justice, and Climate" in the central city drew an estimated 35,000 protesters (Put People First 2009). The activities planned for 1 April included setting up a Climate Camp with some 2,000 participants in the heart of London; a smaller Stop the War Coalition march; and an Alternative London Summit featuring a variety of academics, activists, and politicians. The largest of these events was organized by G20 Meltdown, an anti-capitalist umbrella group (including, e.g., the Anarchist Federation, the Anthill Social, and the Socialist Workers Party) that led a "Storm the Banks" carnival march protesting war, climate chaos, financial crimes, and land enclosures. An estimated 5,000 protesters converged on the Bank of England from four directions, each led by a differently colored "horseman of the apocalypse." Protesters could join the red horse against war, the green horse against climate chaos, the silver horse against financial crimes, or the black horse against homelessness, land enclosures, and borders (G20 Meltdown 2009).

Our analysis focuses on two dominant protest coalitions, PPF and Meltdown, two networks that also pursued contrasting approaches to engaging individuals. In this analysis, PPF represents the hybrid type of organizationally enabled connective action, and Meltdown represents the more conventional organizationally brokered collective action (though it is just one variation of many forms that collective action might take). We also include some measures for the Climate Camp website for comparison purposes, as the Climate Camp represented a more radical network than PPF in its organizing of more direct,

---

[1] Available at www.g20.org/Documents/final-communique.pdf (July 26, 2009).

confrontational actions, and yet it was unlike Meltdown in that it avoided collective action mandates and invited individuals with different ideas about the climate crisis to participate in these actions. Thus, its interactive media repertoire might be expected to fall somewhere between that of the other two networks.

Protest Coalitions and Personalized Communication

Our first task involved investigating whether PPF and Meltdown displayed differences in the ways they communicated to individuals in the mobilization process.[2] Following our definition of personalized communication, we analyzed two ways in which the organizations could personalize communication on their websites: (a) their framing of protest themes and (b) the opportunities they provided to site visitors to use technologies for interactive communication that often enabled personal content to enter the network. Analysis of each coalition's website and related social technologies indicated considerable differences between PPF and Meltdown: the PPF coalition presented a far more personalized thematic and technological interface, enabling individuals to send their own messages to the G20, while Meltdown issued a more rigid call to collective action, including encouragement to "Eat the Bankers" and end capitalism.

Action Framing Differences

The differences in the communication approaches of PPF and Meltdown are instantly signaled by the images that animate their websites. As shown in Figure 2.1, the PPF site featured a banner of feet shod in everyday middle-class footwear and moving together as though in a demonstration. By contrast, the Meltdown site featured a single black horse and rider storming over the Bank of England across ominous skies, as shown in Figure 2.2.

As suggested by the graphics, the PPF site places average citizens at the center of the proposed action and invites them to project their own interpretations on the activities. The phrase that characterizes the site is truly "Put People First." Not only is this the protest slogan, but a statistical content analysis shows it to be the most prominent distinguishing word cluster on the site.[3] PPF emphasizes the priority of "people" while downplaying the specifics of the problem or solution. "Crisis" is the second most prominent word cluster on the site, and

---

[2] We wish to thank Nathan Johnson, Allison Rank, and Marianne Goldin for their research assistance on the studies reported in this chapter.

[3] The keyword analysis was performed using Wordsmith, which identifies words that characterize a text by comparing a research text with a larger research corpus. Dunning's log-likelihood test, a cousin of the chi-square test, identifies words that appear more prominently in the research text. This test identifies not just frequency, but similarity of word ratios. If a word appears in a statistically significant higher proportion in the research text than in the research corpus, it is marked as a keyword. This provides significant word clusters. The complete cluster was "Put, people, first, putting, we, public, essential."

FIGURE 2.1. Put People First coalition homepage, April 2009. Used with permission.

yet details about causes and solutions are kept in the background.[4] PPF requires only that the reader recognize the economic crisis; it avoids problematizing or promoting one economic system over another. The site urges the reform of banking, finance, and trade systems, but it does not detail the direction of such reforms. The presentation instead emphasizes the detrimental consequences of the status quo for "people," letting readers identify the message and action that they wish to endorse as long as it amounts to "putting people first."

By contrast, Meltdown defines its concerns more narrowly and makes it clear that these are not open to negotiation. Instead of associating the crisis and the summit with a plurality of problems and solutions, the website

---

[4] The keyword cluster included "crisis, economic, economies, financial, finance."

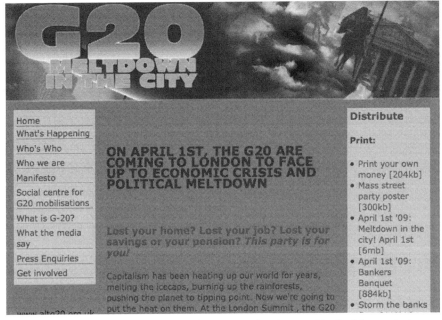

FIGURE 2.2. G20 Meltdown coalition homepage, April 2009. Used with permission.

confronts the reader with a dramatic larger-than-life narrative. The three primary word clusters tell the story that is underscored by the image in Figure
2.2. The first word cluster evokes the characters of the drama (personifying
bankers as the source of the problem and Meltdown's horsemen as the agents
of change),[5] the second cluster emphasizes the crisis,[6] and the third cluster
groups around a drastic solution: overthrowing capitalism.[7] The narrative is
that a group of bankers have caused global economic catastrophe, and a group
of "horsemen" will come to the rescue by "reclaim[ing] the City, thrusting
into the very belly of the beast." While PPF requires only that the reader recognize the existence of an economic crisis, Meltdown insists that the reader
recognize it as a *capitalist* crisis. The goal to "overthrow capitalism" points
both to the source of the crisis ("the dominance of finance capitalism is the
problem") and a drastic solution. The four themes of the "Storm the Banks"
march provide some leeway for personalization (e.g., the opportunity to dress
in costume),[8] and yet the sub-themes are firmly ordered under the collective

---

[5] "Bank, bankers, financial, executives, bankthink, shareholders, shares, horsemen, wave, public."
[6] "Meltdown, crises, crisis, crunch, anniversary."
[7] "Revolution, mobilization, rescue."
[8] The carnival tactics endorsed by at least parts of the Meltdown solidarity network underscore
the power of creative and expressive action at personally adapted levels (see, e.g., Rhythms
of Resistance, rhythmsofresistance.co.uk; accessed August 8, 2012; cf. Cammaerts 2012). We
would note, however, that carnivalesque or theatrical expressions may also entail strategically
depersonalized forms of expression in which individuals take on other personas that often have

action framework of anti-capitalism. The aesthetic is often humorous, but the dramatization demands that participants either accept or reject the message as is.

Technology Interface Differences

In keeping with these differences in framing the protests, the coalition sites differed substantially in the extent to which individuals were offered interactive affordances that invited them to engage on their own terms.[9] Our intention here was to look for features that enable or "afford" opportunities for people to do various things (e.g., to tweet), which may result in interactions with the affordances that are innovative or surprising to the developers (e.g., inserting #, or hashtags, into tweets to help direct and channel them to specific groups or larger crowds). In this chapter we examine affordances deployed by differently organized action networks along a spectrum ranging from organizationally enabled to organizationally brokered protests against the G20 meetings during the early years of the economic crisis. In order to make these comparisons, we first conducted inventories of every interactive digital affordance used across a collection of seven related protests during 2009, beginning with the PPF, Meltdown, and Climate Camp sites in the London protests and continuing with similar "modular" protests later in the autumn at G20 meetings in Pittsburgh (where two different coalition sites were inventoried) and two additional UK coalitions mobilizing public demonstrations ahead of the Copenhagen Climate Change Summit in December. There were many bridges among these protests, including common organizational sponsorships, traveling Twitter streams, and general linking of the economic crisis with climate change issues (e.g., no economic solutions at the expense of climate action).

During the inventory process two trained graduate assistants examined each site for the types and number of potentially interactive affordances, which we defined as features or functionalities that enable people to do things pertaining to engagement with the protests beyond the basic affordances of reading web pages or navigating the sites. A list of all of these items was compiled, and they were sorted by the entire research team (including the authors) in terms of features that seemed to clearly belong together, such as familiar branded technologies (e.g., Facebook, Twitter, YouTube), which we assigned their own separate categories. Familiar generic named technologies (e.g., RSS feeds, email lists) and similar types of technology (photo posting, calendars, maps) were also

historically or dramatically scripted qualities (St. John 2012). We thank Stefania Milan for this comment.

9 Following the discussion of affordances in Chapter 1, we adopt the definition proposed by Earl and Kimport (2011: 10): "the type of action or the characteristic of actions that a technology enables through its design." The idea of interactive affordances implies that individuals may have choices in the way they share in creating, managing, or distributing the content or product offered through the affordance, whether registering a "like" on a Facebook group, forwarding a post on an email list to others, responding on the list, posting a photo, video, or blog, proposing an action, or participating in a denial of service attack.

lumped into their own functionality categories. The many custom, one-of-a-kind affordances (e.g., "Send your own message to the G20," "Buy a Put People First T-shirt") were left as unique items. Using this preliminary list, two new coders again searched all of the protest coordinating sites exhaustively to check the inventory and add anything the first team missed. The teams reconciled the few differences by verifying the existence of items missed on the first pass. This resulted in a total of 106 interactive affordances identified across the seven sites, allowing for multiple counting of affordances such as Twitter that appeared on more than one site.

Figure 2.3 shows the inventory of interactive affordances found in all seven of the inventoried sites. The results indicate a broad spectrum of affordances that enable individuals to make choices about how to participate (e.g., sign petitions, donate money, or come to demonstrations) and/or add content to the communication network (e.g., post videos, photos, blog comments, and calendar events). It is not surprising that calendars and Twitter feeds appeared on all the sites spanning very different types of protest coalitions, from organizationally enabled cases such as PPF to more ideological organizationally brokered networks such as G20 Meltdown. The ubiquity of calendars indicates that a defining purpose of these sites was to help activists know where and when to do things. And in the contemporary protest era, the ubiquity of Twitter indicated that it had already by 2009 become the multi-casting network of choice, spanning the spectrum of protests from the economic and climate summit mobilizations, to the Tahrir Square uprisings, the *indignados* movement in Spain, and the Occupy protests. In Chapter 5 we show the preeminence of Twitter in the networks of networks that helped organize the Occupy protests.

What is equally interesting is the large number of unique affordances that appeared on one protest site but not the others. For example, Put People First offered T-shirts, special badges, and widgets for people and organizations to put on their websites; registration for conference events surrounding the protests; a hotel reservation service; and an "Obama-izer" tool that translated personal photos into the look of the iconic Obama 2008 campaign photo resembling a Warhol silk screen (which later got its creator, Shepard Fairey, into trouble for copyright violation due to his appropriation of a professional photographer's photo). Sites for other protests offered unique affordances for ride sharing and link posting, and one even offered a "bust card" in the form of downloadable instructions that protesters could carry in case they were arrested. The number of unique affordances suggests the availability of tech developer talent distributed across different protest networks. The large number of fancy affordances offered by PPF indicates the relatively resource-rich state of the NGOs in that sponsoring coalition. Perhaps most interesting, however, is that the only one of the seven coordinating sites not to have any custom affordances was the G20 Meltdown site, which also had the fewest interactive affordances of any kind among the coordinating sites we inventoried.

Against this broad survey of types of engagement technology identified across a family of modular economic and environment protests, we now

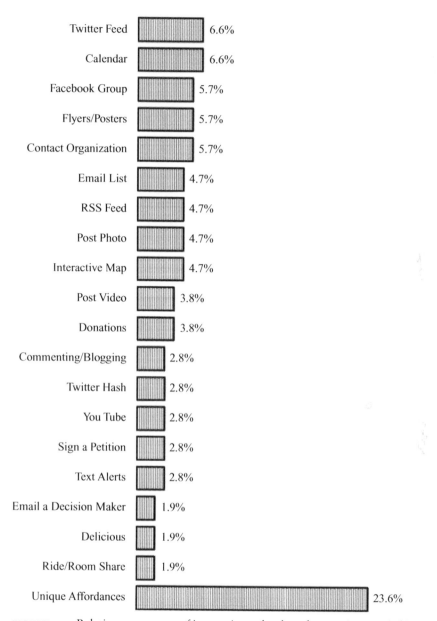

FIGURE 2.3. Relative occurrences of interactive technology features inventoried in seven related G20 and climate summit protest sites, 2009. Affordances appearing on different sites were counted multiple times. For reference, Twitter and calendars appeared on all seven sites, comments or blog features appeared on three sites, etc. Total affordances $N = 106$.

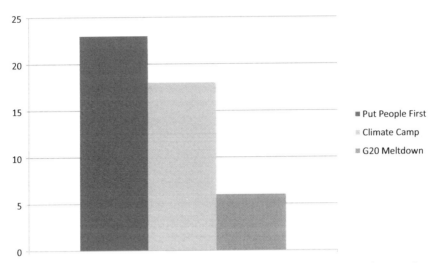

FIGURE 2.4. Number of technological engagement affordances used by three coalitions in the London G20 March–April 2009 protests.

compare the three main cases in this chapter. As can be seen in Figure 2.4, the PPF and Meltdown sites represent the two extremes, with PPF offering 23 personalized digital engagement mechanisms compared with Meltdown's 6 mechanisms. Climate Camp represents an interesting situation in between. For reference, the Meltdown site offered the fewest interactive technologies of any of the seven sites in the affordance inventory, and PPF had the largest number. As previously noted, Climate Camp is a radical organization that advocates direct action (such as setting up camp in the middle of London) but explicitly invites individuals with different ideas about the climate crisis to join such action. Thus, Climate Camp is a network that is more radical than the PPF centrist coalition but less inclined to use collective action frames than Meltdown. It is worth noting that its personalized communication inventory scored between the other two but fell short of the PPF level of personalized engagement opportunities.

The PPF site offered many opportunities for a visitor to enter the protest space. In keeping with the overall approach, the opportunity to "send your own message" to the G20 leaders appeared at the center of the first page under a photo stream of happy and diverse protestors (see Figure 2.1). There were several means of receiving information (via email alerts, Twitter and RSS feeds, and a calendar) and invitations to publicize and organize this information (through ShareThis, Delicious, Twitter, and downloadable posters). Participants were also encouraged to contribute by using the #G2orally Twitter hashtag and by posting personal photos, videos, and audios relating to the protest. Bloggers could link to the featured Whiteband[10] initiative "G20 Voices," through which

---

[10] Whiteband is a broad UK coalition linking the Make Poverty History network to a global anti-poverty network of thousands of organizations claiming to represent some 150 million

50 international bloggers were brought in to cover the summit on-site. As we have seen, followers could also buy T-shirts, use the "Obama-izer" tool to mash up their own photos, install PPF widgets on their blogs or Facebook pages, and post the PPF slogan "Jobs, Justice and Climate" on their own websites, blogs, and social networking sites. Visitors could also join the coalition's Facebook group, which was linked off the main site.

By contrast, the Meltdown site offered only six technological points of entry into the protest space. These included a calendar, an invitation to contact the group, and an opportunity to download posters about the Meltdown event, to follow the organization's Twitter feed and (YouTube) videos, and to read or join the public Facebook group. As noted earlier, there are several possible reasons for the limited set of technological affordances. These include a lack of financial, technological, and skill resources; the possibility that being under surveillance discouraged public information exchange; the belief that over-use of the Internet might impede developing grassroots resources; or the ideological preference for a particular kind of digital repertoire. In addition, Indymedia served as a communication network for many of the more radical G20 protesters, but its equally radical tone made it unlikely that it would engage many beyond existing groups of already committed activists. It was not in any event a medium for personalizing one's protest experience in the sense we mean here. Such possible extraneous factors for the low deployment of personalized digital affordances notwithstanding, a closer examination of the six interactive features on the Meltdown site suggests an overall tone of limiting personalized participation. Indeed, the overall focus of the site was to present information unilaterally to the visitor. Few of the Meltdown affordances allowed users to customize their interaction with the mobilization. Even when information was attributed to people submitting posts, it was unclear who had submitted them or how this could be done. The exception to this one-way directionality was the Facebook group, where users could post not only comments but also photos and posters.

The PPF website meanwhile not only invited individual contributions in several ways, but also tolerated postings straying far from its own organizational themes. For example, although official PPF statements did not focus on events aside from the G20 summit and PPF's own march, various participants using the site raised other issues, such as the death of a bystander at the hands of police at the Meltdown "Storm the Banks" action on April 1. Figure 2.5 shows a post to the PPF/Whiteband blog scroll, which linked to an artist-blogger operating under the name of legofesto (legofesto.blogspot.com/), who created a Lego sculpture of the incident.[11]

It is also important to note that PPF offered points of engagement that were not easily filtered by the central organization. An example of this is

---

people. A white wristband is worn as a personal sign of affiliation. According to the organizers, some 8 million British citizens wore the white band during a national anti-poverty action day in 2005 (www.makepovertyhistory.org/whiteband/index.shtml).

[11] Posted on www.whitebandaction.org/en/g20voice/blog?page=1 (May 15, 2009).

FIGURE 2.5. Artist-blogger legofesto re-creates the death of a bystander at London G20 protests. Copyright legofesto, used with permission.

the #g2orally Twitter hashtag. The organization encouraged supporters to use the hashtag to create a buzz around its march. While the hashtag was predictably used by the PPF organizers to show solidarity and report on the march, it was also used by others for very different purposes. Examples of the latter included critical comments, as in a picture of protesters eating at McDonald's that was retweeted with the following text: "RT @[person's name] & @dothegreenthing Delicious irony of #g2orally anti-globalization protesters lunching @ McDonalds twitpic.com/2j2qb." Other users updated followers on how the news media were reporting the protests: "Just heard – #G2orally not lead story. Spat with Argentina about Falklands is set to bump it." Such examples suggest that the PPF protest space was open to individuals acting in ways showing little programmatic affiliation with the PPF coalition.

In summary, PPF went to great lengths to encourage personalized expression through various technologies deployed on its website. The G20 Meltdown site explicitly endorsed the spirit of solidarity expressed in the Paris Declaration and consequently made efforts to highlight other London Summit protest events as well as provide contact information to the respective organizers (including PPF). Yet its own communication stream was primarily one-way and offered an ideological narrative of the crisis that visitors could either take or leave. The small number of interactive technologies presented on the most visible public face of the coalition reinforced this more bounded collective action framing of its networked activities.

Personalized Communication and Protest Capacity

Having established systematic communication differences between the two main protest groups, we now examine whether there are any notable deficits in the political capacities of organizations and coalitions implementing more personalized communication strategies. In the case of PPF, personalized engagement is facilitated by what we term an organizationally enabled connective action network. In this analysis, we explore the properties of the PPF network in terms of engagement strength, agenda strength, and network strength and stability in order to investigate the three questions about the organizational risks of personalized communication outlined earlier.

Engagement Strength

The first question concerns whether personalized communication undermines engagement strength in a mobilization: Did the more flexible terms of communication that PPF offered undermine its engagement strength – as measured by direct mobilization of participants, indirect communication to general publics, and sustained future mobilization capacity? One of the clearest signals of engagement strength is participation in the protest march itself. As stated previously, an estimated 35,000 people attended the PPF march, compared with roughly 5,000 who turned out for the Meltdown demonstration a few days later (Wikipedia 2009). Were this the only difference between the two coalitions, we might conclude that a more moderate NGO coalition is more likely to mobilize a large turnout than a more ideologically extreme coalition proposing higher-risk actions. However, the size of turnout is just one of the many measures to consider with respect to engagement capacity.

Another measure is the diversity of turnout. While we do not have precise indicators of diversity, the photos of the PPF march posted by participants and sponsoring organizations on various sites clearly show a broader range of people and messages than do those posted from the "Storm the Banks" march organized by the Meltdown coalition. Photos posted on the Indymedia London (2009) and the CAFOD (Catholic Agency for Overseas Development 2009) site show this contrast clearly. Web artifacts from protests and other kinds of activism displayed online offer rich troves of visual imagery: photos, videos, graphic elements, and posters. These aspects of online data are too seldom employed in analyses that continue to rely on text and discourse despite the rich properties of digital imagery.

Yet another way of thinking about engagement strength is to focus on the capacity to reach and engage a public beyond the immediate demonstration. On this point, the mainstream media coverage was also far greater and more positive for the PPF activities than for those of Meltdown. This is documented later in the chapter with respect to agenda strength. What it means is that in terms of secondary engagement (i.e., of people who were not at the protest but who heard about it in the press), the PPF activities reached a far wider audience with more positive messages.

Another useful indicator of engagement capacity is whether those mobilized in this protest were also kept in the communication network for future activities. In the case of the PPF network, many of the same coalition organizations promoted future activities related to climate change and the forthcoming UN

Climate Change Conference in Copenhagen. We will discuss how these networks overlapped in more detail in the section on network strength, but at this point, it is worth noting that PPF continued to link to the topic of climate change and directed site visitors to the Stop Climate Chaos Coalition (SCCC). As we discuss in the following chapter, the SCCC, whose sponsoring membership overlapped considerably with that of PPF, was then coordinating "the Wave" protest leading up to the Copenhagen conference. The Wave demonstrations, which took place on December 5, 2009, attracted an estimated 50,000 people. By contrast, the G20 Meltdown website was discontinued at the end of the summer of 2009, although public communication continued on Facebook and later Meltdown incarnations set up new websites (cf. Kavada 2010).

Related to the issue of keeping participants in the communication network is the importance of what Chadwick (2007) refers to as "sedimentary" digital mechanisms that sustain histories of events and leave behind communication links for people (perhaps people unconnected with the original mobilization) to organize future events. The PPF website was still up and functioning at the time of this writing (more than three years after the protests), with the "Send your own message to the G20" box having been replaced by a scroll of the messages left by people who had used that feature earlier. Other content from that time also remained visible, such as the Twitter stream and the Facebook event page. The Facebook event page of G20 Meltdown remained visible, but the site, as just noted, was taken down in 2009.

Agenda Strength

The second question has to do with whether personalized communication compromises agenda strength. Our conclusion is that it did not do so in the case of PPF. Despite the many invitations in the PPF environment for individuals to contribute to the digital protest space, the PPF coalition policies, demands, and strategies were clearly presented and were not up for discussion. Deep in the site, the coalition presented a 12-point policy platform detailing the goals of the PPF campaign and related London march, which were directed at the UK government. Some points were general, such as "Compel tax havens to abide by strict international rules" and "Work to ensure sufficient emergency funding to all countries that need it, without damaging conditionalities attached." But other claims were more specific, for example, "Deliver 0.7% of national income as aid by 2013, deliver aid more effectively and push for the cancellation of all illegitimate and unpayable developing country debts." This suggests that PPF's flexibility did not unduly compromise the specificity and clarity of its public claims. In contrast, it is interesting that the Meltdown site, which signaled greater rigidity about its message, presented only broad goals directed at the system rather than a specific political target: "1. Participate in a carnival party at the Bank of England. 2. Support all events demonstrating against the G20 during the meltdown period (from 28 March onwards). 3. Overthrow capitalism."

Another measure of agenda strength is the capacity of a protest coalition to communicate to broader publics through various media channels. A common concern about social movements and media is that news stories typically focus on violence or civil disobedience and not on the issue agendas of the protesters. Media coverage is even more problematic for transnational and global justice protesters, who typically represent multiple issues, often leaving news organizations unable to summarize the point of the protest (Bennett 2005). Worse yet, particularly chaotic protests may even be subject to comedic treatments, as in *The Daily Show* parody of the Pittsburgh events mentioned earlier. In our case, we investigated whether PPF's flexible and personalized communication compromised the diffusion of coalition claims and coverage in the mainstream media.

We analyzed reporting of the protests in all English-language print news media in the week of the summit protests (March 27–April 4, 2009). Of 504 relevant items, 225 articles mentioned PPF and 165 mentioned Meltdown. Most mentions of PPF reflected the coalition's own emphasis on the "unified" and "unprecedented alliance" of "mainstream" diversity behind the demand to "Put People First." Mentions of Meltdown, by contrast, highlighted the radical profile of the associated groups and police anticipation of disruptive protests. The coalition's issue claims were seldom featured in the news. The valence of the reporting was more positive for PPF: 46 percent of the total mentions of PPF were positive, 53 were percent neutral, and 1 percent negative. For Meltdown, however, only 3 percent of the mentions were positive, 74 were percent neutral, and 23 percent negative. This general pattern held irrespective of the political position of the news organization (e.g., BBC, *Guardian*, and *The Times*).

Network Strength

The final question concerns organizational network strength, in particular whether it is undermined by personalized communication through digitally mediated connective action networks. We analyzed both the PPF and Meltdown coalitions from the perspective of their organizational network strength and the dynamics of their networks over time. The coherence and stability of protest networks can be thought of in terms of levels of mutual recognition and inclusion of coalition organizations in cross-linked networks. We measured recognition and inclusion in this case through various indicators based on hyperlink patterns among organization websites and campaigns. By these measures, networks that have less strength (i.e., stability and coherence) will display a larger number of isolated organizations that receive few links from others.

In light of the differences in the protest narratives and frames found on the two main coalition sites, it is not surprising that two very different networks were formed by organizations listed as the members of the respective coalitions. As noted earlier, the Meltdown site mostly listed anarchist and anticapitalist organizations (e.g., Rhythms of Resistance, the Whitechapel Anarchist Group, the Haringey Solidarity Group, and the Socialist Workers Party).

The PPF core members consisted mainly of large, well-established national NGOs working in the areas of development, trade justice, and environment (e.g., CAFOD, Oxfam, and Friends of the Earth). The interesting question that moves us beyond these lists of members is how the solidarity networks of the two coalitions were organized. What were their observable patterns of giving and receiving recognition? What is perhaps surprising is that the PPF coalition, which advertised the most personalized affiliation opportunities, displayed by far the stronger network, suggesting that personalization of the mobilization process alone does not necessarily undermine the resilience of the collective action structure.

We should note that given our limited access to participants in these protests, we could not assess network relationships in a fine-grained ethnographic sense (e.g., who regularly calls whom to coordinate actions or what organization leaders or members attend meetings together). We would argue, however, that a finer-grained ethnographic analysis would make it extremely challenging to piece together the extended solidarity networks of hundreds and even thousands of organizations that help communicate the messages of the core organizations and drive participants to their mobilizations. What we are seeking for the purposes of this analysis is a rough assessment of the qualities (e.g., size, organizational composition, and density of relationships) of the extended networks surrounding the core coalitions responsible for organizing the G20 protests. We can get a preliminary understanding of these network properties by assessing one of the most visible ways in which recognition is given or withheld in contemporary protest spaces: through the exchange of links on websites. For explanations of why intentional web linking patterns constitute reliable indicators of network structure in cases like ours, see Rogers (2004) and Foot and Schneider (2006).

It is also important to recognize the limits of the methods that we employ here. Networks do not, of course, reveal all of their dimensions through web linking patterns. Neither al-Qaeda support organizations nor candidates in U.S. congressional elections can be expected to link to their funding sources or to their covert strategy advisers, two important node clusters in their networks. However, web crawls of such disparate organizations may reveal insights into their support and resource networks (e.g., mosques or influential clerics involved in recruitment, in the case of al-Qaeda, or endorsements from respected public officials and organizations, in the case of congressional candidates). More appropriate for our case is that social movement and NGO policy coalitions may signal who their close partners are or where people can go and what they can do to advance mutual goals. Just as important, organizations can choose not to link to others in public even though they may have some agenda overlap. For example, the Meltdown site linked to PPF, but that recognition was not returned, signaling that PPF wanted its public image to be cleanly associated with a financial reform program likely to be recognized by authorities and not linked to a blatantly anti-capitalist message.

More generally, then, the way organizations link (or do not link) to others signals various kinds of relationships in networks that have to do with influence (the degree to which an organization links to others) and prestige (the degree to which other organizations choose to link to an organization). Through this giving and receiving of links, we can detect things such as the number of isolated organizations in coalitions, the density of co-linking among organizations, and the relative equality in the distribution of links among organizations in a network. In order to find out how organizations in our main coalitions positioned themselves in relation to each other through intentional website linkages, we conducted web crawls to assess the co-linking patterns of the two protest networks using a set of starting points that each coalition site defined as core actors. The list of starting points for the Meltdown group was a large one (63 organizations), taken from the "Who's Who" page on the site.[12] That for PPF was much smaller, taken from the list of the 14 organizations authorized to speak to the media on behalf of PPF.[13] Given the differences in the political nature of the two coalitions, there was no obvious way of finding a comparable number of starting points. PPF clearly signaled its lead organizations, while Meltdown (perhaps reflecting its anarchist ethos) categorized all coalition members equally. More important, the relative number of starting points is not as critical as their representativeness, as in this case both sets represented the list of core coalition members. Indeed, as this analysis shows, the network with the far larger set of starting points (Meltdown) produced a far thinner set of co-linkages among those groups, and the resulting network was more or less hijacked by more prominent solidarity organizations, such as Greenpeace, that many Meltdown members tended to recognize but that were not in the core coalition listed on the coordinating website. Since the network

[12] The Labour Party (actually, the "alternative" Labour Party), the Alternative G20 Summit, the Laboratory of Insurrectionary Imagination, Climate Rush, Climate Camp, Stop the War Coalition, Campaign for Nuclear Disarmament, Rising Tide, London Action Resource Centre, People & Planet, Earth First, Radical Anthropology Group, Haringey Solidarity Group, Hackney Solidarity Network, London Coalition Against Poverty, Day-Mer, Aluna, Transition Towns, People's Global Action, Hands off Venezuela, Radical Activist, SchNEWS, noborder network, Network to End Migrant and Refugee Detention, Roadblock, AirportWatch, Climate Crisis Coalition, Plane Stupid, Transport 2000, Airport Pledge, Permaculture, Intergovernmental Panel on Climate Change, Campaign for Nuclear Disarmament, Post Carbon Institute, Campaign Against Climate Change, Greenpeace, Zero Carbon City, Corporate Watch, Corpwatch, The Heat Is Online, the Centre for Alternative Technology, the World Alliance for Decentralized Energy, Biofuel Watch, Carbon Trade Watch, Platform, Simultaneous Policy, International Union of Sex Workers, IFIwatchnet, the Last Hours, Socialist Workers Party, Government of the Dead, Rhythms of Resistance, Barking Bateria, Strangeworks, People and Planet, Whitechapel Anarchist Group, Stop Arming Israel, Anarchist Federation, Class War, the Anthill Social, Reclaiming Spaces, the Land Is Ours Campaign, New Sovereignty, People in Common, Project 2012, the Student Occupation (National Student Coordination).

[13] Actionaid, CAFOD, Friends of the Earth UK, New Economics Foundation, Oxfam UK, Progressio Foundation, Save the Children UK, Stop Climate Chaos Coalition, Tearfund, War on Want, World Development Movement UK, Trade Union Congress, Whiteband/Global Call for Action Against Poverty, World Vision UK.

crawling method that we selected explores all the linking relationships from a set of starting points, network patterns will emerge as long as the starting points are broadly representative of the domain being investigated (in this case, two distinct protest coalitions).

The two respective sets of URLs were placed as starting points, or as a "seed list," into Issue Crawler, a tool made available by Richard Rogers at the University of Amsterdam (for a detailed account of this tool, see www.govcom .org/scenarios_use.html and Rogers 2004). The Issue Crawler identifies networks of URLs and locates them in a relational space (which we will refer to as a "network map") on the basis of the co-link analysis. A co-link is simply a URL that receives links from at least two of the starting points for each iteration (or "click") as the crawler moves out from the starting points. Thus, suppose we begin with site A, site B, and site C, and crawls of the inlinks and outlinks for each turn up site D, which has links from sites A and C. Site D would be included in the network map as co-linking from two of the starting points. Suppose that on the second iteration or click of the crawl, the crawler finds that site D also links to site E, which, in turn, supplies an inlink to site B from our list of starting points. However, site E receives no other links from the members of the expanding network. Under the chosen inclusion method, site E would not be included in the network map. Co-link analysis provides a test of whether networks are more constrained than, say, a snowball or single-link method, which would include more weakly tied organizations such as site E. As with most methodological choices, there are theoretical implications. Thus, we set a somewhat higher bar for network inclusion than other mapping methods would create. The rationale is that since we are interested in comparing networks in terms of density of linking and structural stability, the co-linking criterion puts the spotlight on organizations that emerge in more tightly connected networks.

We set the reach of the crawl at two iterations (or hyperlink clicks) from the starting points. This is the procedure that Rogers (2004) recommends for deriving a solidarity network that includes links among organizations extending beyond a particular issue focus and into support networks for larger categories of concern. For example, in this case, we wanted to capture the solidarity networks surrounding our two clusters of economic justice organizations. This opening to the solidarity network enabled the inclusion of more climate change organizations that advocate linking economic and climate justice causes because they see global warming as having the most severe impact on already-impoverished nations. The question now becomes whether the coalition displaying more personalized engagement opportunities lost network strength in the bargain.

Despite its more personalized appeals to individuals, PPF turned out to have a much more coherent organizational network than Meltdown with its more rigid collective action frames. The crawler visited more than 2,000 URLs in each crawl and rendered a map and a co-link matrix (including directionality of links) consisting of the top sites sharing co-links in each network. The maps

FIGURE 2.6. Core solidarity network of the G20 Meltdown coalition, with nodes sized by relative number of inlinks that organizations received from the network. Map by issuecrawler.net, courtesy of the Govcom.org Foundation, Amsterdam. Used with permission.

of the two networks are shown in Figures 2.6 and 2.7. The sizes of the nodes correspond to the relative number of inlinks that a site received from other organizations. On initial inspection, both networks seem superficially similar, with the crawler returning the core networks of 97 organizations for PPF and 99 for Meltdown. Closer inspection, however, reveals that the networks are vastly different in terms of which of the coalition members ended up in them and which of those ended up at the center of linkages among other core network members. The most dramatic observation is that many members of the Meltdown coalition dropped out of the network altogether, because so few of them were recognized by at least two other members. Even more interesting is that many of the organizations receiving greater recognition from the Meltdown members turned out to be the core players in the PPF network, suggesting that actors in the more centrist coalition garnered important levels

FIGURE 2.7. Core solidarity network of the Put People First coalition, with nodes sized by relative number of inlinks that organizations received from the network. Map by issuecrawler.net, courtesy of the Govcom.org Foundation, Amsterdam. Used with permission.

of prestige (perhaps based on valuable information or other resources) even from many of the more radical Meltdown groups.

Inspection of the linking patterns shown in Figure 2.7 reveals that PPF centered on a tightly knit group of core organizations, including most of those listed in the media contact list. Indeed, most of these PPF starting points remained prominent in the core network, meaning that they received recognition from multiple other members of the network. By contrast, many of the organizations from which we launched the Meltdown crawl dropped out of the network, meaning that they did not receive widespread recognition from fellow members of the organizing coalition list. The contrast is dramatic. Only 1 of the 14 starting points dropped out of the PPF network, because it failed to receive links from two or more organizations in the crawled population. By contrast, fully 30 of the original 63 starting points dropped out of the

Meltdown solidarity network due to lack of recognition among other coalition members.

This, of course, raises the question of who the organizations populating the Meltdown solidarity network are, if not primarily the original coalition members. As previously noted, a number of prominent organizations associated with the PPF network emerge as a tightly linked group in the Meltdown network as well. In fact, a dominant cluster of most inlinked organizations in the upper half of Figure 2.6 turn out to be organizations that also appear prominently in the PPF network in Figure 2.7. In particular, five organizations appear near the center of both networks: Oxfam, Friends of the Earth, People & Planet, World Development Movement, and SCCC. People & Planet and SCCC appear in both the PPF sponsor list and the Meltdown Who's Who list from which the crawls were launched. However, the other three were PPF sponsor organizations that did not appear in the Meltdown starting points.

The asymmetric inclusion of the PPF members in the Meltdown solidarity network does not mean that the two networks were the same. Although many PPF organizations appear in the Meltdown network, they do not dominate the network. Fully 14 of the top 20 most linked-to sites in each network were different. What accounts for this puzzling quality of the Meltdown network, namely that it excludes many of its own coalition members, while affiliating in a solidarity neighborhood that goes beyond PPF to include other organizations? Although environmental organizations that received solidarity recognition from the Meltdown core were a minority of the largely anti-capitalist starting points, they were disproportionately likely to associate with each other and with an extended string of environmental advocacy organizations to provide the core strength of the Meltdown network. Indeed, the top six most linked-to organizations in Figure 2.6 are environmental organizations: climatecamp.org.uk (receiving 33 links from the 99 other organizations in the core network); foe.co.uk (28); campaigncc.org (24); risingtide.org.uk (24); greenpeace.org.uk (23); and peopleandplanet.org (23). Moreover, the top 20 most recognized organizations in the Meltdown network included 17 devoted entirely or primarily to climate change and environmental sustainability issues. Another member of the top 20 was an information network (Indymedia) that carried news and personal accounts from the protests and received 19 formal links from other members of the network. This means that only two core organizations in the Meltdown solidarity network ended up being focused mainly on the economic justice issues that were at the center of the protests, and these were overlapping core members of PPF (Oxfam and the World Development Movement).

This suggests that the formal Meltdown coalition focus on anti-capitalism quickly melted away if we consider the overall network strength of the coalition, which turns out to lie primarily with a subset of environment organizations and their extended network. Without this strong network built around the secondary environmental theme of the protests, there is a real possibility that the Meltdown coalition would have failed to reveal a coherent or stable network at all. In other words, when it comes to network strength, the economic justice wing of the Meltdown network suffered a bit of a meltdown.

Enough Meltdown member organizations linked to the PPF members and/or environmental organizations that the network morphed in surprisingly different directions than one might have imagined just from examining the tone and membership of the coalition site or even from exploring all of the member websites. Perhaps the most striking indicator of the low network strength of the original Meltdown coalition membership (in terms of observed relations among its economic justice organizations) is the fact that even the Meltdown coalition site sits outside the center of its own network (appearing in the lower left of Figure 2.6). The Meltdown site ranked 27th out of 99 nodes in the network in terms of inlinks received from other organizations (13). By contrast, as shown in Figure 2.7, the PPF coalition site is the center of its network, ranking first in recognition with inlinks from 38 other organizations.

The network strength pattern is clear: recognition clearly flows outward from the Meltdown coalition members toward a mix of outside environmental organizations and the dominant organizations in PPF. The reverse is most certainly not true, with the PPF members assiduously not linking to enough Meltdown organizations to include many of them in their network. Indeed, the Meltdown site does not even appear in the network map of the PPF network.

Network Stability and Strategic Adjustment over Time
Another interesting way to think about network capacity is to consider the coherence and stability of organizational network dynamics over time. In this case, following the London G20 Summit protests, the networks around both Meltdown and PPF remained relatively stable throughout the summer of 2009, as indicated by a set of crawls that we did in September at the time of another wave of protests as the G20 leaders again met in London. The core PPF network retained 21 of its top 25 organizations between March and September (and 36 of the top 50 most linked-to organizations), while Meltdown retained 16 out of 25 (and 30 of the top 50 from the April crawl).

The somewhat greater stability of the PPF network is corroborated by another finding: the two networks moved away from each other over this relatively short period of time. By September 2009 the inlink ranking overlap noted in April had disintegrated, dropping from 15 to 8 out of 50. Core PPF organizations such as the Fairtrade Foundation, Christian Aid, and Oxfam disappeared from the Meltdown network. This suggests that our method is sensitive even to short-term changes and that the protest web sphere is not static or neglected; it is dynamic and reflects changes in underlying political arrangements. What is even more interesting is that the shifts we observe in the PPF network seem less a result of entropy or other processes of decline than of strategic adjustments as two protest coalitions (one focused on economic justice and the other on environmental justice) began to coordinate their next political strategies. This dynamic occurred as the stable coalition underlying the PPF protests was repositioning itself to hand off the mobilization of supporters to another coalition in anticipation of a series of demonstrations related to the UN Climate Change Summit in Copenhagen in December. The PPF handed off its network to the Stop Climate Chaos Coalition (SCCC) organizers of the Wave climate protests that occurred in a number of British cities in December prior to the Copenhagen summit. PPF shared nearly half of its organizational solidarity network with SCCC by September 2009: the overlap of prominent organizations in the inlink ranking of the two networks was 10 out of 25 (and 21 of the top 50), with different government agencies accounting for some of the differences in overlap between the economic justice and climate justice protests. SCCC itself ranked third in the PPF inlink rankings in the September crawl. In the next chapter we examine the ways in which the SCCC used social media in coordinating the Wave protests in the United Kingdom, in contrast to the way in which a crowd-enabled network used the same medium (Twitter) during the continuation of the same protest cycle in Copenhagen.

Our analysis of the networking patterns of the members of the PPF network over time also suggests that the PPF protest mobilization network derived from an underlying stable network organization that transcended the London Summit protests. Indeed, we will see in Chapter 4 that most of the core organizations form a stable issue advocacy network centered around fair trade and economic justice both nationally and transnationally. Even more intriguing is that this steady-state issue and policy network features an even more impressive array of personalized (open) digital technologies across the entire network of nearly 100 organizations, with core organizations such as Oxfam receiving more than 300,000 unique monthly visitors. In Chapter 5 we will show how this same core network morphs into various campaign modes to put public political pressure behind many of its policy initiatives, again with impressive levels of personalized engagement and favorable press coverage for its campaigns in the bargain.

To return to the question of network stability in organizationally enabled networks, we are prepared to hazard a proposition that because of their relatively loose configuration around more inclusive public frames, they may be more stable than many organizationally brokered coalition networks that suffer points of contention around the differences that required brokerage in the first place. The ideological and tactical fractiousness of many social movements can result in diverting political capacity through internal rifts, even as the movement tries to present a united front externally. Looking at different views of the UK organizationally enabled economic justice network in different analyses for a six-year span (2006–2012), we find roughly the same set of established development and economic justice NGOs constituting dense core networks in all three of the network configurations we analyze in this book: in protest mobilization modes such as PPF (this chapter) and the Wave (Chapter 3); as a steady-state economic justice issue advocacy network (Chapter 4); or in promoting various public engagement and pressure campaigns (Chapter 5). Indeed, these stable networks recur whether we go backward or forward in time from the protests discussed in this chapter. For example, networks involving many of the same organizations were traced by one of the authors while mapping and analyzing fair trade and development policy activism in the United Kingdom. Analysis of the network maps of the UK fair trade advocacy network in 2006 (Bennett, Foot, and Xenos 2011) with the G20 London Summit and the UN climate summit protests in 2009 shows that a steady cluster of organizations can be traced through the cores of all three. This group includes Fairtrade Foundation, CAFOD, the Trade Justice Movement, the World Development Movement, People & Planet, Christian Aid, and Oxfam. This suggests that a network of large, well-resourced NGOs are cooperating in a string of protest and policy initiatives, developing something of a common brand for their actions. More pertinently, it also indicates that the tendency toward personalized communication already found in the UK fair trade network and continued in the PPF London G20 Summit protest did not undermine the ability of these networked organizations to sustain a stable and tightly knit organizational network. In Chapter 4 we show that these loose public engagement networks are not by any means accidental or haphazardly drawn. To the contrary, they are part of the strategic network design. At other times, the same organizations may split on particular fronts and go it alone or engage in more conventional brokered negotiations over positions and strategies. This organizational hybridity makes fixed category schemes less than helpful in investigating the organization of action in political context.

Overall, this analysis of network strength demonstrates that conventional ideological or collective-identity-based action framing of public activities is not a prerequisite for network coherence (inclusion, stability, and density of relationships) among coalition members. One case surely does not establish a general law, and we expect to see a good deal more variation in outcomes on the collective action framing side of the equation. We know that there are many scenarios in which collective action frames do produce more coherent networks than did the largely anarchist and anti-capitalist Meltdown coalition, which demonstrated relatively low network strength, as indicated, for example, by McAdam's (1988b) work on the U.S. civil rights movement. Our point here is that more loosely configured personalized networking can also produce comparable political outcomes.

Conclusion

The fact that the organizations in the Meltdown Who's Who list displayed relatively low levels of mutual public recognition in their web links while a group of core PPF organizations appeared prominently in the Meltdown network suggests the greater dominance of the PPF network in the London G20 financial crisis protest space. This may partly reflect PPF's resource advantage in terms of providing information, logistical coordination, and a better online communication infrastructure. This sort of resource advantage may also explain why the relative minority of environmental organizations in the original Meltdown coalition turned out to dominate its network structure. The irony, of course, is that the most notable structures in the Meltdown network did not come from the majority of radical economic justice organizations in the coalition, but from environmental and more centrist economic justice NGOs.

There was also a pronounced asymmetry in the levels and nature of recognition between the two networks. For example, Meltdown publicized (and encouraged participation in) the PPF march, but there was no discernible return publicity from PPF for the Meltdown event. Moreover, it was clear from the Indymedia feeds and photos that the Meltdown supporters joined the PPF march without disrupting the peaceful tone, which was a marked contrast to the more confrontational tactics employed by these groups in the later "Storm the Banks" event. This asymmetrical capacity of the PPF network ended up serving it well in terms of getting its message out, both across internal digital networks and in the mass media, which generally gave more and more positive coverage to the PPF activities.

In addition to these network dynamics that helped define the G20 protest space and the activities within it, there were clearly many directly brokered arrangements and understandings that operated beyond the bounds of our observations. For example, the strategic mutual decision reached by the respective coalitions to divide the protest space into different activities and different days greatly enhanced the clarity and (highly personalized) message focus of the PPF activities. Orchestrating separate protests and defining them clearly on the coalition sites and their associated social networks may have appealed to the greater propensity of people to turn out for peaceful demonstrations while contributing to favorable news coverage of a more clearly communicated message in the absence of disruptive noise from more anarchic demonstrators. At the same time, the asymmetry of the networking relationships between the two coalitions reinforced their divisions and provided a stark contrast between our two types of organizationally brokered collective action and organizationally enabled connective action. In other protests in the G20 2009–2010 cycle (e.g., those in Pittsburgh and Toronto) very different networks were intermixed in the same events, and aggressive police tactics set off clashes and violence that quickly drowned out the messages that reached larger publics (leading in the case of Pittsburgh to the *Daily Show* parody mentioned earlier).

One of the most important findings from the perspective of this book is the clear evidence that the coalition that adopted more personalized communication strategies maintained the strongest network. PPF was open to highly personalized affiliation, but it did not seem to sacrifice much organizational control or political capacity in the bargain. The PPF coalition not only dominated the immediate protest space, but also provided clear pathways for people to join in future actions (such as the later climate protests). While the Meltdown site soon disappeared, PPF left various "sedimentary" structures, such as the coalition website, as living memories of the G20 action, complete with messages and photo galleries created by the participants themselves. Thus, the personalization of participation invited citizens into shared environments where they created important content and established interpersonal relationships both on- and offline. At the same time, this individualized communication took place in the context of established messages and action opportunities defined by coalition members whose network relationships indicated strong levels of mutual recognition of action frames and agendas. In short, the PPF coalition opened up the floor for varied individual perspectives (recall legofesto), but the overall effort remained managed and focused.

The analysis in this chapter does not suggest that traditional ideological vanguard coalitions have lost their place in collective action scenarios. The Meltdown coalition mobilized a substantial number of participants who engaged in a highly orchestrated action repertoire of confrontation and disruption of London public spaces. Moreover, the Meltdown plan clearly respected the PPF action, with many Meltdown activists participating in the PPF events without disrupting them. The ability of two such distinct coalitions to mobilize a broad spectrum of participants within the same protest ecology, yet to remain distinctive in terms of messages and actions, suggests a refinement of both strategy and communication.

These findings point toward a richer understanding of communication technologies in the organization of contentious collective action. Our analysis may help balance perspectives that have emphasized collective action framing, mass media, and more formal organizational memberships when thinking about conditions of effective mobilization. While other conditions surely produce weaker and less focused protests, it appears that organizationally enabled connective action networks can harmonize their agendas around message frames that are broad enough to invite diverse individual participation and coordinate this participation through fine-grained digital media applications that result in coherent action.

3

Digital Media and the Organization of Connective Action

The preceding chapter contrasted digital media use and action framing in two differently organized economic crisis protest networks: the organizationally enabled Put People First connective action network and the organizationally brokered G20 Meltdown collective action network. These cases offered something of a natural experiment, as both protests occurred on different days during the same London meetings of the G20 in the early stages of the global economic crisis. With both the protest location and issue focus held constant and with the differently networked events occurring on different days, clear comparisons of action framing and technology deployments could be made.

This chapter examines an equally fortuitous quasi-natural experiment that enabled us to contrast two differently organized climate change protests that occurred later the same year around the 15th Conference of the Parties to the United Nations Framework Convention on Climate Change (COP15). In this pairing, both networks are connective action types, one organizationally enabled and the other crowd enabled. Even more felicitous, the organizationally enabled network that coordinated protests throughout the UK – known as the Wave – contained a number of overlapping members from the PPF network analyzed in Chapter 2. This overlap reflected a demand by many members of PPF that solutions to the economic crisis not come at the expense of the environment. Our analysis looks at the different roles of digital media mechanisms (Twitter in particular) in the UK organizationally enabled Wave network and the crowd-enabled network that emerged around the protests in Copenhagen at the time of the UN summit. Both of these mobilizations were impressive

An earlier version of this chapter was published as "Social Media and the Organization of Collective Action: Using Twitter to Explore the Ecology of Two Climate Change Protests," *Communication Review*, 14, no. 3 (2011), pp. 197–215. Reprinted by permission of Taylor & Francis (www.tandfonline.com).

in size, with turnouts estimated at around 50,000 in the United Kingdom and 100,000 in Copenhagen.

The analysis revolves around Twitter. But we want to emphasize at the outset that we do not single Twitter out as the foundation of either protest. Rather, it is an indicator of how digital media take on different roles in facilitating different types of networked organization. Twitter was just one of many mechanisms (including face-to-face meetings) linking individuals to organizations in the case of the organizationally enabled Wave network and to each other in the case of the crowd-based #cop15 Twitter stream. Yet because it is a piece of a complex protest ecology, Twitter offers a window on the larger mix of actors and technological *actants* (i.e., non-human network agents) with different contextual roles, to use Latour's term discussed in Chapter 1. As we will show, the enabling organizations in the Wave network centrally managed a more or less "official" Twitter stream to rally support and coordinate events, and the organizers effectively turned it off at the end of the protest (insofar as anyone can control a hashtag). By contrast, the crowd-enabled #cop15 stream changed as the crowd shifted among various kinds of activity functions (rallying, information coordination, resource seeking). The #cop15 stream also shifted dramatically in terms of the number of messages tagged with this keyword over time and continued running as a long tail of tweets for an entire year after the Copenhagen summit, until it merged with the Twitter streams around the 16th UN climate summit in Cancun.

The two broad political targets of the protests discussed in this chapter and in Chapter 2 provide interesting institutional backdrops for our analysis. Just as the G20 has been the target of dozens of economic justice protests, UN summits have been the targets of climate change activism. The COP15 was particularly noteworthy for the proliferation of advocacy and activism that converged around it. As world leaders gathered in Copenhagen on December 7–18, 2009, protestors gathered around the world to call for a progressive agreement on climate change. Some of this activity differed from the organizationally brokered action that has characterized environment movement politics, and was characterized to a greater extent by the digital networking and personal action frames typical of different forms of connective action. In some cases this connective action component was substantial, as when the NGO-enabled Wave protests hit London and other British cities displaying a size and structure similar to that of the organizationally enabled PPF connective action networks described in the preceding chapter. In the streets of Copenhagen outside the UN conference, diverse actors and stark ideological divides produced a complex transnational protest space shot through with crowd-enabled connective action. There were, of course, plenty of conventionally organized environmental movement groups in Copenhagen, including ideological collective action networks. However, many thousands of individuals without strong organizational or ideological affiliations also converged on the city and became linked in important ways through media networks. In this chapter we deepen our investigation into how connective action works by focusing on the digital mechanisms that emerged in these differently organized networks.

Technology-Enabled Networks as Organizations: The Case of Twitter

The chapter takes as its starting point the idea of networks as organizational forms, and in particular the action-structuring qualities that may emerge in digital networks. In Chapter 2 we inventoried the networking mechanisms that organizations made available to potential participants and contrasted the personalized communication in a connective campaign with that in a collective one. Here, we are interested in how digital mechanisms embedded in networked action play out under different connective conditions. This tells us something about the organizational role of digital networking mechanisms and also about how connective action types differ.

The two connective network types help us understand network organizations of contrasting kinds, in the sense that one is relatively more intentional and the other less so. Organizationally enabled networks (such as PPF and the Wave) tend to fall roughly into the sphere of intentionally organized networks. In some ways, they accord with the various kinds of (more or less) deliberately constructed networks insightfully studied with respect to sustainable management of common pool resources (Ostrom 1990), economic production networks (Powell 1990), policy networks (Marsh and Rhodes 1992), and global governance regimes (Mueller 2010). Yet organizationally enabled networks may also be less clearly bounded than they tend to be in many of these studies, as shown by Monge and Fulk (1999). In our examination of power and network structure in Chapter 5, we show that it is still meaningful to talk about a core set of organizations in organizationally enabled networks, but the periphery can be rather more loosely organized as core actors open the engagement process to an often large number of organizations and individuals who are neither screened for formal membership nor centrally managed in many of their activities (Bennett 2003).

Crowd-enabled networks, in turn, are less deliberately constructed and even less bounded than organizationally enabled networks. This type in part corresponds to what Mueller (2010) terms "associative clusters" to underline the relative absence of purposeful association, boundedness, and core actors in some networks. Crowd-enabled networks can typically be described in all these ways. However, any approach that views them in poorly specified terms such as clusters or assemblages fails to capture the ways such networks may enable focused and adaptive action and resource mobilization. As we discuss further in Chapter 5 with respect to Occupy, digital technology plays an important role in the organization of crowds. While some crowds may develop with little media infrastructure and may be less organized as a result, our category of crowd-enabled networks points to the growing incidence of connective organization via dense digital media platforms. The key role of social media helps explain why the network boundaries in this type of action are fluid, yet capable of impressive levels of coordinated action and planning, compared with such assemblages as riots.[1]

Digital networking mechanisms play an important role in the network organizations examined in this book. There are, of course, many kinds of digital mechanisms that can help organize crowds, some of which have to do with the way a technology is originally designed and some of which develop through appropriation and use. In a broad sense, Twitter may be thought of as a sort of generic and lightweight networking mechanism, but in practice its uses are quite varied. For example, as we show here, some networks are characterized by organizations heavily managing Twitter streams that can be more or less turned on and off for various purposes, while other streams are less susceptible to central management and, instead, respond to the dynamics of particular crowds. Moreover, different political orientations in organizational networks and crowds (e.g., left–right political orientations) may also affect the levels of structure and routine in flows of information.[2] With so many different organizational patterns available even within one technology, we prefer to look at finer-grained mechanisms available to Twitter users to build their relationships. In this chapter, we consider the organizational effects of two elemental digital mechanisms (hashtagging and hyperlinking) available to users of one technology, Twitter.

To many who view it from afar, Twitter may seem shallow and chaotic – hardly the stuff from which organization might be built. Yet Twitter and other technologies that traverse and connect networks can be important for organizing large-scale connective action in a variety of ways; some of these are illustrated in this chapter, and others are suggested in our analysis of power in networks in Chapter 5. In the broadest generic sense, Twitter is a commercial microblogging service through which users may post messages of up to 140 characters, and the default setting makes messages public. Twitter subscribers can "follow" the updates of other accounts, but several community-generated mechanisms coordinate and spread messages in various other ways.

One of the mechanisms that we consider in this chapter is the hashtag (#), a sign attached to keywords that coordinate and direct traffic for messages around specific themes. Sometimes, hashtags create large highways for different branches of a network to travel in common. At other times, new hashtags enable

---

[1] In an early vision of virtual organizations, Monge and Fulk (1999) refer to "global network organizations." This idea spans our two categories, but we prefer to make the theoretical distinctions between relatively more intentional, organizationally enabled networks and relatively less intentional, crowd-enabled network organizations.

[2] For example, using a novel association mapping method, Conover et al. (2012) analyzed the organizational structure of left- and right-wing Twitter networks in the United States and concluded, among other things, that "the right-wing community is much more densely interconnected, with more users tightly integrated into the right-leaning social network. In contrast, the network of follower/followee relations among left-leaning users exhibits a much more decentralized, loosely-interconnected social structure with far fewer mutually affirmed social connections" (13).

smaller branches for traffic pertaining to specific issues or groups. And some-times, hashtags make it possible to jump across different networks to bridge ideas, actions, or communities. If Twitter is often crowded with traffic, rather like a big city at rush hour, hashtags can direct flows of information to chart paths through the chaos of the crowd. These tags direct tweets carrying various sorts of information and links to resources to designated sub-populations both in and outside of the crowd. Those who receive those resource packets may further direct their paths by adding signals of their own.

Another mechanism that we explore in our analysis of the two different climate protests involves inserting URL hyperlinks (or, simply, links), which is typically done by means of shorteners such as *tinyurl* or *bit.ly* (or Twitter's own T.co, which appeared after we completed this study) to compress long URLs into Twitter's 140-character format. In basic terms, links in messages point users to material beyond the text itself. Such mechanisms allow Twit-ter networks to cross other public and personal networks, both digital and non-digital. More important, as we show in this chapter, many types of links may be introduced into Twitter streams, including links to news sites, activist organizations, streaming sites, fund-raising sites, issue or community blogs, personal websites and blogs, and other places where communities can locate and exchange resources of various kinds in order to grow, stabilize, or aid the work of a crowd-enabled organization (Starbird, Muzny, and Palen 2012).

The importance of crosscutting technology in connective protest ecologies is indicated by the prominence of Twitter in the Occupy movement, which we discuss in Chapter 5, where Twitter emerged as a robust hub with thousands of hashtags and millions of links embedded in more than 100 million tweets. This dynamic meta-network provided something of a connective tissue for Occupy, linking and adding organization to layers that included Facebook pages, Livestream webcasts, and YouTube videos, email lists, SMS trees, phone conferences, and local Occupy websites. Sometimes for better and sometimes for worse, this improvised multi-platform system enabled action plans and related information to flow up, down, and across myriad face-to-face and virtual networks that included millions of people on any given day.[3] While Twitter stands at the center of many contemporary analyses of what we term connective action, it is important to recognize the great complexity of most digitally networked protest spaces. It is also important to point out that Twitter cannot be easily separated in actual practice from numerous other elements of protest organization and that these many elements often include tensions over the use of technology among activists and publics.

This serves to emphasize that sweeping generalizations and assumptions are not helpful starting points for examining the relation between social media and contentious action, much less for illuminating how social technologies operate in specific contexts with specific effects. Looking beyond the obvious function of social technologies as a means of sending and receiving messages, the first

[3] This multi-platform structure of Occupy is sketched in Chapter 5. See also Agarwal et al. (2012).

part of this chapter argues for the importance of analyzing such technologies both as organizing mechanisms in complex action ecologies and as reflections of larger organizational schemes. Precisely because of the crosscutting properties of Twitter networks, we propose that it is both possible and important to analyze them as agents in, and windows on, the wider ecology of the protest space.

Following this conceptual discussion in the next section, the chapter proceeds to trace the emergence of different network organization patterns in our two protest ecologies surrounding the COP15 meeting. In particular, we contrast the London and Copenhagen protest spaces, which were characterized by distinct types of connective action networks, in order to spotlight both the different roles of digital networking mechanisms and their development under different contextual conditions. In the London Wave protest space, an organizational network intent on enabling personalized communication used digital mechanisms to manage a large-scale mobilization. In the crowded protest space of Copenhagen, in which no single organization dominated and technology networks were prominent, the digital mechanisms supported a resource-seeking tendency as the crowd tailed off, and began to pool information and action-related resources to help sustain the crowd-enabled network until the next climate summit a year later.

Contextualizing Twitter Revolutions

The year of the COP15 was the year social media moved to the front line in a variety of national and transnational protests: activists, police, and mass media announced their intention to step up the use of social technology to coordinate, communicate, and monitor the G20 London Summit protests (Ward 2009); Moldova experienced what Evgeny Morozov described as a "Twitter Revolution" in which demonstrators used Twitter to coordinate a challenge pending parliamentary election results (Morozov 2009a); and it was proclaimed that the Iranian revolution would be tweeted (Sullivan 2009). As we now know, the following years yielded a series of uprisings across the Middle East and North Africa that were variously labeled "Twitter Revolutions" and "Facebook Revolutions," while "BlackBerry Riots" flared in the United Kingdom. All of this intensified the debate about the role of social media in contentious politics. The critical discussion has been important, yet it has also been misleading to the extent that it has concentrated on fixed and isolated dimensions of technology or action.

The early commentary about the 2009 Twitter Revolutions focused on two issues: the use of Twitter for communicating information about local causes to distant audiences and its importance in logistical communication among protesters on the ground. Enthusiasts claimed positive effects on both counts; critics played these same claims down. On the first issue, optimistic accounts of protesters' ability to disseminate information to outsiders (thereby providing unprecedented glimpses of events on the ground to journalists and citizens alike) were challenged by those who questioned the reliability and representativeness of tweeted sources (A. Fisher 2010; Morozov 2009b). Moreover, questions remained about the value of Twitter streams in relation to professional journalism (Jewitt 2009; cf. Arceneaux and Schmitz Weiss 2010) and the general public's ability to deal with information overload (A. Fisher 2010; Morozov 2009b).

The other issue revolved around Twitter's ability to facilitate activists' internal communication for the purposes of logistical coordination. The number of active Twitter users and the representative nature of the tweeters were again called into question. Voluble Twitter users may not have been the same people organizing the protests on the ground, who might have preferred more secure means of communication (Esfandiari 2010). Further, it was noted that facilitated coordination is likely to benefit all kinds of actors, from state security forces to pro-regime supporters to genocidal mobs (Cascio 2009; Morozov 2009b; Palfrey, Etling, and Faris 2009). As the early euphoria over the events in Iran was tempered, the debate settled on the questions of whether and how new media have "real consequences for contentious politics" (Aday et al. 2010: 5). In general, "real" consequences were measured in terms of pro-democratic institutional outcomes, and "new media" often boiled down to Twitter: Does Twitter trigger revolutions and are twittered uprisings effective?

Some of this stark framing colored the debate circling more broadly around the building blocks of contemporary contentious action. Following discussions in Morozov (2011) on "slacktivism," whereby a large number of people reap the satisfactions of political intervention from their online actions despite doing little (e.g., clicking to donate, forming a group) to little (or counterproductive) effect, some came to dismiss the idea that digitally mediated action has any role at all. In another much-cited piece questioning the implied links between sheer connectivity, mobilization, and political effectiveness, Malcolm Gladwell (2010) argued that digitally networked activism fails to generate committed collective action when the going gets tough. He characterized social media activism in terms of weak ties and horizontal decentralized organization, and contrasted this unfavorably with the strong ties and centralized hierarchical organization that marked key junctures in the civil rights movement. Digitally networked action, Gladwell concluded, is ill-equipped to bring about systemic change.

It is clear on all sides that we need to develop realistic ways of thinking about the role of communication technologies in the transformation of contentious politics and, ultimately, the effectiveness of such politics. Excellent analyses are emerging to give us greater insights into particular events, such as those of the Arab Spring. Yet it is still important to note that central starting points in the debate have been misleading, and to the extent that these linger, they risk standing in the way of fruitful analysis of contentious connective action.

One of the important analytical fallacies in the debate about social media and contentious politics is that new social media can be abstracted from complex contexts. There are two variations on this fallacy, both of which concern the framing of the debate as much as the dearth of fine-grained empirical analysis. The first is the tendency to isolate social media such as Twitter and Facebook from the broader technological and social contexts in which they operate. This among other things misrepresents the layers of mundane and appropriated technologies (Kleis Nielsen 2011; Earl and Kimport 2011) and mainstream and alternative old line media (Lievrouw 2011; Mattoni 2012) that may characterize a protest. Further, there is a risk that single technologies will become analytically fetishized and that the defining political features of these and other technologies will be assumed rather than discovered. Commentators' periodic cautions in the early Twitter Revolutions debate not to exaggerate the role of facilitated information sharing in regime change (e.g., Eaves 2009) underscored how the discussion tended to approach Twitter as specifically an information communication device, focusing on the quality of the information flows, on the one hand, and its mobilizing promise, on the other. Yet it is not clear what evidence exists for limiting Twitter to the creation of external information flows or the exchange of logistical information among dissidents. Although these are not unreasonable things to look for, they are static rather than dynamic categories.

The second variation on the abstraction fallacy is that social media use can be extracted from the broader political context. On the one hand, it is sensible to recognize that there are likely to be multiple actors, levels, and areas of use to be considered in any particular case. Aday et al. (2010), for example, readily discerned distinct levels at which new media may have mattered in the case of the post-election protests in Iran. Different kinds of actors (including activists, counterinsurgents, states, and technology companies) are likely to be implicated in a digitally saturated protest situation (Askanius and Gustafsson 2010; Morozov 2011; Youmans and York 2012). On the other hand, it is important to note that the framing of the debate about social media and contentious politics at times begs the question of how best to conceive of political action, political effect, and the role of social technologies in particular political events. By neglecting to consider this, not only do we fail to differentiate between different political situations, we also overlook different styles of political action, such as the deliberately episodic, flexible, and nomadic approaches to be found in some contemporary dissent (Juris 2008; Earl and Kimport 2011; Hands 2011; Lievrouw 2011). Pulling any type of social media out of context and asking to what extent it facilitates actions such as those undertaken by the 1960s civil rights movement, as Gladwell does, is far removed from trying to understand contentious politics in late modern societies and the fine-grained communication mechanisms contributing to its organization. As Jussi Parikka (2010) put it:

[W]hile Gladwell is completely correct in saying that the form of politics that is attached to such practices is far from the way we think of politics in the heritage of the social activist movements of 60s and 70s, he himself does not bother mentioning that of course, that should be the start point of the argument, not its conclusion.

The various ways of isolating social media place an undue burden of expectations (e.g., to incite revolutions) on what is just one of many factors in the contemporary political communication and organization repertoire. Moreover, extracting single elements from more complex communication processes involving many actors and technologies may misrepresent the political action and dynamics of the case at hand. By contrast, analyzing social technologies in the context of evolving connective action sequences may enable us to move beyond seeing just a message stream shared among participants, to begin understanding the role of these technologies as organizing mechanisms and using them as windows on the larger protest ecology itself.

The Several Sides of Twitter in the Protest Action Ecology

The following sections focus on Twitter streams. Putting social media "in context" in contentious connective action involves not only mapping ever more technologies, actors, and uses, but also paying attention to the various roles of social media within and across the protest ecology and the differing dynamics that may flow from them. There are at least two important and complementary aspects of a crosscutting social technology such as Twitter from this perspective: its role as both networking *agent* in and *window* on the protest space.

From the first perspective, Twitter is interesting as an organizing element within the specific protest ecology. Networked protest spaces constitute negotiated spheres of individual and collective agency. As discussed in Chapter 1, as digital and social media become more prominent, they too become networking agents within connective action and within the protest space. The presence or absence of digital mechanisms (and discourses) constrains and enables action in networked protest spaces at the same time as they help structure relations among different actors, issues, and events. Twitter is only one of potentially many digital mechanisms that co-constitute and co-configure the digitally networked protest space, and Twitter use introduces several networking mechanisms in turn. The hashtag mechanism, which is central to the analysis in this chapter, was developed by Twitter users to coordinate messages on a particular topic. Appending the # symbol to a keyword makes a message visible for public search (beyond the followers of a particular account or registered users). While hashtags have diverse uses (e.g., emphasis), one of the central functions is to allow Twitter users to cohere around an issue even though they may not be interacting directly with each other (Bruns and Burgess 2011; Bruns 2012). Other notable mechanisms include using @[username] to address and mention specific users (sometimes referred to as @mention), retweeting (resending) messages to highlight or endorse them, and including links to other sites in the message (Honeycutt and Herring 2009; boyd, Golder, and Lotan 2010).

From the second perspective, Twitter streams may reveal interesting features of the protest ecology's wider composition, and in particular something of the organizational scheme in which they are embedded. This may, among other things, indicate something of the larger network of relations involved in a particular event, even if it does not tell the whole story about them (cf. Huberman, Romero, and Wu 2009). One alternative is to analyze the users contributing to a stream (where they are identifiable; boyd and Ellison, 2007); another is to turn the stream inside out to look at who and what is linked to rather than who is posting. The organizations and social media linked in tweets reveal a sample of the organizations, information sources, and social networking sites pertinent to a particular protest ecology. For example, link data from the climate change protests that we discuss later reveal how different organizations (from advocacy organizations to government agencies) and information sources (e.g., the BBC, the United Nations News Center, the Brookings Institution, bloggers) become engaged with activist networks at various stages of protest events. The contexts of these links include participants assessing the mass media effect of real-time actions, sharing think tank material, and recounting their own experiences at events.

This twofold approach to Twitter in digitally networked protests can only be indicative; it cannot roll out a definitive map of the protest space. What is more, Twitter may play very different roles in different ecologies, as our two cases illustrate. With these conditions in mind, we nevertheless distinguish three points of focus that allow us to explore the distinct dynamics of organizationally enabled and crowd-enabled connective action:

- *Twitter streams can be crosscutting networking mechanisms.* Twitter streams can (though do not always) attract diverse players, from individuals to organizations, and include contributors and followers from afar and in the midst of the action. In this light, they may be approached as transmission belts as they cut across and connect diverse networks, actors, and locations in an action space, or specifically a protest space. The networks at play in a Twitter stream may in part be revealed by features such as the links embedded in tweets.
- *Twitter streams embed and are embedded in gatekeeping processes.* There are different modes of managing the flow of links and other inputs embedded within a Twitter stream. A stream may allow glimpses of more classic gatekeeping where, for example, the content of a link is managed by the source of the tweet. More important, however, gatekeeping management is also visible within the stream itself in terms of which (and how many) agents introduce particular kinds of links or amplifying cues such as @mention and the retweet. Although hashtags are open to all users, such management may become more centralized when streams are populated mainly by one or a few organizations whose members have particular organizational uses in mind, such as rallying demonstrators for a specific event. By contrast, hashtags that are dominated by diverse crowds may result in chaotic streams with links and directives that seem not to connect with each other. In still other cases, such in-stream crowdsourced gatekeeping can introduce fairly sustained and rich organizational resources in far-flung protest ecologies.

- *Changing organizational dynamics over time.* As we shift the analytical focus in these directions, it is important to remember that data from Twitter streams contain only a slice of the collective action space and that what the slice looks like may change as other elements of the evolving environment interact with the users and managers of the stream. Depending on where one cuts into a Twitter stream, then, one may find different actors and different kinds of activity going on, from rallying in the midst of a demonstration to debriefing and planning for next events at later stages. In these ways, some streams may operate as relatively long-running communities, rich with information and analysis, whereas others may serve as brief beacons of information and logistics contributing to the orchestration of a particular action within a bounded time frame.

We focus on these three points in turn in the following sections to examine Twitter streams that figured centrally in the London and Copenhagen protests. Our analysis indicates similar yet interestingly different dynamics in the organizationally enabled and crowd-enabled connective action of the respective protests, as well as suggesting different roles for Twitter within them.

Connective Action Surrounding the UN Climate Conference

The previous sections emphasize that social technologies are likely to be deeply embedded in the protest ecologies in which they operate. Recognizing this point may be particularly important when one is dealing with complex protest spaces: that is, contexts in which multiple actors (from individuals to organizations to coalitions to networks) with different political and organizational ideologies co-constitute the protest space and in which social technologies are perceived to offer a flexible means for both organizers and individuals to access and navigate that space. It is in these contexts in which networked layers and the organizing mechanisms embedded in them may become most prominent. As we noted earlier, such complexity characterizes much contentious politics both in late modern democracies and elsewhere. It also specifically describes the protest spaces in London and Copenhagen, which were part of a family of national and transnational protests leading up to the COP15. The two cases illustrate protest spaces that are complex in distinct ways.

The London protest space was dominated by the coalition that organized the Wave – a cluster of UK marches held (primarily) in London and Glasgow on December 5, 2009.[4] The organizer, Stop Climate Chaos Coalition (SCCC), was a large coalition supported by environmental, global justice, humanitarian, and religious organizations such as Tearfund, Oxfam, Greenpeace, the World Wildlife Fund, Christian Aid, and CAFOD. This coalition was well established

---

[4] The protest space was dominated by the SCCC, but there were other protest activities in London during this time. Most notably, a Climate Camp commenced in central London when the Wave finished.

and followed the lead of the earlier Make Poverty History campaign (Rootes and Saunders 2007; Rootes 2012). As noted in the preceding chapter, it also overlapped significantly in terms of organizational membership and solidarity network with the Put People First coalition that organized G20 London Summit protests earlier in 2009, and the PPF website explicitly identified the Wave as the "next event."

As with Put People First, part of the complexity of this case involves the balance of communication between the organizations and potential demonstrators. Like PPF, the SCCC and its supporter organizations used a variety of digital and social media to organize and mobilize participants to urge the national government to hold the line on carbon reduction targets at the Copenhagen conference.[5] As will be discussed further, much of the organizational effort seemed aimed at generating a "buzz" about the demonstration, both to show policy officials that citizens favored decisive action on a climate treaty and to rally support for those activists heading to Copenhagen. As the name of the march implies, the coalition created a broad personal action frame for the march, calling on potential participants to become part of "the Wave." One of the most attention-grabbing sections of the Wave website prior to the demonstration was the invitation to upload home videos to the site to signal support for the demonstration. The video stream showed friends or workmates doing a "Mexican Wave," arranged in such a way that the video stream eventually came to constitute a wave in itself. Participants were encouraged to turn up for the march in blue, complete with painted faces and hands, to emphasize the sky/water environmental focus of this wave of public determination. While there were many homemade placards and diverse slogans (Wahlström, Wennerhag and Rootes forthcoming), the march itself became a sea of blue. Fifty thousand people turned out, making this the largest climate protest to date in the United Kingdom and, in the view of the organizers at the time, "the biggest climate change march in the world ever!" – a boast that would soon be topped in Copenhagen (Stop Climate Chaos Coalition 2009a). The coalition engaged security guards for the march, which remained orderly despite the large number of participants (Rootes 2012). In these ways, the Wave protest fits our model of an organizationally enabled network that has other aspects of organizational management well in hand and uses personal action frames and a variety of digital media to personalize communication with followers.

By contrast, no single organizational actor controlled the protest space in Copenhagen. The conference drew a vast and diverse crowd of local and transnational protest actors, some strictly coordinated and others less so. The

---

[5] The SCCC website did not offer quite as many distinct technological affordances as did the PPF, but it was closer to PPF than Meltdown in this respect. In the website analysis described in the preceding chapter, the SCCC website was found to offer 17 digital mechanisms, compared with the 23 offered by PPF and the 6 offered by Meltdown. (There was also a website dedicated to the Wave linked off the SCCC site.)

protest activities continued for more than a week during the COP15 conference, with numerous events associated with different groups.[6] Clearly, plenty of focused organizational work (and brokerage) took place in and prior to Copenhagen; the protest space was crowded with organizational actors. Yet this meant that no one actor dominated, and there were notable layers of technology-enabled networks beyond the brick and mortar organizations.

Part of the complexity of this case arose from the sharing and partitioning of the protest space among the numerous actors (Reitan 2010; Hadden 2012) and from the variety of protest frames offered and displayed by organizations and individual participants (Wahlström, Wennerhag, and Rootes forthcoming). Organized advocacy and activism against climate change had burgeoned in the years before the 2009 summit. The Copenhagen protest space surrounding the UN conference was thick with ideologically and organizationally diverse organizations and networks that variously overlapped, converged, and kept their distance from each other (Pleyers 2010; Reitan 2010; Hadden 2012). Klimaforum09, an alternative climate summit organized by a broad coalition of almost 100 Danish and international civil society actors in order to offer a forum for meeting and debate, served as a focal point for many groups and individuals in Copenhagen (Klimaforum 2009). Other parts of the protest space were shaped by the transnational network Climate Action Network-International (CAN), which had more than 450 member organizations at the time (Climate Action Network-International 2009). This rapidly expanding but tightly organized NGO coalition aimed at influencing the negotiations from inside the climate talks and was flanked by the Global Campaign for Climate Action (GCCA), which focused on public mobilization. More loosely coordinated transnational networks concentrated on climate justice rather than reform: these included Climate Justice Now! (CJN), a network of more than 200 organizations and movements committed to social, ecological, and gender justice that had been launched at the close of COP13 (Climate Justice Now! 2009), and Climate Justice Action (CJA), a direct action network open to individuals as well as groups (such as various Climate Camp groups, the Indigenous Environmental Network, Kenya Young Greens, and the Danish Climate Collective) that focused on mobilization in line with goals oriented toward climate justice and economic system change (Climate Justice Action 2009). There were plenty of examples of partitioning and sharing just among these four networks – and there were also numerous other actors – with dynamics ranging from outright rejection of goals and campaign styles to negotiated cooperation to organizing the information and action space among them (Reitan 2010; Hadden 2012).[7]

---

[6] For a partial list of events, see www.climateimc.org/en/original-news/2009/11/09/list-cop15-copenhagen-protests-and-events.

[7] As Ruth Reitan (2010) and Jennifer Hadden (2012) discuss, central actors in the reform-oriented and climate justice–oriented blocs for the most part kept their distance from each other, but there were also some coordination and overlapping members between the two (e.g., between CAN and CJN!). Coordination and divisions were also evident within these broad blocs. As an example of the latter, CJN! and CJA remained distinct networks, yet also formed a joint section at the

The protests taking place across the world and the many who followed the events in Copenhagen from afar were also an important part of the picture.

The march that attracted the largest turnout was loosely coordinated by the Danish coalition 12Dec09, which cited a support base of 538 organizations from 67 countries (12Dec09.dk). One of the aims was to attract as many participants as possible. The demonstration, the Climate March at the Climate Summit, which took place on the Global Day of Action, December 12, 2009, drew between 50,000 and 100,000 people (D. Fisher 2010; Wahlström, Wennerhag, and Rootes forthcoming).

One indicator of the importance of crowd-enabled action in this event is that as many as half of those who participated in the march (53.2 percent) were not active in any of the main organizational groupings (e.g., environmental, religious, humanitarian, global justice, trade union, political), compared with 31.3 percent in the organizationally enabled London march (Wahlström, Wennerhag, and Rootes forthcoming). A variety of slogans were visible throughout the march. The innocuously named 12Dec09 initiative's website simply stated "Planet first, people first" in one corner and "Climate March at the Climate Summit" in the other. Although organizationally endorsed slogans about global justice, climate justice, and system change also appeared, these themes were not the most dominant among the individual protesters: when surveyed about solutions to the climate crisis, most respondents identified solutions related to policy action and individual lifestyle changes (Wahlström, Wennerhag, and Rootes forthcoming). The Copenhagen protest space was thus crowded not just with actors but also with action frames.

As in London, several of the organizing actors in Copenhagen used a variety of commercial and alternative digital media platforms to communicate with potential participants in Copenhagen and the wider public abroad, with various degrees of success (Askanius and Uldam 2011; Gavin and Marshall 2011). Aside from using social technologies to communicate the message, mobilize, and provide real-time coordination for action on the ground, some also encouraged the use of various (often generic) technologies and mechanisms to connect participants with each other and to involve their personal networks.[8]

December 12 demonstration under the banner "System Change not Climate Change," and CJN! supported the CJA-organized "Reclaim Power: Push for Climate Justice!" demonstration on December 16, which drew an estimated 3,000 people. So it is not unexpected that CJN! appears, if only peripherally, in the CJA digital "solidarity network" at this time (as does SCCC and Never Trust a Cop, but not CAN).

[8] The CJA provides a good example of this broad encouragement. Its website, which offered the same number of affordances as the SCCC, was updated shortly before the summit week with a tab to "get connected," which listed places to obtain and contribute news (linking to Climate Indymedia, Danish Indymedia, and Danish Modkraft); instructions on how to sign up to get SMS updates about the street demonstrations; and the instruction to tag messages on, e.g., Flickr, YouTube, and Twitter with the hashtags #CJA, #climatejustice, #cop15, #COP15IMC, #badcop (Climate Justice Action 2009). The official CJA Twitter profile feed @ClimateActivism echoed this information regularly throughout the week.

Connective action networks emerged in both London and Copenhagen, yet different connective action types characterized the protests in the two cities: the former was more organizationally enabled while the latter was more crowd enabled. Digitally networked action surrounded the central demonstrations in both cases, but examining the two cases reveals connective action in which organizations and technology played somewhat different roles and different dynamics emerged.

Organizing Mechanisms in Two Protest Twitter Streams

Our analysis focuses on the Twitter hashtag streams that were most prominent in the respective demonstrations in London and Copenhagen.[9] We do not claim that either hashtag was the central organizational backbone in terms of, for example, planning the logistics of each march, but we do find that their use patterns reveal differences in the role of social media in such networks.

The first hashtag in our analysis, #thewave, was launched by the SCCC as part of a wider campaign to mobilize and publicize the Wave march. The number of tweets sent with #thewave amounted to more than 2,500 from the point at which it trended in the United Kingdom on the morning of the protest to its dying out a few days later. This is a modest number compared with the number of tweets sent during other protests (e.g., Occupy; see Chapter 5), but it reflects the more centrally managed uses of Twitter found in short-term strategic deployments by organizationally enabled networks. Such streams typically pale in comparison to many crowd-generated Twitter hashtags, which clearly do more core organizational work in the crowd-enabled networked organizations. Indeed, our technology overview indicates that the Wave stream was a relatively small element of a larger battery of digital media deployed by organizations to engage a diverse array of individuals. As previously noted, we documented some 17 different digital engagement mechanisms available on the SCCC event coordination site. Reflecting its short life during the demonstrations, the use of the hashtag ceased shortly after the protest (but was later reactivated in a non-related context).

By contrast, the other hashtag, #cop15, was an emergent stream that was not centered on one organization or coalition. This multi-language hashtag of unclear origin became one of the most highly used and tracked streams relating to the COP15 conference as well as the associated protests (Boynton 2010). It was used prolifically for various purposes and in different locations by diverse actors, including the Danish government as conference host, individual protesters, bloggers, and advocacy organizations around the world. It was in use months before the conference and continued (at a far lower volume) for a full year afterward. By the end of December 2009, roughly 100,000 #cop15 hashtagged tweets had been logged (Twapperkeeper.com).

[9] We are very grateful for the research assistance of Nathan Johnson, Marianne Goldin, Allison Rank, and Sofia Tahko on the studies reported in this chapter.

Because there were thousands of tweets in each of the streams, we took random samples. Every tenth tweet was sampled from each stream for the dates selected. One clear difference in the two streams was that #thewave involved a burst of activity around the day of the protest, whereas #cop15 had a much more extended life before, during, and after the main protest day. Thus, we were able to compare the two streams on the day of the protest marches and also sample #cop15 on other dates to assess dynamics over time. On the day of the main demonstrations, #cop15 included 3,251 tweets, giving a sample of 325. Because #thewave was dedicated primarily to the protest day itself, we sampled the single trend line that included the day of the protest and the few tweets of the days after, for a total of 2,529 tweets, which resulted in a sample of 253.

Twitter as Crosscutting Networking Mechanism

As we suggested at the beginning of this chapter, a Twitter stream can be conceived as a crosscutting transmission belt connecting diverse users, uses, and temporal and spatial regions of the protest space. Hashtag streams are particularly interesting from this perspective, as they suggest the contours of networks cutting across (and beyond) the protest space (Bruns and Burgess 2011; Bruns 2012). Hashtagged messages – and their retweets – may disperse widely in combinations across a variety of feeds and networks bringing messages to users with various levels of interest in an issue. The mechanisms of retweeting and of including mentions and links in messages all enhance the crosscutting capacity of the hashtagged stream. We did analyze the use of @ and retweeting in the streams, but because of space limitations we focus in this discussion on linking.

In line with the perspective sketched in the preceding section, we suggest looking at links not just with respect to information flow but also in their role as organizing mechanisms and, more abstractly, as windows on surrounding players and links among diverse information flows. In the first instance, this entails viewing links from the perspective of how they may structure and alert members of social networks to particular slices of the protest space. This draws on previous work that has explored how links on organization websites can play a structuring role, enabling and constraining action in protest space, and how they shape a protest space in the way they are used to construct and advertise alliances between actors (Rogers 2004; Foot and Schneider 2006). It also entails approaching links in Twitter messages with attention to what they reveal about the networked ecology of the agents involved. Although information about user profiles may reveal important sides to the protest ecology, we here turn the Twitter stream inside out to shed light on actors and sites that in this manner are revealed to be or are brought in to become part of the protest space.

This dual approach can be applied to the two hashtag streams related to the London and Copenhagen protests. Both protests involved a variety of organizations and individuals operating in the midst of the demonstrations as

TABLE 3.1. *Breakdown of Tweets Containing Links Sent on Day of Protest, by Media Levels*

Link Type	#thewave[a]	#cop15[b]
Mass	15.15% (15)	18.18% (36)
Middle	34.34 (34)	56.56 (112)
Micro	33.33 (33)	10.60 (21)
Other/broken	17.17 (17)	14.64 (29)

[a] Data gathered December 5–8, 2009. Number of tweets sampled: 252. Tweets containing links: 99 (39.0%).
[b] Data gathered December 12, 2009. Number of tweets sampled: 325. Tweets containing links: 198 (60.9%).
Chi-square = 26.0, $p < .01$.

well as from a distance. Our question here concerns what was made of the stream: What kinds of sites were linked to and what do the different patterns of links tell us about the underlying organizational logic of the protest ecology?

Links are major elements of both streams on the day of each protest, but there are important differences in their volume and distribution. As indicated in Table 3.1, links appeared in 39 percent of #thewave tweets and fully 60.9 percent of the #cop15 tweets (as we discuss in the dynamics analysis later, linking in the latter stream was in fact higher on other days). The volume and nature of linking in the Copenhagen protest stream as compared with that of the London stream suggests interesting things about the two protest ecologies in which the streams are embedded and, as we shall discuss later, the differing roles Twitter plays in the two cases.

Our analysis tracked the different types of links that emerged in both streams. In the case of the continuing #cop15 stream, we also followed how they may have changed over time. We discovered a media world that places the mass media at the margins and elevates purveyors of social technology, from NGOs to Flickr, into prominent roles. The breakdown of links on the day of the two protests also appears in Table 3.1. We categorized the links in terms of whether they pointed at mass media sites (e.g., BBC, *Le Monde*, the *New York Times*), middle media sites that exist primarily or only online yet receive a large number of users (e.g., alternative and activist news media, NGOs, government and corporate sites, environment and climate information sites, and prominent blogs such as Real Climate), or micromedia sites that reflect individual-level sites that are clearly personal in nature. In keeping with our focus on what elements were brought in through links, we made borderline decisions on the basis of where the content was created rather than who posted it (e.g., Al Jazeera on YouTube would be coded as mass media; an NGO-posted twitpic would be coded as middle media; and a personal or anonymous twitpic would be coded as micromedia). This scheme builds on the model suggested by Peretti (2002) for tracking media flows across increasingly intertwined communication networks.

In contrast to what has been found in other types of political hashtag streams (Small 2011), links in the two protest streams for the most part do not point toward mass media. As Table 3.1 shows, actors in the realm of middle media represent the dominant action and information sites in both these slices of protest ecology. Yet a notable difference between the two streams has to do with how links were distributed within the middle media and micromedia categories. Within the middle media categories, links to NGO and activist organization websites and their uses of social media rival links to mass media news actors in both streams: in #thewave, this NGO pattern constitutes 19.19 percent of all links, and in #cop15 on the day of the protest it constitutes 17.67 percent of all links. In #cop15 a similarly large number of links led either to alternative and activist news and information media (e.g., Indymedia, *Huffington Post*) or think tanks and various kinds of climate information sites or institutes (e.g., the Scientific Public Policy Institute, the Amazon Environmental Institute, Think Progress). Together these kinds of links add up to 18.18 percent of the total number of links, also equaling the mass media linking rate in this stream. Meanwhile, governmental sites such as the conference host Denmark's COP15 website accounted for 13.13 percent of all links. Contributors to the #cop15 hashtag in this way pooled organizational and information resources using the networking potential of middle media sites.

The links in #thewave, by contrast, underscore the ways in which this hashtag centered on a physically co-present demonstration in which the organizational capacity of the central coalition was well established. Mid-level linking in this stream primarily led back to the coalition coordinating the march and its sponsoring organizations, and the micro-level links primarily presented depictions of the march itself. As we shall discuss further in the next section, #thewave hashtag was used strategically by the SCCC to personalize the mobilization for the planned protest. As noted, participants were encouraged to paint their faces and hands blue to echo the climate theme when they waved at cameras and then to post photos from the demonstration. This seems to explain the strong linking to micro-level sites in this stream. Almost all of the micro-level links in this stream led to twitpic or yfrog photos from the street march itself. A number of the middle-level links also went to coalition organization photo pages, resulting in fully 44.32 percent of all links in #thewave going to photos or photo galleries. This high rate can be compared with the lower presence of personal micro-level linking in the #cop15 stream, which also had fewer photo links overall (only 14 percent). This seemingly reflects how the Wave was oriented to a community of protesters who shared both geographic and ritualistic elements in their protest identifications via high levels of personally expressive content, but it also indicates that the organizational capacity was already beyond doubt.

All of this suggests that linking as a crosscutting element of the Twitter messages may play out differently in the context of different protests, even ones belonging to the same family of collective action events (i.e., addressing the same issue, happening in the same time frame). Thinking about links as revealing elements of the protest ecology, we see a more personalized and expressive co-present experience reflected in the Wave, echoing the encouragement by NGO facilitators to share personal experiences. The lower level of NGO links in the Wave reflect an organizing coalition of NGOs that did not need to link back to themselves, but rather encouraged those being mobilized to link to each other. That participants then did so underscored the personal and person-oriented tone of the communication and the protest itself. By contrast, the stream associated with the more crowded protest ecology did seek out organizational and informational resources. The large number of Copenhagen demonstrators and people following their activities from afar seemed to find it more useful to point to diverse NGOs, activist organizations, and middle media information sites as resource hubs, thereby also extending the network beyond the Twitter stream.

Gatekeeping Processes in the Twittered Protest Space

A further important point of comparison between protest ecologies has to do with the gatekeeping that distributes actionable information to participants. While there is little agreement about the meaning of gatekeeping (Barzilai-Nahon 2009), it here refers to the filters operating in a communication system, the agents that control them, and the information they screen out and let through. Unlike the Twitter profile feed, in which the messages are controlled by the owner of the account, anyone may attach a hashtag for any tweeted message and no contributor can control a hashtag stream in the sense of deleting messages. However, actors can contribute positively to the shape of a stream by, for example, contributing posts and links or amplifying others' contributions by mentioning them or retweeting messages (cf. Honeycutt and Herring 2009; boyd, Golder, and Lotan 2010; Bruns and Burgess 2011; Bruns 2012). Here, we continue to focus on in-stream management in the form of linking. Broad comparisons between the two Twitter streams suggest that very different in-stream processes were at work: #thewave reflected a far more organization-centered and centrally managed protest space, while #cop15 reflected a more decentralized crowdsourced scheme. What is remarkable is that both stayed fairly consistently on topic and displayed little violent disagreement.

As already indicated, #thewave hashtag was launched and largely managed by the coalition coordinating the march, the SCCC. It and its supporter organizations used several digital technologies in a strategy of personalizing the mobilization around the march, enabling users to fill in details in the protest narrative and to customize their digital interactions with the coalition. As part of this, the SCCC initiated several "Twitter storm" campaigns before and during the demonstration, which involved encouraging supporters to tweet on a specific topic during a given period in order to make it "trend" in the general Twitter traffic. One storm on November 5, 2009, highlighted the official launch of the Wave website. The organizers encouraged followers to "Tell all your friends and retweet, retweet, retweet! See you on #TheWave" (Stop Climate Chaos Coalition 2009b). The hashtag trended to second place among all Twitter streams in the United Kingdom during the march (Twirus UK). After the march, the SCCC no longer actively encouraged use of the hashtag, and its use died out within days.

As with the PPF in the preceding chapter, the SCCC strategy of personalizing its public communication meant running the risk of losing control over its message and brand. Yet #thewave is a surprisingly orderly stream. The SCCC apparently did not try to discipline the contents of the stream aside from, say, encouraging retweeting. As expected, then, some of the sampled tweets publicize other actions, for example, those that couple #thewave with #copout (referring to the direct action protest organized by Climate Camp London, which was scheduled to start at an undisclosed location at the close of the Wave). Yet there were only a few of them, and there is only one explicitly critical tweet in the entire sample: "People on #thewave screaming bloody murder are the same kids who used to take the piss out of my family for growing veg & mending clothes." Again, #thewave clearly reflected its function as a rallying and mobilizing mechanism centered on the physically co-present demonstration. As discussed in the preceding section, links predominantly led to the sponsoring organizations or the photos of people attending the demonstration. Coded for content, the stream scored high in tweets that were either describing the real-time event (68 percent) or expressing solidarity with the protest (28.9 percent). Logistical information (where to go, what to do) was less prevalent (11.1 percent), suggesting that logistical support was being provided through other sources. It is interesting to note that there was little "self-promotional" use of the hashtag (Small 2011): the coalition and its supporter organizations contributed only 11 percent (28) of the tweets in our sample (and only in four cases did they link to their own organizational site), but this proved enough to shape the arc of the stream.[10]

In contrast with #thewave, the #cop15 stream was not driven by a dominant actor, and yet it too turned out to be surprisingly ordered. We have not found evidence of any attempt to launch this hashtag among the central organizations related to the conference or the protest march. The conference host government's Ministry of Foreign Affairs used #cop15 consistently in its profile feed @cop15 from the summer of 2009 onward but did not indicate any sense of ownership. The 12Dec09 coalition, the coordinators of the march, created a profile Twitter feed (@12dec09), yet posted few entries (barely filling one page) and did not use any hashtags on this feed. The CJA instructed participants to tag messages on various social media with #cop15, and the profile feed @ClimateActivism used it fairly regularly. None of these appear as dominant contributors in our sample.

---

[10] This dynamic can in some ways be seen to be similar to military swarming tactics, which combine centralization and decentralization in the form of central command and self-organizing targeted strikes (see, e.g., Arquilla and Ronfeldt 2000).

Despite strategic deployment by a few prominent actors, the bulk of the stream reveals a general absence of dominating gatekeepers around the time of the protest. The day-of-protest sample includes a wide variety of contributors, with the largest grouping being "individual" Twitter account profiles.[11] In contrast to the SCCC and its support organizations in #thewave, relatively few identifiable organizations are found in the sample tweeting in #cop15 under its own name on this day. In other words, the #cop15 management during the protest seems to have been more crowdsourced, with links to a wide variety of governmental and civil society organizations, as discussed in the preceding section, and with few account holders linking to themselves here either (5 percent). Moreover, #cop15 also did not seem to serve the steadily managed role of rally mechanism that was seen in #thewave. Coded for content on the day of the protest, #cop15 scores fairly high for real-time descriptions of the event (61.2 percent) but low on expressions of solidarity (13.2 percent) and logistical messages (6.2 percent). The low level of logistics suggests once again that the real-time orchestration of demonstrations occurred elsewhere and that #cop15 instead offered windows on the events and other resources for the actors to share.

This comparison suggests that in-stream gatekeeping in a crowdsourced stream need not be less coherent than more centralized organization management of the sort we find in #thewave. It also appears that different streams can serve different organizational roles and stay focused. The #cop15 tweets tend to keep to the general issues at hand: climate change, the conference, protesting the conference. Few messages express criticism of the other tweets being disseminated through the hashtag. Some of the environmental information sites belong to climate skeptics, yet there is little disagreement or abusive language voiced within the stream about earlier contributions or the issues at stake. This finding is in line with other work on crowd management in Twitter hashtags (Bruns and Burgess 2011; Lindgren and Lundström 2011). As we found in a separate study, however, it is unlike the character of the #G20 stream used during the G20 Pittsburgh Summit protests in the fall of 2009, in which protesters, anti-protesters, and disgruntled locals struggled via Twitter over the rightful uses of the streets of Pittsburgh.

The crowd-organized character of the stream also reveals how various social technologies can adapt to the temporal frame of contentious political activities. One clear difference between #thewave and #cop15 is that the latter ran alongside the 10 days of protest activities, including various direct action and civil disobedience events, several educational forums, religious services, and the main demonstration. Figure 3.1 shows that there were several days with thousands of tweets, indicating that #cop15 was far more

[11] The coding of contributors noted only information provided in the account profile. A user was coded as "individual tweet profile" if no other information was given (e.g., if no indication of affiliation with an organization, collective, institution, or business was provided) or if it was explicitly stated that the user's views were her or his own.

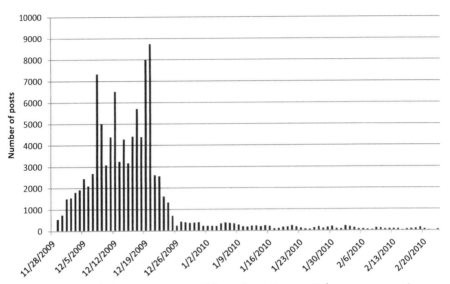

FIGURE 3.1. Posts in #cop15 over time (November 28, 2009–February 22, 2010).

than just a rallying or logistical communication aid during the demonstration itself.

The crowd-as-gatekeeper (in the sense of emphasizing particular themes and creating particular resource and organizational links) also repurposed the #cop15 stream after the conference ended. Unlike #thewave, the #cop15 stream did not come to an abrupt halt. Running as a "long tail" for a year after the Copenhagen events, the stream gradually merged with others in a kind of handoff to the COP16 activist network focusing on the next UN summit in Cancun. Although the number of tweets dwindled, the relative level of linking increased after the protest (even as the diversity of users seemed to decrease). It appears that a kind of resource-seeking process was created with links to a variety of organizations and bloggers offering information and organizational resources across a global network.

The two streams raise different points of comparison. They were similar in terms of their remarkable focus on the protests with very low levels of noise or hijacking by spam or so-called trolls. Yet they differed markedly in terms of the high level of organizational management in one case and the shifting crowd dynamics leading to the organizational resource-seeking dynamics in the long tail of the other. The very different dynamics of the two cases highlight our final point: the importance of recognizing the potentially changing nature of hashtag streams (and the role of the hashtag mechanism) embedded in different collective action contexts and at different points in those contexts over time.

How Twitter Reflects Changing Dynamics in Protest Ecologies

Another clear organizational feature of Twitter streams in protest ecologies is their capacity to shift organizational functions over time. As Herwig, Kossats,

TABLE 3.2. *Tweets in #cop15 by Date and Type of Use*

Type of Use	December 3[a]	December 12[b]	January 12 and 19[c]
Description	24.4% (47)	61.2% (199)	25.3% (21)
Solidarity	5.2 (10)	13.2 (43)	3.6 (3)
Logistical	10.9 (21)	6.2 (20)	6.0 (5)
Link	78.2 (151)	60.9 (198)	88.0 (73)
Other	4.7 (9)	9.8 (192)	6.0 (5)

Note: Multiple coding for each tweet was permitted.
[a] Total number of tweets: 193.
[b] Total number of tweets: 325.
[c] Total number of tweets: 83.
Chi-square = 160.3, $p < .01$.

and Mark (2010) observe in the case of the 2009 #unibrennt student protests in Vienna, these twittered network patterns appear to be "permanently beta," open to change in organizational character (cf. Neff and Stark 2003). In the case of some streams, such as #thewave, that rally participation in a particular event, the organizational sponsorship results in the stream disappearing as the central "driver" stops encouraging its use when its immediate function is outlived. In other cases, such as #cop15, the stream evolves through several different organizational phases in the time before, during, and after the Copenhagen demonstrations.

Different patterns of use emerge depending on where one cuts into the stream. However, one general difference emerges. The long tail of the #cop15 stream, embedded in a dense, crowded, and wide-ranging protest space, increasingly "seeks out" resources as the remaining users link to blogs, organizations, and institutional sites. This resource seeking in a way stabilizes the structure of the stream as it merges into other streams. By contrast, the more centralized coalition facilitating a demonstration via #thewave may have provided support resources directly through member organizations communicating with their affiliated publics. In other work in progress at the time of this writing, we observe similar resource-seeking behavior in the long tail of Occupy networks in the United States, as Tweets become more densely linked to the city websites of the protests, rather as if pointing to lifeboats in a sinking movement.

As previously noted, we traced the #cop15 stream from one week before the December 12 protest to one month after the protest. Shortly after December 12, it decreased to a small but steady stream and underwent various organizational transitions reflecting the changing ecological context of the protests. Table 3.2 shows the level of linking in different time periods, with a notable increase in links as activity tails off. (Note that multiple codes were permitted, so that a tweet could, for example, contain a solidarity message and a link, just a solidarity message, or just a link.) After the protest, the number of tweets containing links rose to an extraordinary 88 percent (fully 73 of our late stream sample of 83 tweets). As noted, the relative absence of central coordination in the Copenhagen protests and #cop15 stream may account for the higher levels

TABLE 3.3. *Tweets in #cop15 by Link Type over Time*

Link Type	December 3[a]	December 12[b]	January 12 and 19[c]
Mass	21.19% (32)	18.18% (36)	17.80% (13)
Middle	68.87 (104)	56.56 (112)	65.75 (48)
Micro	4.60 (7)	10.60 (21)	8.20 (6)
Other/broken	5.29 (8)	14.64 (29)	8.20 (6)

[a] Total number of tweets: 193. Total number of tweets with links: 151 (78.2%).
[b] Total number of tweets: 325. Total number of tweets with links: 198 (60.9%).
[c] Total number of tweets: 83. Total number of tweets with links: 73 (88%).
Chi-square = 14.2, $p < .05$.

of links embedded in the tweets; participants increasingly point each other to organizations and other resources after the protest as well.

Table 3.2 suggests that there are several types of organization being produced by the crowd in different phases of the protest. There are understandably more descriptions of ongoing events on the day of the demonstration actions.[12] Logistical coordination is highest during the period before the action. Perhaps most interesting is the use of the long tail of the diminishing stream to share resource links with other activists following the action. As shown in Table 3.2, fully 88 percent of tweets a month after the protests contained links.

Table 3.3 shows the types of sites linked in tweets at different points in the arc of the stream. This view gives a more nuanced picture of such resource sharing. Even as the organizing character of links changed over the arc of the protests, the predominant media level was that of the "middle media" of NGO, activist, and alternative information sites. The consistent emphasis on this level of media seems to be in accord with the impression that crowd-enabled connective networks focus on sharing content that may offer more interactive potential than generally found at either the mass media or the personal website level. This is an interesting contrast to the Wave tweets, which displayed a high use of micromedia and photos, again suggesting perhaps that richer organizational linking was less important, due to fact that these protests were to a greater extent managed by the coalition organizations.

The end of stream dynamics that we observe with #cop15 also bears on the earlier gatekeeping discussion. The linking in the later stages of the stream remains focused on middle-level sites, evenly divided between NGO and activist organizations, on the one hand, and alternative information sites or think tanks, on the other. As we traced these developments, however, we noted a shift in the balance of actors in terms of who contributed at what rate. Analysis of the stream one month after the protest revealed a continuing diversity of actors, even as there were some shifts within and between the categories. By this time, "individual" profiles and middle-level contributors jointly dominated the

[12] The coding of "descriptions" included only events in the city of Copenhagen. It would have been higher on the day of protest had the coding included, e.g., descriptions of the parallel events in Australia.

stream, and within the middle category, information and action organizations had been joined by green businesses as the government actors faded. For the most part, the users were still not linking to themselves: 12 percent of all messages at this point included a link to the account holder. In contrast to this earlier variety, analysis by "What the Hashtag?!" indicates that by the time almost a year had lapsed, a few single actors had come to dominate the stream. In October 2010, What the Hashtag?! reported that 80.3 percent of the 71 #cop15 tweets in the preceding week had come from the "top 10" contributors to the stream, chief of which was @Climatebloggers, a profile feed aggregating the posts of a delimited network of bloggers covering the COP15 (including *Huffington Post* and Oxfam).

The balance shifted yet again at the end of the life of #cop15 as participants apparently shifted to other hashtags, such as #cop16, in anticipation of the next conference. The #cop16 hashtag had not only a greater volume of tweets during the same October 2010 time period (994), but a far greater number and proportion of unique contributors (512). Only 20.8 percent of these #cop16 users came from the "top 10," chief of which was @cop16 (What the Hashtag?! 2010). The transition to #cop16 may thus have marked a return to the more distributed, crowdsourced management pattern described in earlier phases of #cop15. Nevertheless, the dominance of the late phase of the old stream by higher-resource actors (e.g., middle-media bloggers) seems important both for stabilizing a weak stream and facilitating its handoff to the next.

This resource-seeking pattern is one we see echoed in the long tail of other crowd-enabled connective contexts. One example is the #globalchange stream during the global change demonstrations related to the *indignados* and Occupy Wall Street on October 15, 2011, as this stream subsided and blended into other streams (see also Vicari 2012 on the related Italian #ott15 stream). As noted, a similar pattern developed in the multiple Twitter streams connected to the larger U.S. Occupy movement. In this case, linking soared markedly after many Occupy city encampments were displaced in November and December 2011. In particular, links to organizations, and especially Occupy city websites, increased as links to individual sites diminished.

In the case of the climate change protests, the development of the two hashtag streams over time illustrates how digital mechanisms may reflect the distinctive character of the connective action networks in which they are embedded, and how they play out in different ways within them. While the trajectory of hashtag use and linking in #thewave amplified its organization-centered base, #cop15 reflected the absence of dominating organizations in its crowded protest space. At the same time, the linking in #cop15, which was widespread, constituted something of an external spine that stabilized the long tail of the stream and facilitated its merger with other networks and other streams.

Conclusion

The Twitter Revolutions of 2009 ignited the question of whether new social media have any real effect on contentious politics. This chapter has argued that critically examining the relation between transforming conditions for communication and collective action demands recognition of the ways in which social technologies infuse specific protest ecologies. The immediate question from this perspective is neither what Twitter does to contentious politics nor what specific actors do with Twitter. Rather, this approach looks at the roles of social technologies as organizing mechanisms (as organizational agents) and how the traces of these technologies may reflect larger organizational schemes in a protest ecology, while serving as a window on that ecology for researchers.

Treating the network as an organizational unit opens up important dimensions for analysis. It directs attention to network-level mechanisms that emerge when a large number of participants move through the digitally dense contexts characterizing many networked protest spaces. In particular, it looks to the roles of social technologies as organizing mechanisms that are contingent on how various actors from organizations to crowds deploy them. Moreover, elements such as the link patterns in streams offer windows on the larger protest ecologies, on what resources and further networks are brought into play by what actors from which locations using what sorts of technologies. Through this dual perspective we also catch sight of differences and similarities in the dynamics of different connective action networks.

Although protest ecologies can be expected to differ in a variety of ways, three dimensions facilitate analysis and comparison of connective action in different cases: the way Twitter streams represent and involve networking mechanisms that cut across the protest ecology; how they embed and are embedded in various kinds of gatekeeping processes; and how they reflect changing dynamics in the ecology over time. Tracing these dimensions in the context of the two protests, we observed some of the specifics of the respective ecologies and their dynamics, as well as differing roles played by tweeting within these ecologies. Most significantly, while #thewave was successfully harnessed as an amplifying mobilization and publicity resource by a set of central actors in the organizationally enabled connective action in London, the #cop15 hashtag in the crowded Copenhagen protest space suggested how primarily crowd-enabled connective networks may seek resources in different and more pronounced ways than organization-centered ones.

As a note of caution, it should be stressed that the approach applied here yields indications rather than full descriptions and that the illustrative analysis presented is limited. Completing the picture of what happened at these protests would require delving even deeper into the hashtags, including reintroducing users more fully into the analysis to ascertain who did what and helped create what kinds of resources. This among other things means that developing ethnographic understandings of relations and events remains essential. Further, as noted at the beginning of this chapter, in most episodes of contentious connective action, a Twitter hashtag is just one of many digital and non-digital mechanisms operating to bring publics together to act in concerted or less organized ways. Networks of people and technologies may operate differently in terms of coherence, sustainability, and effectiveness of associated actions, and this invites further attention to how collective action spaces develop under different conditions (cf. Langlois et al. 2009): filling out the picture would require re-embedding these hashtags into the complex contexts of digitally networked action in which they appear.

An overarching point in this chapter is that viewing a technology such as Twitter primarily as an information update service may not distinguish its most intriguing dimensions in contentious action. Twitter reveals a variety of interesting clues about different kinds of protests: what kinds of actors and resources are operating in the environment, how the players organize different gatekeeping mechanisms, and how those gatekeeping processes may help explain changing linking and user dynamics of hashtags over time. Yet such features may be difficult to evaluate if we too closely follow unexamined assumptions about where and what the politically relevant effect ought to be. Will the revolution be twittered? This is an ephemeral question. It is more important to ask how social media embed and engage different ecologies of dissent.

4

How Organizationally Enabled Networks Engage Publics

The preceding chapters analyzed protest actions mobilized by different types of connective action networks. As defined in Chapter 1, connective networks rely on digital technologies to help people personalize their political participation and focus the attention of policy makers and broader publics on hotly contested issues. Beyond taking to the streets to display popular concern, there are many ways in which activists and organizations seek to promote their causes in public. Organizations and concerned citizens spend time and resources helping to educate people about issues and showing them how to incorporate acts of issue awareness into everyday life. Issue advocacy organizations also help citizens join in more collective forms of political influence, such as petitions, campaigns, election canvassing, and networking with friends. In undertaking such public action, organizations often form networks with others to coordinate and amplify their political strategies. Such networks may be more or less (or not at all) connective. This chapter examines the conditions under which organizations do or do not form connective action networks, the very different ways in which those networks can be organized, and how different organizational patterns reflect the role of digital media in enabling personalized public involvement in large-scale action over time.

Digitally networked action is often suspected to be unsustainable in the long term. Similarly, action via the menus of online digital action that organizations offer is easy to dismiss as mere "clicktivism." We want to see if there exist more stable and robust public engagement opportunities surrounding the clicks. Just as technologies should not be artificially isolated, as we argued in Chapter 3, so also actions should not be taken out of context. Seemingly isolated acts of engagement such as sending an email to a politician or signing a digital petition may be embedded in far richer political contexts. Often these small acts are part of long-running campaigns that have many fronts, including election canvassing, lobbying politicians, and getting others to work on projects such as making homes, churches, and schools more energy-efficient or turning local communities around the world into "fair trade towns." Clicking on a link to send a message may be one of many actions a person undertakes in a campaign. And if clicking on a personally comfortable response to an issue is someone's only action, that act may nonetheless add to thickly layered networks of engagement, both online and face to face, that extend far beyond a particular click. It is thus interesting to examine engagement across networks.

Rather than extract any single activity out of these larger contexts of engagement, we seek to assess more holistic engagement patterns. This entails finding ways to observe how a large number of organizations relate to each other and how they deploy (or fail to deploy) different kinds of digital tools across networks to engage publics in their causes. In making such broad assessments we examine the most visible public faces of organizations, their websites. NGO websites can attract a large number of visitors.[1] Some who connect with organizations through their websites may already follow an issue through the activities of a particular organization or through referrals from other known organizations; other visitors may be newcomers who find organizations in searches for information about an issue. Yet we caution the skeptical reader to think beyond intuitive reactions to websites such as "How many visitors do they have?" Beyond the question of the sheer numbers of those attracted to given organizations is the more important question of how the broader networks are organized and whether their organizational signatures reflect how they use various kinds of personalization strategies (issue frames and digital technologies) to engage those followers. Looking beyond individual organizations enables us to see that networks can be greater than the sum of their organizational parts. This holistic principle of networks operates in many ways. On the one hand, smaller organizations in the "tails" of network action (e.g., organizations that link to the larger organizations but that may not receive much recognition in return) may gain from sharing in the activities fueled by more resource-rich organizations at the head of a network. On the other hand, those larger organizations may gain from the spreading engagement of the fine-grained "tributaries" in the tails of a network linking distribution, much as a large river contains the many smaller ones that flow into it.

Organizational and network properties can be measured in different ways – for example, by means of micro, ethnographic analyses based on observing and interviewing officers in specific organizations about what they do, how they do it, and with whom who they do it.[2] However, for our present purposes, we

---

[1] High traffic volumes are most common for large NGOs such as Oxfam, with UK web traffic consisting of around 400,000 unique monthly visitors, and the Royal Society for the Protection of Birds, which topped well over a million unique visitors for the month in 2010 for which we were able to get data. These numbers, along with the data in Chapter 5, were provided by Hitwise. Our point here is that traffic alone is not the main (or even a particularly good) measure of engagement. In order to understand how publics may engage more broadly with issues, we need to look beyond the number of visitors to more holistic network properties that point both to off-site activities and network-wide activity levels.

[2] Ethnographic studies are valuable complements to the methods we employ here, but the methods we pursued were more central for addressing the questions at issue in this chapter. We have

developed a particular method of web network analysis in order to seek broad generalizations about how large issue networks are organized and how they attempt to digitally engage publics. This method allows us to document and map how organizations display their relationships with other organizations by granting or not granting recognition through more or less prominently featured hyperlinks. It also enables us to assess the kinds and densities of various technologies that are deployed across entire networks to enable people to engage in personal ways with various causes.

This chapter examines the organization and public engagement strategies of issue advocacy networks in an effort to understand not only how they engage publics, but also when (under what political conditions) they do or do not engage publics to advance their causes. Connective action networks may succeed or falter in different contexts. More important for this chapter, they may also shape up differently in contexts that entail different political constraints and opportunities for the organizational actors involved. The importance of political conditions becomes especially clear when we consider organizationally enabled connective action.

We here focus specifically on the type of connective network organization that was presented as the hybrid or middle type in the framework we introduced in Chapter 1 (Figure 1.1). As our theoretical framework suggests, a key distinction between the two types of connective action involves the differing roles of conventional organizations, particularly NGOs. Both forms of connective action display the properties of personal action frames shared over digital media networks. In cases of crowd-enabled action, however, formal organizations are either relatively absent or maintain stealthy profiles, leaving the crowd to mobilize the necessary organizational resources, from communication and technology development to fund-raising, event coordination, and information sharing. As we discussed earlier, this type of connective action best fits cases such as the Tahrir Square uprisings in Egypt, the *indignados* protests in Spain, and the Occupy protests in the United States. The cases we examine in this chapter are examples of connective action that is organizationally enabled by often-familiar NGOs, such as Oxfam and the World Wildlife Fund. Such organizations may behave differently in different strategic contexts, as noted by observers who have documented this kind of "organizational hybridity" (Bimber, Flanagin, and Stohl 2005, 2012; Chadwick 2013). They may, among other things, form issue advocacy networks – loose networks of advocacy organizations working together on a common cause – without developing strong connective action properties. When organizations do embrace connective action strategies, however, the key is the formation of loosely linked cooperative networks that share broad action programs to get publics and policy makers engaged with their issues. This requires that the organizations refrain from trying to own, control, or tightly brand issues and actions.

shown our analyses to NGO workers to get their reactions about validity and have often noted their surprise to learn things about their networks that they either did not know or that they suspected but had no way of confirming.

This chapter explores organizationally enabled networks as they mobilize personalized public engagement with the family of economic justice and environment/climate change issues that we follow throughout the book. The aim is to examine the connective action properties of various issue advocacy networks and how these may be shaped by the political contexts in which the networks operate. We continue to focus on action in the areas of economic justice and environment/climate change politics, and we compare issue advocacy networks in different national political contexts (the United Kingdom and Germany) at different levels of governance (national and EU levels).

Personalized Politics, Complex Issues, and NGOs

What are the typical organizational properties of issue advocacy networks, and how do they connect with ordinary people, particularly those who prefer personalized forms of engagement with issues? Connecting with people who seek to personalize their political engagement can be a different order of business than, say, recruiting and cultivating membership supporters.[3] This does not mean that people seeking to personalize their politics are less serious or less aware of the co-presence of others who share their concerns than are activists driven by particularistic ideologies or mutual support for established organizations that represent them. To the contrary, many citizens take a serious personal interest in issues that help them feel connected to social and environmental realities beyond their private lives. Those connections can become integral parts of people's lifestyles, from doing small things about everyday energy consumption and "carbon footprints," to altering personal relationships to the production and consumption of food, clothes, computers, and other elements of the "good life" (Micheletti 2003).

As noted in the introduction, many of these politically independent citizens feel that governments and businesses neither care about nor do enough to address problems they could be doing more about. And due to the globalization of so many human systems, action must be taken at different levels and in different political arenas (Smith and Wiest 2012). Into this political situation have come legions of NGOs: thousands upon thousands of non-profit, non-governmental organizations taking positions on a wide array of issues. One of the most interesting aspects of the rise of NGO-centered issue advocacy is that on some issues publics may trust them more than they trust government or business. Public opinion trends in many nations over recent decades reveal an erosion of trust in established political and economic institutions (varying in different countries), in some cases accompanied by a growing trust in issue-oriented NGOs. Surveys of opinion leaders in different democracies ranging

---

[3] There are many membership-oriented citizens still out there, and many organizations are happy to sign them up and receive their membership fees. However, the generational changes in society and identity that we discussed earlier make for fewer joiners among the new generations of citizens that have entered the polity since the 1990s. As Bimber, Flanagin, and Stohl (2012) explain, this creates interesting challenges for conventional organizations.

across Europe, North America, Latin America, and Asia indicated that this was the case even before the financial and environmental crises reached the levels they attained while this book was being written (Nelson 2007).

It is no accident that the explosion of NGOs has broadly tracked the arc of globalization. Radical changes in markets and societies have made many policy problems more complex. And policy processes have in many cases spilled beyond old political boundaries between nations and the outer world. Indeed, many of the same NGOs operate in local, national, and transnational arenas as they engage policy processes at different levels (Lang 2013). One early observer of this trend has even likened its importance for the politics of our times to that of the rise and preeminence of the nation-state in the 19th century, noting that the shift in the number and importance of NGOs corresponds to the decline of traditional national institutions that are losing their monopolies over citizen engagement:

From the developed countries of North America, Europe and Asia to the developing societies of Africa, Latin America and the former Soviet bloc, people are forming associations, foundations and similar institutions to deliver human services, promote grass-roots economic development, prevent environmental degradation, protect civil rights and pursue a thousand other objectives formerly unattended or left to the state.

The scope and scale of this phenomenon are immense. Indeed, we are in the midst of a global "associational revolution" that may prove to be as significant to the latter twentieth century as the rise of the nation-state was to the latter nineteenth. The upshot is a global third sector: a massive array of self-governing private organizations, not dedicated to distributing profits to shareholders or directors, pursuing public purposes outside the formal apparatus of the state. The proliferation of these groups may be permanently altering the relationship between states and citizens, with an impact extending far beyond the material services they provide. Virtually all of America's major social movements, for example, whether civil rights, environmental, consumer, women's or conservative, have had their roots in the nonprofit sector. The growth of this phenomenon is all the more striking given the simultaneous decline in the more traditional forms of political participation, such as voting, party affiliation and union membership. (Salamon 1994)

The scope of activities embraced by these organizations is as impressive as their rapid rise. While some NGOs advocate global markets that are fairer for producers and consumers alike, others challenge those demands by promoting the human freedoms and economic growth created by unregulated business markets. Where some work to educate publics and officials about the perils of global warming, others deny the scientific evidence for human causes of the problem.[4] It is not surprising that, as they have grown in number and influence,

---

[4] Our comparisons of opposing networks on issues such as fair trade and climate change suggest that challenger networks (e.g., those that deny global warming) are less transparent in terms of their policy agendas, less densely networked in publicly visible ways, more likely to have corporate funding, less well known among broader publics, and more likely to simulate public support using so-called astro-turf methods. These underlying properties of many conservative

NGOs have become contested politically at many levels, from governments regulating and even outlawing some of their political activities to challenges about their legitimacy, often in the form of "Who do they represent, anyway?" The fascinating politics of NGOs is part of another story that has been told in detail by others (e.g., Keck and Sikkink 1998; Lang 2013).

Yet an important question for evaluating the democratic properties of NGOs and their networks is whether they seek to engage publics and what kind of engagement they enable (Bennett, Lang, and Segerberg 2011; Bennett, Lang, Segerberg, and Knappe 2011). Indeed, a long-standing contrast in democratic theory is the divide between theorists who define democratic values around institutional processes such as elections and representation and those who focus on participation in more diverse forms as central to a healthy democratic sphere (Pateman 1970). As the analyses in the previous two chapters and later in this one suggest, NGOs can straddle this divide in that they often attract publics to forms of action that fall outside of conventional institutional processes, and they also target various kinds of influence and pressure on institutional decision making. From the perspective of understanding how digitally networked action works, it becomes important to examine how NGOs navigate this divide and how different political contexts infuse both their opportunities and their goals.

Organizations, Networks, and Public Engagement in Different Political Contexts

This chapter seeks to determine how well the model of organizationally enabled connective action fits issue advocacy networks in our core cases of fair trade and environment/climate change as they operate in different political contexts. In particular, we examine how these networks differ in the density of digital engagement mechanisms deployed across organizations in loosely organized advocacy networks and how those digital engagement "signatures" compare among different issue networks within and across political settings. This analysis entails developing original methods and measures for assessing the personalized engagement signatures of various issue networks. The goal is to illuminate the political conditions that are more and less conducive to organizationally enabled connective action based on measures of how the issue networks enable individuals to find different ways to participate in causes. This means that we are equally interested in finding issue networks that have low engagement signatures and understanding why that may be the case.

In drawing comparisons between the engagement capacities of different issue networks and political contexts, we anticipate that network organizational

oppositional issue networks in the economic justice and climate change arenas make them harder to analyze using the methods we develop to measure democratic public mobilization. Indeed, public "demobilization" may be closer to their goals. These generalizations surely differ across issue areas. For example, Christian values networks in the United States have demonstrated remarkable success in mobilizing publics and should be more accessible using our methods.

structures will differ in interesting ways. For example, networks that are oriented toward engaging publics in their causes are likely to have a greater density of connections and more evenly shared distribution of power among organizations than are networks that do not have this orientation. As we explain shortly, this network pattern of "density without dominance" is likely to arise because large-scale mobilization is better accomplished when many organizations form loose affiliations that enable them to share followers and that enable those followers to communicate easily with each other. As a result, individual participants get the sense that they are joining something big – but joining on their own terms. By contrast, networks that score low on public engagement capacity should be more hierarchical and sparsely clustered. We also identify broad political conditions that alternately favor or stunt the network structures and engagement potential of issue networks. For example, we show that political opportunity structures in the European Union can turn NGOs into what Lang (2013) has called "proxy publics," or organizations that neglect public engagement despite advocating public causes. The next step in elaborating this analysis is to explain how we selected our cases and what they offer for comparative purposes.

Putting Advocacy Networks in Comparative Perspective

We have two empirical aims in this chapter: (a) to establish how large-scale advocacy networks can be measured reliably for their connective action potential and (b) to examine how that potential may be shaped by differences in the political contexts in which those networks operate. In particular, we analyze how issue advocacy networks operate in two very different national political contexts: Germany and the United Kingdom, both of which have strong traditions of public advocacy in economic justice and environmental protection, including our core cases of fair trade and environment/climate change. Following methods explained later, we derive comparable networks in each country and then inventory the digital media public engagement mechanisms deployed across the organizations forming those networks. We also trace and inventory parallel issue networks for Germany and the United Kingdom that link to the EU civil society process.

We introduce several methodological innovations into these inquiries, including a method for identifying issue networks through a web crawling procedure and a method for inventorying all organization websites in a network with respect to the digital mechanisms they offer to engage publics in their causes. We address these digital engagement indices of issue networks in two ways: (a) as direct measures of networked public engagement capacity and (b) as indicators of the level of commitment among member organizations in a network to mobilizing publics as part of their core political mission or strategy.

The comparison of issue networks in different political systems enables us to see if patterns of engaging publics vary with differences in political contexts.

For example, does the strong institutional state of environmental politics via the presence of the Green Party in Germany affect the organization and digital engagement profile of the environment/climate change network, in contrast to the parallel network in the United Kingdom, in which environmental politics is less firmly institutionalized? We also trace the same issue clusters to the EU level, noting that as networks of economic development and environment NGOs get closer to the center of power in Brussels, the more likely they are to shed mechanisms for engaging publics in their issues. This is suggestive of the much-discussed EU "democratic deficit." At the same time, we do not go as far as those critics who dismiss NGOs as taking the place of or ignoring publics in staking issue claims in policy arenas. In this analysis we follow the work of Lang (2013), who shows that things are far more complicated than the often-sweeping generalizations swirling around NGOs would suggest. It is too simplistic to either laud or condemn the way they advocate for the many issues in our contemporary political scene. Political context matters for understanding both the degrees to which and the ways in which organizationally enabled connective action networks engage publics.

Putting the Analysis in Theoretical Context

In the theoretical context of the book, this discussion strengthens the notion that political conditions play into the way connective networks develop. Our analysis shows that there are interesting trade-offs among the different methods of organizing contention around a particular issue and that the way networks (and actors in networks) handle such trade-offs is sensitive to political opportunities and constraints. Several of the organizationally enabled networks that we have sampled (particularly at the national level) are clearly capable of mounting sustained initiatives to promote their issues and causes, and they signal clear commitments to mobilizing large-scale publics through impressive batteries of personalized digital media affordances. However, in other networks in the same issue areas, especially at the European level, such connective commitment is much less forthcoming.

An obvious question is whether digitally enabled networks are politically effective in achieving various outcomes, and this question becomes even more pressing when organizations argue that rejecting connectively oriented organizing allows them to better pursue their political goals. We addressed some of the political impact questions surrounding the organizationally enabled protest networks in the London financial crisis mobilizations in Chapter 2. The overall profile in terms of Tilly's WUNC criteria (worthiness, unity, numbers, commitment) was by and large more impressive than in the more conventional and particular ideological mobilizations operating in the same settings.[5] Beyond the

---

[5] It is important to note that not all protest organizers aim to achieve WUNC in their demonstrations. Moreover, some organizers may not value high turnout as much as, e.g., ideological commitment in participants.

obvious outcomes of sustained focus and mobilization strength, our analysis in Chapter 5 shows that different ways of organizing and focusing political power in both organizationally enabled and crowd-enabled networks can produce surprisingly comparable outcomes.

However, before further pursuing such questions about power and political outcomes, as we do in Chapter 5 and the concluding chapter, we need to address several more fundamental questions about the nature of organizationally enabled and broadly networked public engagement:

- How and under what conditions do organizations form large-scale, loosely affiliated issue networks?
- What kinds of conflict and dysfunction may occur in these networks?
- How and under what conditions is personalized, digital engagement a signature property of organizationally enabled networks?

The following sections discuss each of these in turn.

Incentives for Flexible Issue Networking across Different Organizations

Studies of issue advocacy organizations suggest that they face a host of challenges even beyond the obvious ones, such as fund-raising and making strategic choices about staffing and agenda priorities. Even when agendas and resources are established, organizations operate at a power deficit when facing often better-funded business lobbies that have easier access to politicians. In addition, organizations in the same issue sector may defeat each other if they clamor too noisily for attention and end up competing for ownership of similar issue agendas. The depth of the NGO political challenge comes through in the words of a director of a regional association of Southern African NGOs:

> NGO leaders face extraordinary challenges which are very distinct from those faced by leaders in government and the private sector. They often function in isolated and unsupported circumstances, and are faced with a set of complex and interrelated challenges relating to NGOs' social change mission, increased pressure for accountability and transparency, the need for unquestioned integrity and to maximise limited resources, and the ability to network and position their organisations in an uncertain external and political environment. (Barnard 2008)

The difficulties of networking and positioning are heightened by strategic questions of what to do about followers who support causes and may contribute financially to the resource base of organizations through membership payments or contributions. Pooling efforts with other organizations in an issue sector may also mean mingling and pooling followers who are counted as organizational resource capital. The membership/followership challenge is particularly interesting in light of notable changes in personal preferences for affiliation discussed earlier in this book and elsewhere by others, most notably by Bimber, Flanagin, and Stohl (2005, 2012). If people are less likely today than in earlier eras to formally join organizations as members, it may be that keeping publics affiliated with causes is better achieved through other means. For example, creating a loose but highly networked and interlinked web sphere around issues may attract people through a combination of communication outreach and web searches. The deployment of digital technologies of the kinds we inventory later on invites the co-production of engaging activities that enable people to activate relationships through their own social networks while remaining within the overarching political sphere created by the networked organization.

All of these factors offer incentives for organizations to band together to form loose coalitions to raise the visibility and reduce the noise surrounding their pressing concerns. Not all organizations are willing to give up their brand imperatives or to join with organizations that may be rivals for funding or that advocate competing political goals. However, the appearance of large, digitally linked organization networks in many issue areas suggests that loose-tie networking is becoming a popular model. Organizations that enter into these kinds of networks may pay the price of stepping back from the branding process, although brands can still be inserted in different ways into campaigns and membership messaging in other areas. Nearly everyone in the advocacy sector has tales to tell about the challenges of working together, but in many areas we see stable networks recombining around initiatives to advance common goals.

The key question in loosely knit network formation is what kinds of issue frames and public activities are likely to endow the action of a network with WUNC. An insight into this is offered by Yanacopulos (2009) in her study of NGOs involved in two of the most enduring and successful economic justice networks: the Jubilee 2000 debt relief coalition and Make Poverty History. Her question is neatly related to ours: How did those coalitions "structure themselves to appeal to a wide range of organizational members and publics?" (Yanacopulos 2009: 67). Her interviews with organizers of these networks show how a complex and poorly understood issue (the fact that poor countries were burdened by back-breaking levels of debt to international lenders) was transformed within a few years into a widely embraced popular cause. This transformation entailed the loosely linked publicity and public engagement efforts of more than 70 organizations in Britain and hundreds more in other nations as the network spread worldwide. Public pressure through various campaigns, protests, and other tactics aimed at G7 meetings and national government leaders resulted in the forgiveness of hundreds of billions of dollars in debt for poor nations.

The networking process behind these activities straddled the gray boundary between a loosely knit network and a brokered centralized alliance. While Yanacopulos (following others in the field of transnational network analysis) makes a distinction between networks and coalitions, we think that this obscures a central issue: that all of the formations spanning the spectrum that we identify in our model in Chapter 1 are networks. What makes them distinctive is the underlying associational logics that organize them. The Jubilee 2000 debt relief and the Make Poverty History coalitions are both interesting examples of our hybrid organizationally enabled network type. Although Jubilee came into being before the advent of Web 2.0 made interactive technologies a central part of political engagement,[6] it displayed the important feature of developing easily personalized issue frames that enabled both organizations and individuals to buy in and share their engagement easily with others.

Achieving this kind of organization does not happen automatically – far from it. A good deal of analysis by organizers of the network was required in order to arrive at what may seem to be the simple frame of making the international economic system fairer and more effective for more people. Among the array of other possible framings, this position was a long way from the more radical but also more particular action frames challenging the system's legitimacy and demanding its overthrow of the kind we saw in our discussion of the G20 Meltdown in Chapter 2. Although many at the core of the Jubilee campaign may have identified with stronger and more specific challenges to the system, they foregrounded political practicality in the interests of broadening the participatory base and public appeal of the network. The public ideals of the Jubilee network were expressed in a broad language of fairness and justice with an appeal to broader publics and gave political targets a relatively comfortable bridge to policy change. While the framing enabled a loose network with wide appeal, the inside analytical process of arriving at this point was anything but automatic or easy. Indeed, one of the early organizers of the Jubilee network likened that framing process to cutting a diamond:

The analysis was worked on for two years. The working out of the analysis is like cutting a diamond. You look at a diamond for two years if you are a diamond cutter. And when you cut it, you cut the problem in such a way as to maximize the reflection of the problem, enabling a lot of people to see themselves in the analysis. When you've done that, you then test the way you've cut this diamond is actually attracting light, is actually reflecting light, is actually credible. (Ann Pettifor, quoted in Yanacopulos 2009: 73)

In this chapter we explore how our fair trade and environment/climate change networks are organized, how they engage publics (and when they do not), and how they operate in different political systems in relation to the incentives and power configurations of the environments that affect their outreach, internal coherence, and power. Because organizations may disagree on how to "cut the diamond," not all networks come together or function very well. Before looking at some that function well, we consider why some others do not.

Conflict and Dysfunction in Networks

We should be clear at the outset that not all networks are harmonious, stable, or effective. Indeed, our interest is in examining variations in network

---

[6] In Chapter 5 we analyze the Robin Hood Tax (RHT) campaign that emerged from the Jubilee era but continued to build network ties during the next decade as Web 2.0 became fully established via interactive media. The result was that RHT became a large hyperlinked network that utilized a full range of digital technologies to engage publics and win considerable support from diverse public officials.

organization and public engagement. It is clear that some networks are divided, often around powerful organizations that seek their own political strategies and wish to brand their activities around particular styles of participation. Earlier work (involving one of the authors) on fair trade networks in the United States showed that there were considerable divisions and gaps in network organization due to very different framings promoted by different organizations (Bennett, Foot, and Xenos 2011).

Fair trade advocacy begins with educating consumers about their place in their respective commodity chains and showing them simple ways to make a difference by exercising their consumer choices. However, there are dozens of more complicated issues ranging around this core of citizen consumerism, including how goods such as coffee, bananas, or soccer balls must be produced in order to be labeled fair trade, how big companies like Starbucks and Proctor & Gamble should be licensed to participate in selling fair trade items, and whether consumers should be encouraged to engage in stronger forms of activism that might lead them to pressure or boycott the very companies that, if certified, end up paying an important part of the cost of the labeling and monitoring and development systems underlying fair trade.

In the more than 20 nations that belong to the international Fair Trade Labeling Organization (FLO), one core organization in each country is granted a franchise for licensing the use of the preeminent international fair trade mark. This does not stop many other organizations from calling themselves or their products fairly traded, and even proclaiming that they have different or even higher standards to back that claim. However, there are obvious advantages in sending clear "brand" signals that do not confuse consumers, and even clearer advantages in concentrating resources in a global system that can aid farmers and other workers in developing local sustainable economies on a large scale.[7]

The history of trouble in the U.S. network reflects how difficult it can be to cut the diamond so that often-diverse organizations might enter a network that shares issue framings, political goals, and strategies for engaging publics. In the United States, the FLO product labeling and certification license was granted in 1998 to an organization called Transfair USA. In the coming years, Transfair set out on a course to cultivate large businesses such as Starbucks and other household brand companies in different product sectors. The accompanying public engagement model placed a low-key emphasis on being a conscientious consumer. Transfair steered clear of promoting much other overt political activism that might raise corporate concerns about their brands being contaminated with political messages. Many other organizations (often smaller companies that were directly working in partnership with producers and communities in the global south) felt that consumers should become more involved

---

[7] Information about this trademark and its background can be found on the leading UK site, Fairtrade Foundation UK: www.fairtrade.org.uk/what_is_fairtrade/fairtrade_certification_and_the_fairtrade_mark/the_fairtrade_mark.aspx. It is ironic that Transfair USA, the initial licensed labeling organization, never adopted the same international trademark logo used by other members in the national federation due to the rift in this network.

in the politics of trade and development, and that a fair trade system that catered too much to corporations would compromise its principles. These disagreements on how to cut the diamond kept many organizations out of the international FLO fair trade system. Such rifts grew over the years and showed few signs of being resolved. Ironically, Transfair, which had been the flash point within the U.S. network, eventually left the FLO system in late 2011, changing its name to Fair Trade USA. One issue in this network disruption was a dispute about the basic FLO model of community-based development anchored in farmer cooperatives. Among other things, Fair Trade USA (under the direction of its founding CEO, Paul Rice) favored including plantation-scale "factory farms" in fair trade classification. At that point the rift became a rupture, and dozens of issues surfaced about the very nature of fair trade and how to harmonize the engagement of consumer publics, southern producers, and northern corporations.[8]

What is interesting is that cutting the diamond on fair trade was far more successful in the cases of the United Kingdom and Germany that we examine in this chapter. Even more remarkable, the different frames of conscientious consumption and justice activism have been nested effectively within many organizations across the fair trade networks in both countries, so that individual citizens have considerable choice over how to participate in adding social and political value to the goods that make up their lifestyles. It is also worth noting that both the German and UK networks pursued different strategies for doing business with retailers, including creating large fair trade corporations to buy, process, package, and sell commodities. The main point, however, is that cross-organization harmonizing of the very different framings of fair trade made it possible for more coherent networks to emerge in Germany and the United Kingdom and for those networks, in turn, to deploy an impressive array of ways for people to personalize their learning about fair trade and to share their engagement with friends, family, neighbors, schools, churches, local communities, and fellow citizens in their own countries and beyond. This networked organization was achieved to an important extent through rich varieties of digital media mechanisms for personalizing popular engagement with the cluster of issues related to trade, development, and, more generally, economic justice.

How Do Organizationally Enabled Networks Engage Publics?

This brings us to the key analytical question of the chapter: How and under what conditions do organizationally enabled networks engage publics? We

---

[8] Various reactions to Transfair's leaving the international FLO system ranged from the polarized to the diplomatic: "United Students for Fair Trade Withdraws Support from Fair Trade USA/Transfair," usft.org/node/373; "Action Alert: Show Your Support for Authentic Fair Trade," www.equalexchange.coop/fair-trade; "FLO Overview: Fair Trade in the USA," www.fairtrade.net/overview-usa.html.

predict that higher levels of public engagement can be achieved with fewer resources in large-scale connective action networks (compared with the conventional organizationally brokered kind) when organizations manage to frame their common issues in ways that are easy for individuals to adopt. That is, issue framings will favor loose-tie networking when they do not seriously compromise either organization-level mission and brand considerations or individual-level personal comfort levels. To put it simply, it has to be possible for individuals to personalize these framings without being required to adopt particular political values or identifications. Clearly, other paths to engagement and activism work very differently than this, and there are signs in our networks that those paths are there for individuals who seek higher levels of involvement.

Once networks emerge around an issue, what helps hold them together is whether they gain recognition from stakeholders such as policy makers, businesses, and publics. Attracting publics requires offering people accessible mechanisms that help them engage. These mechanisms are not always online. For example, shoppers may encounter kiosks of fair trade items or energy-efficient lightbulbs in local stores. At the same time, they may also search online for places to find those products, or even buy them online. Moreover, many of the engagement mechanisms that characterize contemporary issue networks are online, in such forms as menus of "things you can do" on websites and stand-alone campaign platforms; photo- and story-sharing spaces and networking affordances on organizational websites; news and action feeds in Facebook groups, Twitter alerts, or email lists; and many other types of digital connective mechanisms we identify later. In order to analyze how organizationally enabled networks engage publics, we need first to consider how we can identify such issue networks and how we can reliably measure and categorize the engagement mechanisms they contain.

Measuring Issue Networks and Digital Media Use

How can we find and describe issue networks? How can we understand their public engagement orientations involving digital media? And how do these networks and their engagement orientations change in response to political contexts that offer different constraints, incentives, and opportunities for mobilizing publics?[9] We explore these questions by mapping large national and transnational issue networks in the two broad areas featured throughout the book: networks of environmental organizations broadly focused around climate change policy, and economic justice and development networks that are

---

[9] The methods and some of the data we use to address these questions draw on a series of earlier reports, including Bennett, Lang, Segerberg, and Knappe (2011) and Bennett, Lang, and Segerberg (forthcoming). We are grateful to the research assistance of Sheetal Agarwal, Michael Barthel, Scott Brekke Davis, Marianne Goldin, and Allison Rank in the studies this chapter builds on.

challenging the neo-liberal world trade regime by advocating fair trade policies and practices.

The broad rationale for looking at economic and environment issues was outlined in the introduction to the book. Here we point out some additional advantages for the comparative purposes of this chapter of looking at the networks in these areas. First of all, these issue clusters are among the most ubiquitous policy concerns in NGO communities of many nations and transnationally. This provides opportunities for locating national and transnational networks and for making broad comparisons. In addition, the two issue clusters tend to be organized differently, which enables us to see if certain network properties affect how those networks engage publics and use personalized approaches in the process. For example, fair trade organizations are loosely organized around a federation of fair trade labeling and certification organizations in more than 20 nations. These gatekeepers provide some structure to the terms of engagement with fair trade (by subscribing to common definitions of fair trade and promoting similar norms for production and consumption). This sort of federated structure still leaves a lot of room for national differences (and even national dysfunction, as noted earlier in the U.S. case), so we regard fair trade networks as interesting cases of loosely structured coalitions that reflect national political contexts. At the same time, they may have more commonly shared orientations toward publics than do less structured networks such as those around environment and climate change policy.[10]

Another interesting advantage of looking at these two issue clusters is that different political contextual factors – one might even call them opportunity structure differences – make for a critical comparison between the UK and German environment networks. Because environmental politics is more institutionalized in Germany, with among other things the Green Party having been a political force in government for many years, there is a greater potential for prominent national environmental organizations to defer some degree of direct public engagement in favor of channeling engagement into governing institutions, both through elections and through direct access lobbying and consultation.[11] Such an institutional effect might diminish direct public engagement in the German national environment network. By contrast, the trade justice / fair trade networks in both the United Kingdom and Germany operated at the time of our study (spring of 2010) within the contexts of labor and centrist governments that, although relatively sympathetic to some of the aims of fair trade advocates, had struck neo-liberal bargains with business and world trade regimes. Thus, we might expect a more direct public engagement focus in fair trade networks than across environment networks in Germany.

---

[10] We will refer to such networks as "environment networks" in this chapter.
[11] This does not preclude continued grassroots mobilizations. However, we are here more concerned with broader national and transnational network patterns.

As just noted, the national/transnational dimension of our two broad issue clusters makes for another level of comparative analysis. In particular, we also chart comparable NGO issue networks at the EU level, where broad issue-based "civil society platforms" have long existed in Brussels with the aim of creating policy dialogue and various kinds of resource exchange between the European Union and its national civil societies. We inventoried the memberships of the environment platform (the Green Ten) and the relief and development platform (CONCORD).[12] We are thus able to see whether different kinds of network organization reflect differences in issues and in political contexts. This analysis proceeds in several steps: (a) we identify national-level and EU-level issue advocacy networks, (b) measure the public engagement orientations of the issue advocacy networks at each level, (c) assess the public engagement contributions of the overlapping organizations that operate at both national and EU levels, and thus (d) separate out the public engagement effects of the organizations that operated in both national and transnational networks. This enables us to compare engagement capacities across issues, nations, and network levels from national to transnational.

Sampling Issue Networks
The first step is to identify the respective issue advocacy networks. Our two broad categories of issue networks present different sampling challenges and opportunities. Since fair trade operates nationally with gatekeeping organizations that control the international fair trade label, it makes sense to see how broader national networks emanate from those organizations (bearing in mind that there is considerable room for different networks, as we discovered in the U.S. case). Although these gatekeeping organizations are rather differently constituted from country to country, they offer starting points for network crawls to establish larger issue networks on trade and economic justice. We conducted web network crawls (as explained in Chapter 2 and reviewed in the next section) using the member lists of the German and UK national fair trade labeling organizations: the Fairtrade Foundation in the United Kingdom (www.fairtrade.org.uk/) and TransFair in Germany (www.transfair.org/).[13]

---

[12] These platforms served mainly to identify NGOs that made Brussels a focus of political attention. For comparison purposes, we sampled national NGOs that belonged primarily to EU issue networks. Since some of the organizations in these networks were also in the national-level networks sampled from other starting points, we could compare the engagement orientations of the national and the EU networks both with and without overlapping memberships. This creates an interesting test of the hypothesis that much of the engagement capacity of the EU-level networks will be provided by national organizations with established patterns of engaging national publics in causes. We expect that those engagement patterns are not as politically useful or welcomed by the EU in dealings between the commission and NGOs, and will not be as evident in organizations that operate primarily through the EU with little national public presence.

[13] In the UK national sample, the web crawl starting points were taken from the website of the UK Fairtrade Foundation (www.fairtrade.org.uk), including the Foundation itself. The Foundation names 15 "charity shareholders." The German national fair trade sample began with the 36

In the case of the environment networks, there was no such obvious national-level starting point. However, at the time of our sampling in the spring of 2010, many national climate and environment organizations had organized large networks ahead of the December 2009 UN Climate Change Conference in Copenhagen, including the 15th Conference of the Parties (COP15), which we analyzed in Chapter 3. The Stop Climate Chaos Coalition that helped mobilize the Wave protests in Britain ahead of COP15 was the UK coalition used in the crawls in this chapter. We located a comparable national climate change coalition (Die Klima Allianz) that focused broad attention in Germany on the Copenhagen meetings. We initiated co-link web crawls (as introduced in Chapter 2 and elaborated in the next section) from the coalition member lists.[14] The organization memberships of these environment networks remained stable in the few months between their launch in late 2009 and our network mapping in April and May of 2010.

The starting points for the EU-level networks were drawn from the relevant civil society platforms as identified in the EU civil society contact group website. The two respective environment networks were drawn from the German and UK members of the Green Ten (environment) platform. The two economic justice / fair trade networks were drawn from German and UK members of the CONCORD (relief and development) platform.[15]

members of the gatekeeping organization TransFair (www.transfair.org) plus Transfair itself. There is no reason to keep the number of starting points the same, as small networks may result from a large number of starting points, and a large network may result from a small set of starting points when the co-link methods described later are used. What does matter is that the selection of the origin of the starting points should be comparable in the networks that are to be compared.

[14] The national-level samples for the national environmental advocacy networks were drawn from the following sources: The British national sample was taken from the UK Stop Climate Chaos Coalition (www.stopclimatechaos.org), a broad NGO umbrella coalition that organized the largest protest in the United Kingdom on the eve of the UN Climate Summit. The protest known as "the Wave" took place in London on December 5, 2009, and was attended by an estimated 50,000 people. The crawl was initiated from a list of 104 organizations that joined this coalition. The German national-level sample was drawn from the Copenhagen protest coalition Die Klima Allianz (www.klimagipfel2009.de/cop15/organisationen/) as a starting point. We gathered all 56 member organizations of klimagipfel2009.de and entered them into Issue Crawler, as explained in the next section.

[15] At the time of our mapping, the contact group was located at this web address: www.act4europe .org/code/en/default.asp. The group has since fallen into disarray, and the members of the various platforms can be found by searching each platform on its own. The starting points for the two networks were derived as follows.

1. EU-level fair trade / development networks: The *UK EU-level sample* began with the British national coordinating organization in the EU CONCORD network, the Bond organization. Bond is a broad coalition of development, relief, and trade organizations that range well beyond fair trade issues to include disaster relief, clean drinking water, and other issues. We thus sampled and screened this list for a focus on trade and economic justice. The sample of the Bond UK network was created by selecting 10% of the 360 member organizations of Bond UK (www.bond.org.uk/index.php). We selected the starting points by picking every 10th organization from the members list on the Bond website. We started with the first

The carefully considered differences in starting points for generating the fair trade and climate change network maps offer a useful contrast between (a) two long-standing fair trade networks in Germany and the United Kingdom and (b) two environment networks working to raise awareness about a critical political conference and to mobilize various kinds of protest actions. Tapping into the German Klima Allianz at the time of the Copenhagen mobilization provides a tough test for our hypothesis about lower levels of personalized public engagement in the climate change network in Germany, since the Copenhagen climate summit would seem to invite direct public engagement rather than just the posting of news items on organization websites. As it turned out, we learned that enduring engagement orientations define network organization in ways that are little changed by externalities.

Since the research design and the research team were assembled in the winter of 2010, we deemed it important to test our mapping, digital engagement inventories, and comparison methods before conducting final network mapping, coding, and measurement. We also decided to hold the time period more or less constant in crawling and comparing the fair trade and climate change networks. Thus, all the networks reported here were crawled in April and May 2010.

Drawing the Network Maps: Web Crawling Methods

The next step in identifying the respective issue advocacy networks was to see how the starting points established for each network linked to other organizations in ways that might fill in larger issue networks. We used an automated method to search for links from the starting points to other organizations. The methods we followed here are essentially the same as those used to derive the maps of the Put People First and G20 Meltdown protest networks that we compared in the analysis of the London financial crisis mobilizations in

organization and then went down 10 organizations, picked the 10th, went down another 10, and so forth, resulting in 36 orgs. The *German EU-level sample* was drawn from the German coordinating organization named Venro. Starting on the Venro homepage, we went through the Venro member list (www.venro.org/mitglieder.html). Venro has 118 members, making it considerably smaller than Bond in the United Kingdom. We picked every fourth member until we gathered 30 organizations, which we then screened for a focus on trade and economic justice.

2. EU-level environment samples: The *UK EU-level sample* consisted of UK organizations ($N = 48$) listed in the EU civil society platform for the environment (Green Ten) member organizations/networks: BirdLife International, CEE Bankwatch Network, Climate Action Network Europe, European Environmental Bureau, Friends of the Earth Europe, Greenpeace European Unit, Health and Environment Alliance, International Friends of Nature, Transport and Environment, WWF European Policy Office. The UK members or partners of each of the ten organizations/networks were selected. The *German EU-level sample* consisted of a list of 25 starting points generated by collecting the German affiliate organizations from the same Green Ten member organizations/networks. We screened the environmental organizations for a general focus on climate issues, following the same procedures as for the fair trade sample.

Chapter 2. The full method of analysis is described in detail in that chapter. In brief, we placed the respective sets of organization URLs for each network as starting points into the tool Issue Crawler (see Rogers 2004) in order to render a network map on the basis of co-link analysis. As noted, a co-link is a URL that receives links from at least two of the starting points for each iteration (or hyperlink click) as the crawler moves out from the starting points. Co-link analysis includes only tightly connected actors, and thus sets a higher bar for network inclusion than other mapping methods that also include more weakly tied actors. As in the analysis in Chapter 2, using co-link analysis is important in this case because we are interested in comparing networks in terms of density of linking and structural stability that gives their engagement efforts some coherence.

In contrast to the procedure described in Chapter 2, we set the reach of the crawl in this analysis at only one iteration from the starting points. This is the procedure that Rogers (2004) recommends for deriving a network that includes mainly organizations concerned with the same issue (as opposed to a "solidarity network" of the kind that we analyzed in Chapter 2, which reaches beyond a particular issue focus and into support networks for larger categories of concern). We set the crawler to a crawl depth of 3, which instructs it to drill two pages beyond the homepage to follow any outlinks on those pages. In our experience, this crawl depth generally catches most network links that matter to the mission of organizations.

The crawls produced network maps for each country, and these networks became the populations from which we drew our network samples for measuring public engagement orientations. Space limitations prevent us from showing all of the maps; instead we will illustrate the overall results with one national-level civil society issue network map and one EU-level map. Figure 4.1 shows what a national-level fair trade network in Britain looks like. It is a dense and highly interconnected network, in which many organizations link to each other. We have followed this network for more than five years and note that it is remarkably stable, with most of the core (densely linked) organizations remaining at the core and only peripheral organizations moving in and out of the network. Since we screened all the nodes in the network for issue relevance, some of the peripheral organizations did not make it into the set of network members coded for digital engagement tools.

By contrast, the EU-level networks had little density or cross-linking among organizations. We had to employ two different crawl methods to determine this result. The initial co-link crawl method produced cluster maps that on first inspection appeared similar to that shown in Figure 4.1, although with more dispersion and different satellite clusters. On closer inspection, we realized that the most dense and issue-relevant of these clusters was populated largely by the outreach efforts of a small number of national network organizations that overlap with the EU-level networks. Even closer inspection revealed that most of the other EU-level organizations dropped out of the maps altogether, meaning they did not receive link recognition from even two other organizations.

FIGURE 4.1. UK national-level fair trade and development network showing dense co-linking among organizations. The size of each node reflects the number of organizations in the core network linking to it. Map by issuecrawler.net, courtesy of the Govcom.org Foundation, Amsterdam. Used with permission.

Thus, most of the network structure existing in co-link networks drawn from EU-level issue organizations was, in effect, already captured by the national level networks.

In other words, using the co-link method resulted in little or no insight into what kind of networking, if any, was going on among the hundreds of national NGOs that were unique members at the EU level (i.e., that did not show up on maps drawn from the national-level starting points but that were clearly listed as German or British members of the relevant EU civil society platform). The idea that a small number of overlapping organizations reconstituted networks that we had already mapped at the national level meant that we would be duplicating the national-level network and effectively missing the chance to examine most of the EU-only organizations when examining the public engagement orientations of EU networks. Of course, we wanted to assess the contributions of the national-level overlapping organizations to the overall engagement profiles

FIGURE 4.2. EU-level fair trade and development network in the United Kingdom, showing a hierarchical or "star" structure with little co-linking among organizations. Map by issuecrawler.net, courtesy of the Govcom.org Foundation, Amsterdam. Used with permission.

of the EU networks, but we did not want to miss the unique EU-level organizations in calculating the overall engagement scores of their networks. Thus, the co-link crawl told us that the overall EU-level network was rather weak and must be approached by other means if we wanted to include its organizations in the engagement analysis.

In order to determine whether the unique EU-level actors formed any sort of network, we entered members of the CONCORD platform affiliated with the UK coordinating organization (Bond) into an interactor crawl, which relaxes the criteria for network inclusion by mapping any single links between any two organizations. Figure 4.2 reveals a "star" or hub-and-spoke network, with Bond (the lead UK NGO in the EU economic development platform) at the center and other organizations linking to it, but not to each other. This is a textbook case of a "star" network of the sort not often found so perfectly in nature. This picture tells us that the EU-level development organizations are associated in a rather hierarchical way and do not share many close, cross-linking relationships insofar as the public face presented on their websites goes. A subsequent interactor analysis was based on the set of UK development organizations more narrowly defined around fair trade initiatives (e.g., excluding relief or health organizations). That map revealed that the star formation around Bond was joined by a second, more densely linked cluster of the overlapping national-level organizations found in Figure 4.1, again suggesting that the national- and EU-level issue networks are organized very differently. NGOs that focused primarily on political relations with the EU were relatively unconnected with each other, while the overlapping members that we had already found in the national network crawls provided most of the relationships that form a dense interconnected issue network.

These notable mapping differences between the EU- and national-level networks led us to choose different methods for selecting the sites to be coded for public engagement at the different levels. For the national-level networks that displayed the more densely clustered structures, we screened all the organizations identified in our network crawl to select the ones that had a general focus on trade or development policy.[16] For the national-level environment networks we screened for a general focus on environmental protection and climate change.[17] The same screening was done for the samples drawn from the corresponding EU platforms. However, as already noted, when we attempted to generate samples based on co-link maps of the EU-level networks, we found that unique EU-level organizations tended to drop out because they were not linked to from multiple other organizations (suggesting very weak – or more competitive – relations among EU-level NGOs). Thus, we decided that the only way to gather a coding sample of these more hierarchically networked EU NGOs was to sample directly from lists of UK and German member organizations in the relevant EU platforms. The initial samples drawn from the EU environment and development platforms were screened for having a general focus on climate change / natural environment and fair trade / economic justice, respectively. Organizations that did not fit these classifications were replaced randomly and screened until the original sample numbers were met.

---

[16] Through this process, we eliminated various nodes that existed mainly in the tails of the networks. These included organizations far afield from trade or economic justice, such as disaster relief or health organizations that found their way into the network due to the often multi-faceted activities of huge NGOs like Oxfam and CAFOD that were in the starting list. We also eliminated social media sites such as Facebook and Twitter because they are not codable in their globular forms, and we were coding each organization separately for their presence. The screening produced 46 issue-relevant organizations from a beginning network of 96.

[17] We dropped organizations focusing on workplace environment, environmental health policy, etc., leaving a coding sample of 56 issue-specific organizations from an initial core network of 96. As with the fair trade sample, most of the included climate change organizations were closer to the head of the network inlink distributions, suggesting that they were also regarded as more "relevant" by more of the organizations in our starting point list, which provides an independent measure of validity for our screening.

The resulting sample sizes that we used to code public engagement opportunities among organizations ranged from 58 organizations (UK national-level environment network) to 23 (EU-level German environment network). The differences in sample sizes for the EU-level networks reflects the fact that although those networks spanned broader ranges of policy issues within the very general civil society platform categories, they had fewer unique organizations in the relevant categories of our study.[18] The smaller number of issue-specific organizations operating exclusively at the EU level may reflect the greater competition among fewer organizations for scarce institutional resources, contrasted with the greater proliferation of grassroots organizations. We standardized these differences in sample size by reporting the percentages of organizations in each network that displayed each measure of public engagement.

Measuring Public Engagement

Following earlier work on varieties of online engagement (Bennett, Wells, and Freelon 2011) we drew a distinction between two broad varieties of engagement: (a) exchanging *information* about issues and (b) suggesting or enabling *actions* that people could take to promote goals and causes. We reasoned that, reflecting the spectrum of digital media forms, both of these types of engagement could either be passive, through directives sent by organizations, or interactive, through the use of technologies that invite people to contribute to information streams and the planning and implementation of action. We inventoried public engagement mechanisms on the websites of all organizations in each network. These digital mechanisms ranged from newsletters to downloadable organizer toolkits, from photo-sharing tools to live Twitter feeds from demonstrations, and from making donations to aiding the orchestration

---

[18] The sample characteristics of the various networks are as follows:

1. Environment: The *UK national network* included 96 sites in the crawled network, leaving a codable sample of 58 after screening for relevance of policy focus. The UK climate crawl was conducted May 9, 2010. The *German national network* included 100 sites in the network crawl and 57 codable sites following the screening. The German climate crawl was conducted on May 9, 2010. The *EU-level environment network in the United Kingdom* began with 48 Green Ten partners, of which 24 were left after screening for relevance (sample gathered May 25, 2010). The *EU-level German environment network* resulted in 25 German-based organizations found in the Green Ten and 23 left following screening for relevance (sampled on June 6, 2010).

2. Fair trade networks: The *UK national-level network* included 96 organizations in the crawl and an N of 46 codable organizations after screening (crawled April 16, 2010). The *German national-level network* included 93 organizations, of which 37 were coded following screening (crawled April 20, 2010). When the *UK EU-level network* was screened for relevance, 19 of the 36 Bond members dropped out due to falling outside the policy bounds. Since this was a large network with many British member organizations, the disqualified organizations were replaced by random selection of new members from the Bond list until the original N of 36 relevant organizations was reached (April 30, 2010). The *German EU-level network* drawn from the original sample of 30 Venro members resulted in 16 dropping out after screening and being randomly replaced with relevant organizations (May 9, 2010).

or co-production of protest actions. These engagement mechanisms not only are indicators of the orientations of each organization to engaging publics, but constitute actual means of engagement. This approach misses various public aspects of issue networks such as the fact that some organizations are too small or poor to have websites (or to have resource-rich websites) or that some organizations engage people largely offline. In addition, our methods are likely to reveal far more about how transparent policy networks engage publics than how less transparent networks such as terrorist networks do. However, since we are seeking broadly reliable indicators of national and transnational public policy engagement, we believe that the networks we have sampled represent central players in national and transnational issue advocacy and that the comparisons offered by our approach generate useful input for building general theory.

We next operationalized the two broad categories of public engagement opportunities on organization websites (information and action), along with the two modalities of each type (passive and interactive). For example, information can be observed moving in largely *one-way* flows from an organization to its publics (e.g., via newsletters, closed calendars), or it can emerge through *interactive* information sharing among publics themselves (e.g., via calendars open to public posting or Flickr photo pages). Similarly, we can observe two kinds of action opportunities: those that are *highly structured* and managed by the organization (e.g., formally joining an organization or donating money) and those that were significantly *co-produced* by the organization and citizens who made creative contributions (e.g., by participating in protests or hosting events at home). We identified eight broad measures based on different digital media for each dimension of engagement. (Two interactive information measures were dropped due to poor coder reliability, leaving six measures in that category.) The resulting scheme for measuring public engagement is shown in Figure 4.3 in the form of the website coding template used by coders.[19] In the next section, we will report all of the coding results for an issue network to help the reader become more familiar with the component measures that make up each of the categories of engagement. We will thereafter report only the summary scores for the four engagement dimensions, along with a summary score for the sum of the four engagement dimensions across all coded organizations in the network. Thus, the process of coding the engagement levels of each organization and summing the scores across all the organizations in an issue network shows what percentage of organizations in the network offer each form of engagement to the public. In this approach, the websites not only serve as proxies for looking at the engagement orientations of each organization in a network, but also represent actual communication media through which networks are structured, information flows, and action is coordinated.

---

[19] The coder reliability coefficients (simple percent agreement, given the use of a "presence or absence" coding protocol) ranged from .98 to .7 on individual items, and the average for each of the four dimensions was above .8.

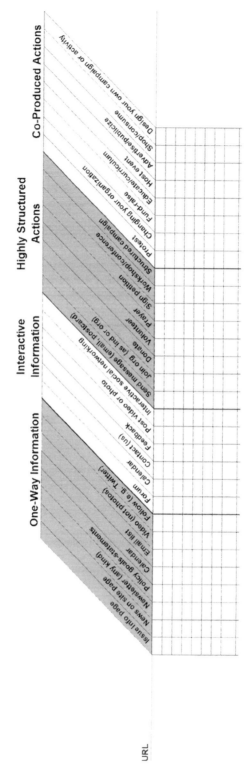

FIGURE 4.3. Four dimensions of public engagement measured by component indicators across organizations in issue networks.

Network Organization and Digitally Mediated Public Engagement

In general, we found that the national-issue networks produce substantially higher levels of engagement across all four engagement dimensions than do the EU-level networks. This pattern holds true for both the fair trade and environment networks in the United Kingdom and the fair trade network in Germany. The German environment network presents an interesting contrast by offering significantly lower direct engagement opportunities than the corresponding UK network, which we will address later.

We began by establishing a baseline measure of high levels of digitally mediated engagement, using the British cases. The national-level networks in the United Kingdom are interesting because they register the highest engagement levels of any networks in our sample (also scoring as high or higher than the economic, environment, and gender issue networks in other countries not reported here due to space limitations). It is also interesting that the two UK national-issue networks are roughly comparable in terms of engagement patterns. As shown in Table 4.1, both networks offer a broad array of engagement opportunities, and they are not significantly different on the five summary measures that we will use for the remainder of the analysis. These measures are the mean percentage scores for the items in the four separate engagement categories and an overall engagement score obtained by summing those four scores. They are handy for comparing different issue networks (e.g., fair trade and environment), as well as the national level and the EU levels of those networks, and for interpreting deviant cases, such as the low engagement scores in the German national environment network.

Table 4.1 makes clear that the average of the items in each of our four engagement categories is remarkably similar in the two British national issue networks. In fact, *T*-tests on the four overall scale scores and the sum of the four engagement scales shown at the bottom of Figure 4.1 showed that the differences were not statistically different and could have resulted from random chance. A casual item-by-item inspection suggests that there are, as one would expect, some differences between particular types of digital engagement in the two networks. For example, the significant presence of church organizations in the fair trade network results in a higher level of encouragement to pray for a more just world. There are a few other item-by-item differences that may reflect such things as the maturity or resources of the network, or externalities in the environment at the time we did the network mapping and engagement inventory. For example, the UK environment network was mapped around the time of the Copenhagen climate conference, and the Stop Climate Chaos Coalition, which provided our starting points, was involved in mobilizing large public protests. It is not surprising that the opportunities to engage in protest activities were significantly higher for organizations along that network, with 22 percent of the organizations displaying specific protest opportunities, in contrast to the fair trade network, where only 11 percent of the organizations

TABLE 4.1. *A Comparison of Four Categories of Public Engagement in UK National-Level Environment and Fair Trade Networks*

Category	UK National-Level Fair Trade Network[a] (%)	UK National-Level Environment Network[b] (%)
INFORMATION VARIABLES (ONE-WAY, INTERACTIVE)		
Site: Recently updated?	87	98
One-way: Issue information page	93	93
One-way: News on site page	89	94
One-way: Newsletter (any kind)	61	63
One-way: Policy goals, statements	89	70
One-way: Calendar	52	54
One-way: Email list	63	44
One-way: Video (not photos)	59	63
One-way: Follow (e.g., Twitter)	48	59
Interactive: Forum	37	37
Interactive: Calendar	20	15
Interactive: Contact (us)	98	94
Interactive: Feedback	20	44
Interactive: Post video or photo	24	15
Interactive: Interactive social networking	52	67
ACTION VARIABLES (HIGHLY STRUCTURED, CO-PRODUCED)		
HS: Send message	61	52
HS: Join org	67	50
HS: Donate	52	59
HS: Volunteer	52	43
HS: Prayer	20	9
HS: Sign petition	30	24
HS: Workshop/conference	26	37
HS: Structured campaign	57	76
CP: Protest	11	22
CP: Changing your organization	17	48
CP: Fund-raise	39	26
CP: Educate/curriculum	46	35
CP: Host event	35	22
CP: Advertise/publicize	54	46
CP: Shop/consume	46	46
CP: Design your own campaign or activity	30	35
OVERALL RESULTS		
One-way information (summary score)	0.69	0.68
Interactive information (summary score)	0.42	0.45
Highly structured actions (summary score)	0.46	0.44
Co-produced actions (summary score)	0.35	0.35
Overall public engagement score (sum of four component scores)	1.91	1.92

Note: Item scores represent the percentage of organizations in each network displaying each engagement mechanism. Summary scores represent averages of item scores for each engagement dimension.

[a] $N = 46$.
[b] $N = 58$.

TABLE 4.2. *Engagement Levels in UK Fair Trade Networks Comparing National-Level and EU-Level Networks (with and without Overlapping Organizations)*

Category	UK National Level vs. EU Level (with Overlapping Organizations)	UK National Level (with Overlapping Organizations) vs. EU Level (without Overlapping Organizations)
One-way information	0.12**	0.18**
Interactive information	0.10*	0.14**
Highly structured actions	0.10*	0.17**
Co-produced actions	0.09***	0.13**
Overall public engagement score	0.40**	0.62**

* The difference is significant at the $p < .05$ level.
** The difference is significant at the $p < .01$ level.
*** The difference is significant at the $p < .10$ level.

displayed protest opportunities.[20] For some purposes, fine-grained analyses may compare different issue networks along specific engagement items, and even locate the organizations in the network that are contributing most to particular item scores (e.g., which organizations are more focused on social networking, protesting, or co-producing events with followers). However, since our interest is in understanding the political organization of broad public engagement across entire networks, we concentrate primarily on the summary scores for the four categories of engagement and the sum of those four scales to generalize about the overall engagement orientation of an entire network.[21] This is what we refer to as the engagement signature of the network.

In addition to being similar in terms of the four engagement scales and the overall engagement measure, the scores for both of these UK issue networks are the highest observed for any of our networks, whether compared with their national counterparts in Germany or with any of the EU-level networks for both countries. As such, they provide a baseline for comparing the engagement orientations of other networks. Indeed, the plot thickens when we compare both of these national-level UK networks with their EU-level counterparts for the United Kingdom and discover significant engagement score differences. The EU fair trade / economic development and environment / climate change networks offer far lower engagement opportunities across all four categories of engagement. Consider, for example, the case of fair trade. Table 4.2 compares the national and EU levels of these networks for the United Kingdom; one

[20] This suggests interesting possibilities for mapping and assessing engagement profiles in networks over time and in response to events. However, in one-time analyses such as this one, we recommend using the summary scores to reduce the dominance of any single engagement item such as protests.

[21] If all of the organizations in the network displayed all of the component mechanisms making up a particular engagement category, then the network score would be 100%, or 1.0 for that scale, with the highest possible summary score 4 × 1.0, or 4.

TABLE 4.3. *Engagement Levels in German Fair Trade Networks Comparing National-Level and EU-Level Networks (without Overlapping Organizations)*

Category	Difference in Means
One-way information	0.17**
Interactive information	0.09**
Highly structured actions	0.02
Co-produced actions	0.18**
Overall public engagement score	0.45**

** The difference is significant at the $p < .01$ level.

comparison is based on the overlapping organizations that appear in both networks, and another comparison shows just the EU-oriented NGOs by excluding from the engagement score calculations for national-level organizations that belong to both networks.

The networks differ significantly even when we include the organizations that appear in both networks (e.g., Oxfam, Fairtrade Foundation), suggesting that even the national-level organizations are not sufficient to boost the public engagement levels of the generally hierarchical EU networks. To see just how much of the total engagement signature those organizations brought to the EU network, we removed them and recalculated the engagement comparisons. As shown in Table 4.2, the engagement gap between national- and EU-level economic policy networks grows considerably larger. This pattern also holds generally true for the German fair trade networks. Table 4.3 compares the national- and EU-level fair trade / economic development networks and shows that for three of the four engagement dimensions, the national-level network is significantly higher than the EU-level network and that the overall engagement scores are significantly different as well. The one category without a significant engagement difference is the collection of highly structured actions, where we find that the EU network organizations were more active in seeking members and donations. This is interesting, since these activities are commonly associated with conventional organizations that tend to regard publics in membership terms – an orientation that reflects a civil society format that is being challenged by individuals seeking less formal relations with particular organizations. By contrast, the national-level network was much more active in engaging citizens in campaigns and petitions, which reflects an important difference in the kinds of engagement operating at the national versus the EU level. A similar pattern holds for the United Kingdom as well, particularly when we control for the overlapping membership of national-level organizations.

The British environment networks follow much the same pattern, with the national-level network displaying significantly higher public engagement profiles than the EU-level network for all four categories of engagement, all of which are significant at the $p < .05$ level, and for the overall engagement score ($p < .01$).

The German environment networks provide interesting exceptions to this pattern of networked public mobilization through digital media. To begin with, these networks displayed no significant public engagement differences between the national and the EU levels, even when the overlapping national organizations were removed from the EU network.[22] Even more striking is that the German national-level environment network was significantly lower than the UK network on all the four engagement scales and on the overall summary score based on summing the four scales across all the organizations in the networks. The UK network scored 1.92 out of a possible 4, in contrast with a score of 1.32 for the German national network. The summary scores and all four sub-scales differed significantly ($p < .01$) between the German and British environment cases.

We attribute this to the institutionalized and professionalized character of environmental politics in Germany, where the environmental movement has effectively organized to incorporate public engagement into governing institutions through voting and elections, and the success of the Green Party has helped harmonize policies between the social movement community and political institutions.[23] The current state of institutionalization is far removed from the active grassroots movement of the 1970s, which centrally figured independent local citizens' initiatives trying to address the side effects of industrialization and with it the core credo of the German model: a higher standard of living through industrial progress (Brand and Rink 2007: 502; cf. Markham 2008). Local activists and their alliances (Buergerinitiativen) carried much of the message of green politics at the time, before helping to launch the Green Party on the local and state levels and to get it elected into the national parliament in 1983. The surge in the environmental movement and the rise of the Green Party created an environmental agenda for other political parties, political dynamics that are reflected in both legislation and executive actions, such as Chancellor Angela Merkel of the Christian Democrats supporting a pullback from nuclear power after the 2011 Fukushima disaster in Japan.

The institutionalized representation of environmental issues opened up opportunities for cooperation and funding resources for NGOs, resulting in an arc of transformation that Brand and Rink summarize in terms of the "institutionalization, differentiation, professionalization, and internationalization" of the environmental movement (Brand and Rink 2007: 505–507; cf. Markham 2008). Even as environmental protests continued (Rucht and Roose 2003), many "Protestakteur" transformed into professional advocates of environmental causes and sought out more cooperative partnerships and client

[22] There was a surprising level of overlap in the two networks, with fully 14 of the 23 sites appearing in both networks (which we take to be a sign of greater institutionalization of these networks). However, even with the overlapping sites taken out of the EU-level network comparison, the engagement levels were not significantly different (although the Ns were small at that point).

[23] We are grateful for the research assistance of Curd Knüpfer in this discussion of the German environmental movement.

relationships with governments from the local to the transnational level (Roose 2003; Brand and Rink 2007: 502; Markham 2008; Brand 2010). The financial base of German environmental NGO networks compared with those of similar networks in the United Kingdom offers an indicator of the institutional transformation during this era. One study shows that, in the United Kingdom in 1997, 71.1 percent of environmental NGOs had a yearly budget of less than 5,000 euros (calculated from 1997 equivalents), whereas in Germany only 12.2 percent had such a low budget at that time (Roose 2003). This professionalization and resource distribution accelerated with the Red–Green coalition on the federal level between 1998 and 2005, when funding could be better achieved through cooperation with private and state institutions rather than through membership fees or donations.[24]

The "professionalization dilemma" (Brand and Rink 2007: 512) of the environmental movement seemingly produced a trade-off between institutionalization and mobilization. As the Green Party gained influence and other parties and policy institutions became more receptive to environmental initiatives due to various forms of influence from within and below, the expanded opportunities for NGOs for direct political access may in turn have helped reshape their coalition alliances and how they choose to cut the diamond. This does not imply that grassroots environmental politics in Germany is dead. As various kinds of environmental activism in Germany suggest, people are also finding ways to engage by other means. For example, the intense protests surrounding the controversial Stuttgart train station development project offer a glimpse of how personalized lifestyle issues still activate protest networks (although, ironically, the majority of citizens voted to continue the project and elected a Green local government around the same time). Nevertheless, the greater political harmony among German NGO environmental advocacy networks across national- and EU-level networks has come at the cost of a weaker promotion of everyday public engagement with the issues.

The larger moral of this story is that NGOs and their networks, when embracing the institutionalization of their agendas, may turn away from a focus on public engagement (Lang 2013). The result of the institutionalization of the most visible German environment network as well as the EU-level issue networks in our study seems to be an emphasis on strategies of institutional influence at the expense of public engagement. For the environmental NGOs

---

[24] A further indicator of institutionalization is the number of formal institutionalized coalition networks that appear as members of the larger network, which signals that the network is more strongly characterized by organizationally brokered lobbying and insider politics than organizationally enabled public engagement. The largest coalition in the UK network was the Stop Climate Chaos umbrella network, which was clearly a loosely tied network that coordinated various public actions such as the series of protests ahead of the Copenhagen UN Climate Change Conference. The other large coalition in the UK network was the Put People First network, which, as discussed in Chapter 2, was also loosely organized to enable broad inclusion and personalized engagement. By contrast, the German national-level network included seven large professionalized umbrella organizations, including an organization of state governments, a network of professional policy NGOs, a network of 1,200 German cities, and a European city network with nearly 500 German cities out of 1,640 total members.

in the German issue advocacy network, the opportunities afforded by insider politics seemed sufficient to divert attention from high levels of direct public engagement. A similar story is associated with the EU issue advocacy networks that have established institutional niches in Brussels. The opportunities and trade-offs in the political environment affect how issue networks are organized and how citizens are included or excluded by that network organization. When the political context offers institutionalization, issue advocacy networks seem less likely to develop or sustain connective action.

Conclusion

The similarities and contrasts among the issue advocacy networks examined in this chapter suggest several things for the purposes of understanding how connective action works, and in particular what factors may play into the development of organizationally enabled connective networks over time. There are clearly many ways "to cut the diamond," as the director of the Jubilee 2000 debt relief network put it. What is more, the structuring of political opportunities, incentives, and constraints affects how these network diamonds are cut. When they are cut to favor greater refraction of the distribution of light (in our case, public engagement), we begin to see changes in how organizations enter into alliances and how those alliances regard broader publics.

To begin with, the more the organizations involved seek to engage publics, the more an organizational network becomes loosely fashioned (and the flatter its power curve becomes, as discussed in the next chapter). These organizationally enabled cases of connective action are best represented in the three high-engagement national issue networks analyzed here. In those cases, the loosely linked relationships among a large number of organizations enable individuals to find personally comfortable ways to engage with issues on- and offline. This generally means that as the terms of networked association among organizations are relaxed (i.e., as coalitions move from brokered to less heavily managed associations), the variety of personalized engagement opportunities offered across the network tends to increase. Indeed, the way in which we have categorized and scaled the four categories of digitally enabled engagement mechanisms means that relatively high scores indicate greater levels of interactive and more personalized engagement. We found no cases of low engagement based primarily on the interactive forms of information and action, and, conversely, we found no cases of high-engagement networks based primarily on one-way information and action items. While particular externalities and organizational histories may create exceptions, it is generally true that some less interactive media affordances (e.g., newsletters, email lists, information pages on websites, donation links, petitions) are relatively more common across different network types, while the more interactive engagement forms tend to cluster in organizationally enabled networks defined by a large number of densely linked organizations.

The lower public engagement profiles of the other networks, meanwhile, were also reflected in stark differences in network structure: the EU-level networks were sparsely interconnected and hierarchical. In the exceptional case in which a low-engagement network displayed more densely clustered interrelationships, as was the case for the German national environment network, far more of the member nodes were umbrella organizations representing large professional or technocratic networks that were clearly organized more for institutional access than for public mobilization. This finer-grained analysis is a reminder that our networks are heuristic representations in part based on actual, in-the-world relationships (e.g., linkages that signal recognition) and in part abstracted from more complex contextual realities. These maps are rather like satellite photos of installations on the ground in that they make some things perfectly clear, while interpreting other things requires more contextual interpretation and local knowledge.

The analysis in this chapter helps us understand some of the dynamics of organizationally enabled connective action networks. Yet we should also note that in the wider perspective such network patterns do not speak for themselves. For example, many organizations forming centralized, low-engagement issue advocacy networks would argue that they may not be achieving connective action but that the way they are doing things better serves their political goals. Why should they spend time mobilizing publics if they have more direct ways to advance goals that stand to benefit those publics in the long run? This refrain ran through interviews with leaders of EU women's policy networks reported by Lang (2013), and a similar refrain can be heard in the debates on the institutionalization of the German environmental movement. One answer to the defense of NGOs without publics is that participation is a valuable outcome in itself and that when institutionalized politics, in effect, replaces a participatory civil society some important degree of democratic experience has been lost (Pateman 1970; Habermas, 1989, 1998; Tarrow 2001; Lang 2013). It could also be argued that the relative absence of direct participation in, for example, EU politics contributes to a democratic deficit that affects its legitimacy (Tarrow 2001; Risse 2010; Bennett 2012).

If we step back from these theoretical debates, we see that they have some ironic real-world variations. For example, some of the most institutionally successful NGO networks find themselves on the defensive in regard to the democratic representation question of "Whom do they speak for?" or "Whom do they represent?" What is ironic is that such questions are often directed at progressive NGOs (such as the environment or economic justice organizations in our network cases) by business lobbies that already have disproportionate access to many decision-making arenas and feel that their own legitimacy is not subject to question. It is also notable that the EU Commission in Brussels has begun to conduct democracy audits on some of its NGO networks in the civil society platform, outsourcing the task to accounting firms that may be even less well equipped for the task. This said, it is true that if held accountable to conventional electoral-institutional criteria of democratic accountability and legitimacy, it is often hard for NGOs and NGO networks to justify their representative standing. Nevertheless, such criteria, as conventionally understood, are elusive to apply, measure, and evaluate in national and transnational contexts. In earlier work with Sabine Lang that is more centrally focused on this issue, we argue that public engagement, by contrast, is an important dimension of democratic accountability and legitimacy that can be meaningfully applied also to contemporary advocacy networks as political network organizations (Bennett, Lang, and Segerberg 2011; Bennett, Lang, Segerberg, and Knappe 2011; Bennett, Lang, and Segerberg forthcoming).

Still, NGOs do not always help their own cause when challenged about legitimacy. NGO officers do not typically see public engagement as an automatic standard that they either can or should promote within their organizations or networks. And even when they do value public engagement, they may have a model of that engagement based on formal membership and more tightly bounded organizational ownership of their issues and causes. In a conversation with a high-level official in the EU civil society platform, we asked about the difference between most of the civil society platform members and more visible national-level NGOs depicted in our network maps. He characterized the nationally networked NGOs as "campaign organizations," using a tone that suggested they were playing an entirely different game. This distinction implies that something of a wall may exist between different types of organization within the EU networks. What may be lost in this distinction is the possibility that organizations that are not oriented to engaging publics might boost both their political capacity and legitimacy by joining loose networks with more public-minded organizations.

An important point to observe is that the network configurations examined in this chapter, and the stark differences among them, are only partly the result of conscious design choices by organizations. Organizations (and their officers) nested in the EU civil society system may have strong ideas about their organizational priorities, just as actors operating within dense national mobilization networks may sense this as their natural proclivity. It is not surprising that the ways in which networks are constructed and how those networks regard publics are partly the result of contextual factors (power and opportunity) that condition the design process itself. To power and opportunity, we add another contextual factor: the nature and proclivities of publics themselves. To the extent that publics seek personalized and mediated forms of engagement and to the extent that they find solidarity less in forming collective identifications than in sharing personal content with their social networks, affiliation preferences also become a conditioning factor in how issue networks organize themselves. Perhaps this is why cutting the diamond takes so much time, why it remains so difficult, and why it often reveals so many flaws.

5

Networks, Power, and Political Outcomes

Earlier chapters in the book have examined the political and organizational capacities of different types of connective action. Comparing the protest mobilizations in Chapter 2 showed that organizationally enabled connective action can perform surprisingly well in terms of maintaining political agendas and gaining positive recognition from news media and acknowledgment from public officials, while a more radical brokered mobilization fared poorly in terms of public "worthiness."[1] Chapter 3 showed how another organizationally enabled connective action network also managed a large and well-received demonstration, while a crowd-enabled sub-network of the Copenhagen climate protests displayed robust organizational capacities in response to short-term events and longer-term adaptive patterns such as a marked resource-seeking capacity when the continuing existence of the network became tenuous. In Chapter 4 we found that organizationally enabled issue networks operating at the national level in the United Kingdom and Germany displayed dense mechanisms for personalized, digitally mediated engagement as part of their efforts to attract popular support for their initiatives at the same time as they exerted pressure on institutional politics and policy.

Such findings suggest that large-scale connective action networks need not always be mere lightweight versions of more traditionally brokered collective action coalitions in which players negotiate alliances and allocate resources such as money, professional staff, memberships, skilled leaders, and other levers of power. Indeed, in some respects and in some contexts, the flexibility of connective action networks may offer some clear advantages over more formally constituted coalitions.

[1] As noted previously, it is important to acknowledge that not all protest organizers aim to achieve the same goals. We thus do not wish to imply that the more militant anti-capitalist and anarchist groups were necessarily seeking respect from those quarters. They may well have measured success by other standards, such as publically disavowing the system or inserting their preferred messages into public spaces.

The findings also suggest an interesting proposition about power in networks: power can be organized very differently, using different kinds of resources, and still produce comparable results. Manuel Castells (2009, 2012) and others have suggested that there has been a general shift of power in the so-called network society away from hierarchical organization and political institutions toward loosely tied, flexible citizen networks. Yet, as we discussed earlier, there is persistent skepticism about the political capacity of connective action. Underlying this skepticism is the worry that organizational structure and capacity play against each other. The familiar concern is that the gains of connective action such as rapid scalability and adaptability may be paid for by a loss of capacity to set agendas, achieve policy change, and continue to mobilize and coordinate action in the face of adversity over time. However, we cannot simply reject or accept this generalization without considering some of the often-contested ideas about power itself: how it is and should be organized most effectively (Tarrow 2011).

In this chapter we address the question of how power operates in different kinds of connective action networks. We pursue empirical investigations that offer clearly established points of comparison, from which we may learn about different kinds of power and different kinds of political outcomes. Our analysis focuses on two differently organized connective action networks, both of which aimed to get discussions of economic inequality and justice onto the public agenda. One case is an organizationally enabled connective network operating in the United Kingdom to promote the idea of a tax on financial transactions, which would limit the level of financial speculation and return a portion of the proceeds of that speculation to development and redistributive economic policies. It was named the Robin Hood Tax campaign in an effort to "cut the diamond" in ways that would reflect many organizational and individual points of engagement. The contrasting case is the Occupy protests in the United States, which generated the crowdsourced "We Are the 99%" personal action frame in drawing attention to multiple questions of social, political, and economic inequality. Occupy is an example of crowd-enabled connective action. The protests under this personal action frame, along with hundreds of creative "occupations" of politicians and places, also shifted elite and media discourses on inequality and fairness.

The two case studies present different configurations of power in very different connective action formations. Most connective action networks do not have the observable successes of the cases presented here, but some do. We focus on cases with relatively positive outcomes in order to show that different kinds of network power can produce similar outcomes. This suggests that differences in success and failure cannot be pinned easily on different configurations of power in networks. The question to be addressed in developing this point is this: Under what conditions do different configurations of power in action networks have what kind of political capacity? To answer this, we must first explain what we mean by power in networks.

Contested Conceptions of Network Power

In an attempt to dispel the popular misconception that all political networks are alike (and necessarily egalitarian), scholars of action networks similar to the ones we discussed in the preceding chapter have made the important observation that these may develop different structural forms and that their power distribution varies (Cowhey and Mueller 2009; Mueller 2010). Yet a more focused examination of how networks evolve in different power terms and how they function is necessary for our purposes.

In order to approach our cases, we need to conceptualize and characterize different ways of thinking about the organization of power in political networks. A good place to start is to question the proposition that loosely configured connective networks are inevitably inferior to more tightly organized coalitions in terms of success in challenging their targets and managing the activities of their followers. Under some conditions this assertion may be true, but it distracts from seeing other ways in which effective power can be organized. Tarrow's account of a politically effective hybrid movement organization in which loose umbrella organizations help to coordinate the activities of more autonomous socially networked groups presents an example of one such way (Tarrow 2011: 136–139).[2]

However, analyzing network power is challenged by the breathtaking empirical scope of possible cases and contexts, as is richly illustrated in Scott's work on peasant resistance in oppressive regimes (Scott 1985). A good deal of research shows that how one thinks about the trade-offs between organizational power and outcomes depends on such factors as the political arenas, the issues, and the opponents being contested. Considering this Rubik's Cube of contextual factors, we quickly see that distributed terrorist networks might have a greater chance of success against hierarchical targets such as states with powerful militaries than would more formally organized hierarchical networks (Arquilla and Ronfeldt 2000). Even when we control for political contexts and targets and look at relatively democratic institutional contexts such as policy processes, the basis for empirical hypotheses about the advantageous organization of power are still not self-evident. We must, for example, account for different incentives (and other opportunities) offered by institutions and different political goals sought by those contesting political outcomes. This is illustrated by the issue advocacy networks that we tracked in the preceding chapter, which showed less public mobilization at the EU level than at the national level.

If conceptualizing the permutations of power and outcomes in networks is empirically problematic, it is equally challenged by normative perspectives that run a similarly broad gamut of complexity. For example, there is the

---

[2] This account is similar to that of our organizationally enabled hybrid type, although we distinguish our ideal type by specifying the key linkage mechanisms as personal action frames and digital engagement tools.

familiar standpoint of "means and ends" that one often hears from NGOs operating in client relationships with governments: if outcomes benefit some general public good, then whether we organize hierarchically, use our clout to get to the bargaining table, or choose not to mobilize publics should not matter (see Lang 2013 for interesting examples of this). However, there are equally strong ideas that distributing power more evenly across organizations and broader publics is an essential ingredient of democratic politics, such that the absence of conditions that favor equal participation casts a shadow on the legitimacy of political outcomes and the processes that produce them (Pateman 1970; Habermas 1989, 1998).

Given the complexity of factors affecting how we think about power and outcomes, it is not surprising that much research has focused on network power in tightly circumscribed political arenas. While such work has produced rich results, the overall effect is that different research fields seem to be operating in parallel universes using different conceptual vocabularies that may result in an overall discourse that may obstruct the forest for the trees.

Part of the trouble is that different bodies of literature tend to analyze network power in different ways, often depending on which aspect of the network is in focus (Kahler 2009). One important body of work has focused on the power of (i.e., the impact of) networks. Scholars interested in political agency and capacity often concentrate on the ability to shape political outcomes in terms inherited from research on policy networks and social movements: agenda setting; achieving policy change; and achieving behavioral change in targets or others in the network by getting them to adopt issues, represent viewpoints, or make lifestyle changes (see Sikkink 2009; cf. Keck and Sikkink 1998).

In different reaches of the network universe, other scholars draw on network theory and social network analysis to focus on relationship patterns internal to the network structure. The emphasis here is less on the forms of political agency than on the structural properties of a network and the implications for particular actors and their strategies. Taking an interesting technology-focused perspective, for example, Castells (2011) highlights the power of technology codes that embody cultural rules of inclusion or exclusion, with a focus on the particular roles of "programming" and "switching" in network construction. Zeroing in on communication networks in specific events (e.g., across different phases of a protest), others examine the centrality and influence of the different kinds of actors involved (González-Bailón et al. 2011; Theocharis 2012).

Many of these different research areas in fact study much the same kinds of action formations, and there is great value to be gained in bringing the various perspectives together. As both Kathryn Sikkink and Mario Diani observe in different ways, an urgent question emerging out of such work is how power *in* a network organization relates to the power *of* the network (Sikkink 2009; Diani forthcoming). This is where it becomes important to question assumptions about a straightforward relationship between how power is organized and how this translates into political outcomes. Common assumptions circling around the idea of powerful networks include the following: that more effective and powerful networks tend to be deliberately arranged by a set of purposeful actors with clear goals; that they tend to be centralized; and that they tend to concentrate resources (or resource-rich actors) at their core (cf. Diani forthcoming). By contrast, our theoretical framework, as applied in the studies described in Chapters 2–4, suggests that many connective action networks have different internal organizing structures and processes but that these differences do not necessarily translate into significantly different or weaker outcomes. In this chapter, we develop a more deductive approach drawn (with modifications) from network theory that makes it possible to generalize across different fields and, in our case, to understand the processes through which networks with different power configurations are organized, while pointing toward ways of thinking about outcomes.

Network Power Signatures

We propose that action networks display what might be termed "power signatures" and that the different types will tend toward different signatures. We use the term *power signature* to refer to the degree to which recognition (prestige and influence) is concentrated or dispersed among actors in a network. Measures such as the inlink rankings of organizations in a network crawl reveal the degree to which power is concentrated or dispersed across organizations in the network. Such measures indicate which actors others perceive as central and whom they join in protests, campaigns and other actions. The idea is to assess whether networks cohere strongly or not as measured in terms of cascades of recognition accorded to leading organizations by less highly (peer) recognized organizations below.

In some networks, cascades of recognition may be steep, with many lower-ranking organizations demonstrating allegiance to larger, more highly recognized organizations in the network. In other cases, the cascades may be more moderate, with a number of organizations sharing ties more evenly with other organizations in the network, yet still conforming loosely to some hierarchy of relative dominance among organizations. In addition to these steep or more moderate hierarchical networks centered on backbones of organizations, however, there are also more disjointed systems of action in which the power signature reflects the absence of a coherent coalition structure. We find in our crowd-enabled type a dispersed "network of networks" in which different clusters of activity may be scattered both geographically and socially. Despite the lack of centralized leadership or other resources, networking technologies may join these distributed centers of activity, sometimes resulting in a surprisingly large capacity for action. Such networks of networks have dispersed power signatures.

The first two power signatures of steep and moderate network hierarchies can be modeled using a core principle of network theory: the "power law" of networks. By contrast, the dispersed "network of networks" power signature entails a qualitatively different approach to thinking about network power, more in terms of dynamic circulation and surges in content and action than as a steady connection. The challenges are how to model these different configurations of power and then to understand how they work in actual political conflicts.

Varieties of Network Power Signatures

One of the most interesting principles of network theory is the power law. The basic idea is that there is a remarkable tendency among networks of very different types (from river systems to status-oriented social circles to bloggers to political activists) to link to, and thus concentrate their associations around, established high-capacity or high-popularity nodes (Buchanan 2002). This gives such networks a curious but robust "scale-free" pattern, which means that growth in network size seldom seems to change the pattern of association linking bottom nodes to larger, or more widely recognized, nodes (Barabási and Bonabeau 2003; Barabási 2009).[3] This has been termed the "rich get richer" principle of networking after Pareto's observation that in most societies wealth tends to become disproportionately concentrated. In fact, Pareto noticed his famous 80–20 principle in many kinds of distributions, from wealth in society (where 80 percent of wealth tends to be owned by 20 percent of the population) to peas in his garden (where 80 percent of the peas were produced by 20 percent of the pods).

The power law and the influence of larger network hubs on smaller ones help explain how people negotiate the vastness of both offline and online social worlds. For example, the power law underlies the "small-world" phenomenon of being able to get from one point to another, even in a vast network such as the population of the United States, in, on average, six moves (Watts 2003). When the world being navigated is smaller, as in the network of people in Hollywood, past and present, the average number of moves connecting people is smaller still. For example, in the game "The Oracle of Bacon" (also known as "The Six Degrees of Kevin Bacon"), it takes only three links (a Bacon number of 3) to get from silent film star Mary Pickford to contemporary actor Kevin Bacon.[4] The small-world idea was popularized by psychologist Stanley Milgram (1967), who sent letters to random people in Middle America and asked them to forward the letters to a friend of Milgram's in Boston. He did not give the friend's address but suggested that the people forward their letters to people who might be more likely to know someone who might know someone who would know how to get the letter to its destination in Boston. The stunning

---

[3] More broadly, power laws are also observed in distributions of more discrete events (or events that display less well understood principles of linkage) such as earthquake magnitudes, sizes of solar flares, or infrared spectrum emissions from the Magellanic Clouds.

[4] To see how they are connected and to enter your own nodes in the small world of Hollywood, see oracleofbacon.org/help.php.

result was that it took on average fewer than six jumps or forwards to reach the destination. This seemingly incredible pattern in networks left to their own random processes was later formalized by mathematicians Duncan Watts and Steven Strogatz (1998), who developed a mathematical model showing how this was in fact a systematic pattern in different networks.

Steep power law distributions (a small number of nodes getting most of the links and traffic) can be observed in many kinds of social and political networks, and the importance of these network "heads" has been widely discussed. Shirky (2003) argued that the concentration of followers around a few highly visible bloggers in the blogosphere (in which smaller blogs link up and thus feed audiences to larger ones) not only is inevitable, but explains their impact in terms of influence or prestige. An important caveat for our story about crowd-enabled connective action is that the "tails" of these steep power distributions can also serve important roles that may not be intuitive when one is thinking about the bottom end of a power distribution. For example, the tails of those blogger networks drive many of the followers of the blogs to the top, aggregating audiences among otherwise unstructured online populations. Indeed, sometimes tails can have independently important effects in networks depending on how access to them is organized or what positions they may occupy in other networks. Anderson (2006) argued that tails in the merchandise offered by online shopping sites overcome conventional constraints of brick and mortar organizations. For example, online retailers such as Amazon can offer far more obscure merchandise than any brick and mortar retailer can afford (or has space) to stock. As a result, those online retailers reap substantial sales from the tail of their inventories that are sold in smaller numbers than the "best sellers" found in stores. Comparable arguments about long tails making a difference can be made for some kinds of social and political action occurring exclusively online, such as initiating petitions in which low costs and available technologies allow lone enthusiasts to persist with few resources (Earl and Kimport 2011).

Both the heads and the tails of (more and less hierarchical) networks can interact in complex mobilizations, each contributing important elements to the activation of participants. The mobilization effects of such combinations can be impressive. An example of this was seen in the Internet piracy protests against the U.S. Congress described in Chapter 1.[5] Moreover, the importance

---

[5] Wikipedia (in English) and thousands of smaller online sites went dark on January 18, 2012, in protest against online piracy bills pending in the U.S. Congress. Facebook and Google also rallied their communities in the protest. Google claimed that the petition it sent to Congress contained more than 4.5 million signatures. Wikipedia announced that there had been more than 160 million page views of its political message and said that its links to members of Congress produced more than 8 million messages, which shut down congressional switchboards and "melted their servers" (Lee 2012). The contested legislation was withdrawn (at least for a time) in both legislative chambers, and a number of prominent political supporters went on record as withdrawing their backing. While the action was widely reported in the conventional press and online media, the real-time monitoring and updating of activity among social media

of heads or tails may shift over the course of events even in the same network. An insightful study of the activation of Twitter streams in the early period of the Spanish *indignados* protests shows that the early Twitter users on the topic could not be predicted in terms of whether they had more or fewer followers. However, the word spread to a large number of others largely because of those early messages being picked up and retweeted by people more central in Twitter networks as measured by their larger number of followers (González-Bailón et al. 2011).

The power law of networks and its applicability across so many kinds of networks have led some researchers to posit an explanation based on "preferential attachment" to already established nodes (Barabási and Albert 1999). Such attachment may be seen in the preference of many people for Google as a search engine or in the core of the algorithm that the Google engine uses to rank results. However, many variations on attachment in networks do not seem so free or natural. This is where we suggest a modification in thinking about power laws in action networks: the "natural" distribution of association patterns in networks can be altered dramatically through intentional interventions, such as laws regulating the redistribution of wealth downward (or even further upward) or the genetic engineering of peas to produce more uniform yields. Thus, we note that different political networks may have different power slopes that reflect some combinations of natural order (jockeying for position, resource seeking), external constraints (opportunities and incentives in the political arena), or intentional intervention (norms and rules applying to members and their relations). In the online world, entire networks may tend toward particular power signatures based on underlying values that become embodied in network design and communication affordances (Benkler 2011).

It is not likely that most action networks conform to true power laws in the sense of associating around a single or a few dominant players, as we may see in unregulated industrial sectors dominated by a few firms or in national population growth, where people tend to migrate to a few megacities while leaving a long tail of tiny villages. Network actors often try to set conditions on how power is organized. When players overstep the norms or rules, others may react by disciplining the wayward player, reducing the player's cooperation, or leaving the network altogether. Moreover, the interesting thing about political networks, at least ones that embody some degree

---

users was notable. For example, tweets about the protests and the parallel bills (the Stop Online Piracy Act and the Protect Intellectual Property Act) numbered more than a million a day for several days and topped 2 million on the day of the blackout (Courtesy of Topsy Social Analytics). This mobilization involved layers of all three of our ideal types. There were some very large organizations that created affordances for their visitors to use in contacting officials, but each organization tended to offer people its own rationale for action, and few linked to each other in the process (though there was surely coordination among them). At the same time, the network-crossing at the individual level was dense, as people activated their personal networks using all manner of communication to share both action options and real-time monitoring with friends and contacts.

of free association, is that the actors in them jockey for political position based on, among other things, visions of ideal political organization forms. Those ideals may reflect combinations of perceptions (negotiated among individuals and organizations) about what works best to obtain desired outcomes. There may also be added network tensions about just what the desired outcomes should be. At an even more fundamental level, there may be network power tensions about how best to "walk the walk" in displaying common values about democracy, hierarchy, gender balance, or other principles that people want to introduce. In some cases, organizing principles clash, as we discuss further in the concluding chapter. When fundamental clashes occur, we find exploding networks, as in the case of the U.S. fair trade community discussed in Chapter 4 in which one dominant actor polarized the national network and eventually split from the transnational network over differences of political and market values.

However, if we are right about ways in which organizationally enabled networks cut the diamond so as to best accommodate diverse principles and realities (the individuation of publics, the proliferation of political arenas, the intersection of issues, etc.), then there may be a tendency to seek an optimal power distribution in such networks. This optimal distribution should look less severe than a classic power law but more hierarchical than a "distributed" network. This is the distribution we might expect when organizations such as NGOs, SMOs, or other civil society groups attempt to join in efforts to engage publics and mobilize action in a connective way.

A network's power signature may be more finely described with other structural properties such as centrality, betweenness, or structural holes, and such design elements of coherent networks may also reveal aspects of the political opportunities, market forces, resources, and other factors in the ecologies in which they form and function (Monge and Contractor 2003). However, a more basic analysis of network power signatures provides useful points of comparison in examining different types of connective networks and their outcomes.

We suggest that it is possible to assess the dominance and coherence in relations among actors involved in a large-scale action network according to whether their association tends toward (a) a classic power law of networks with an exponentially steep power curve (of which, for reasons already explained, we expect to find relatively few stable examples), (b) a moderate variation that breaks with the power law tendency by establishing more loosely tied power sharing to achieve stable coalitions (which we expect to find among organizationally enabled networks), (c) a dispersed power signature reflecting recombinant network-of-network power dynamics (which we expect to find among crowd-enabled networks, as discussed later), or (d) little or no discernible capacity to organize power effectively at all. These alternatives can be found in our three types of large-scale contentious action. In their pure form, our connective types can be expected to conform to alternatives b and c above. In the case of the organizationally brokered networks, the picture is less clear.

Power Signatures in Organizationally Enabled Networks

Strictly defined, power law distributions tail off rapidly and steeply, reflecting a sharp cascade of association from lower to higher nodes in the network. By contrast, what we expect to find among hybrid organizationally enabled network types is a tendency to display what might be called a *moderate power signature* – namely a less steep network curve with a more gentle slope, indicating more organizations sharing recognition (as well as resources and technologies) with others in the network. While these moderate power signatures are technically not power laws, they can be contrasted to those more highly concentrated forms as they reflect intentional design dynamics aimed at keeping them from reverting to that natural concentration (or breaking apart altogether).[6]

A useful feature of this idea of moderate network power signatures that may be measured by inlink distributions is that we can apply it to very different networks and standardize aspects of their inlink distributions for comparison.[7] Following our discussion in Chapter 4, this reflects the idea that these organizationally enabled networks are typically configured to cut the diamond of issue framing and organizational affiliation norms in ways that create the broadest possible engagement among other organizations and individuals, yet still wield enough focused power to raise their issues on the public and institutional agendas. This latter part of the organizationally enabled model pertaining to the intentional focus of power is critical. Like networks with more concentrated power relationships, organizationally enabled networks still aim to wield power in purposeful ways, though sharing the construction of political intentions more broadly than in networks with steeper power signatures, indicating rule by a smaller number of more dominant lead organizations. As we show next, all of the organizationally enabled networks analyzed in this book – including that

---

[6] It is important to note that in some scientific fields such as physics, there are debates about just what a power law is, due in part to the problem of inferring the principles of association underlying the phenomena being observed, as well as the effects of measurement methods on the distributions themselves (Stumpf and Porter 2012). It is ironic that the social sciences tend to employ power law analyses relatively less often than the physical sciences, despite the greater understanding of the things being observed and their associational nature. Even more ironic is the tendency to transform distributions of data in ways that eliminate potentially interesting outliers that may conform to power laws. One observer (Crawford 2012) goes so far as to say that many social organizational phenomena have fewer normal distributions (despite the overwhelming use of Gaussian statistics) and many more power law relational patterns than conventional observation admits. The familiar normal distributions described by Gauss work fairly well to describe things like height and weight (which are not suited to power law calculations) but do not work well for something like the concentration of dominant companies in most industrial sectors, or in our case the affiliation patterns in political networks.

[7] For example, it is possible to standardize and compare what percentage of the inlinks in a hyperlinked organization network go to different slices of the top organizations, and what the inflection points are at which tails begin developing, and what the fatness of the tail is in terms of interlinking (and sharing other measurable resources). We are indebted to Michael Barthel for helping us see these possibilities.

of the Robin Hood Tax developed in this chapter – have network association curves with remarkably similar moderate slopes.

The top half of Figure 5.1 shows the classic steep power law curve, and the bottom half shows a family of more moderate network power curves. The moderately sloping inlink plots represent four of the British organizationally enabled networks analyzed in this book (including the Robin Hood Tax network). The two German national networks analyzed in the preceding chapter fit the same basic pattern.[8] We also note that the two campaigns that we discuss (Put People First and the Robin Hood Tax) have relatively steeper inlink drop-offs after the first organization at the head of the network, reflecting that in both of these cases the top organization exists only as a website that coordinates activities, displays key coalition members, and provides overall information about the campaign.

When we look beyond the top clusters of organizations traveling down the tail of inlinks in each network, we see that the tail in each case drops slowly, indicating rather sustained levels of recognition across the network. Such patterns would not exist in strict power laws, which quickly tail off to a baseline of little or no mutual recognition, as in the hypothetical case in the top half of Figure 5.1. We think that this moderate power signature is a defining characteristic of organizationally enabled networks that cut the diamond to include a large number of points of view in framing issues and to enable personalized engagement beyond the organization level. As noted earlier, this power signature fits Tarrow's (2011) account of hybrid mobilization networks in which loose umbrella networks enable relatively autonomous activities beneath them. The twist in our analysis is that an important part of what keeps those autonomous activities coherent are the digital media mechanisms that activate personal networks and feed them back into the larger issue, campaign, or protest mobilization network.

Power Signatures in Organizationally Brokered Networks

If the hybrid organizationally enabled network type tends toward a moderately concentrated power curve, what can we say about more conventional collective action networks of the organizationally brokered type? What is interesting about those networks is that since they reflect brokerage among particular ideological and collective identity frames of member organizations, they can take on a very wide range of power signatures, from classic steep power hierarchies

---

[8] We note that although the German climate change network discussed in the preceding chapter displayed less public engagement orientation than the other organizationally enabled networks, it was also by far the most federated, with large nested organizations within organizational umbrellas aimed at exploiting formal institutional linkages to parties and state institutions. This suggests that the political opportunity structure of state environmental policy in Germany favors a moderately concentrated issue advocacy system that has shed much of its national public mobilization capacity. There are, of course, grassroots networks that may operate with different power signatures that fall outside of our study.

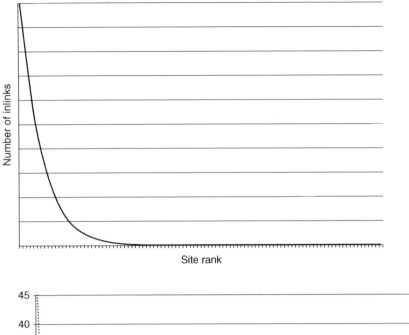

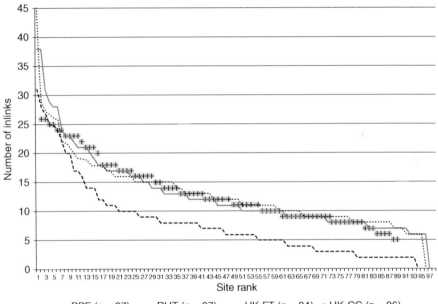

PPF (n = 97) ······ RHT (n = 97) ---- UK-FT (n = 94) ✦ UK-CC (n = 96)

FIGURE 5.1. Two ideal-type network power curves. Top: Classical steep power law showing strong upward cascade of nodes receiving most of the links from the network. Bottom: More moderate power signatures with less steep upward cascades of links. Shown at bottom: four organizationally enabled digitally mediated networks (Put People First mobilization network from Chapter 2; UK fair trade and climate change issue networks from Chapter 4; and Robin Hood Tax campaign network, this chapter). All four networks show a similar pattern of gentle power curves with many nodes sharing links from other organizations and gentle tailing off due to many organizations in the tail also receiving links from others.

to rather flat distributions. However, as conflicts over issue framing or political tactics intensify, there may be a tendency for resource-rich organizations to try to impose their imprint on brokered networks, resulting in either hierarchical (but potentially unstable) networks or fragmented networks with many disconnects and breakaway networks, as happened with the U.S. fair trade network discussed in Chapter 4.

Another pattern is suggested by the relatively egalitarian anarchist and anti-capitalist network we examined in the G20 Meltdown protests in Chapter 2, which had no clear network power signature at all, as the network ended up rather fragmented and melted into a default network of environment organizations that received independent links from a number of organizations in the G20 Meltdown coalition. Although this network succeeded in producing a demonstration during the G20 London meetings, it did not regroup or continue as a sustained network in the way that the Put People First coalition did (shown in Figure 5.1). Indeed, one by-product of the moderate power configuration in organizationally enabled networks is that it may represent a relatively stable solution for coalitions operating in the heated arenas of contentious issue politics.

In any coalition network, a variety of factors from social engineering to natural disarray can force a political distribution out of a power law altogether. And, as we shall see in the next section, networks without strong organization coordination are likely to display completely different power signatures.

Power Signatures in Crowd-Enabled Networks

Configurations of dense "networks of networks" that depart from conventional network organization may appear so disjointed that they seem incapable of concerted action (Tarrow 2011: 136–139). Yet numerous action networks are capable of effectively pursuing their goals even though their dispersed structures reflect fuzziness in collective intentionality, boundaries, and power sharing. It is clear that when systems of association are to a significant degree organized simultaneously by many different networks and network layers – as is often the case in many crowd-enabled networks[9] – it does not makes sense to analyze the overall action network in terms of power curves or other network metrics. However, we suggest that although these complex formations require different representational and analytical approaches, they can nevertheless be discussed and meaningfully compared in network power terms.

The question is what kind of power signature they display. We argue that crowd-enabled networks will tend to display a *dispersed power signature*, in which the relations of recognition will be multi-centered, multi-tiered, dynamic, and dispersed. The dense layering of distinct networks with limited overlap

---

[9] All action networks involve multiple networks to some degree. However, crowd-enabled connective action is characterized by the networked elements bearing relatively more of the overall organizational burden.

implies that although there will likely be recognizable power curves in pockets or layers of the overall network, relations throughout the action network taken as a whole will be granular and dispersed. Moreover, these relations may shift as the overall network surges in undertaking various actions. The dynamic character suggested by the high degree of circulation of content between network layers and the surges of action in the network is an important distinguishing mark of this power signature.

To get to this point, we need first to consider how one can represent and analyze the loose configuration of "networks of networks" that often characterize crowd-enabled action. One approach is to reduce the crowd to one of its networks, often resulting in an abstracted study of either the organizations or the social media networks that may be involved without putting them back into the larger context. We argued against this in Chapter 3. Even if one were to take such an approach, however, it is not obvious how one would think about power relations even when dealing with only one social media network. In an impressive study, Cha et al. (2010) examined some 6 million Twitter accounts and concluded that inlinking alone is a very poor indicator of actual influence as measured by such things as retweeting or mentions of the names of account holders. More realistic measures of influence are the authority of sources and the interaction between topics and authority. This means that CNN may be more influential in breaking news from particular parts of the world, but tweets from the long tail may drive more traffic to an anonymous YouTube video showing the death of a protester in a place where journalists cannot go. According to another impressive study of patterns throughout the Twitterverse, different ways of parsing followers, reciprocal followings, or distributions of tweets and retweets reveal that Twitter is a rare social network that does not display any clear power law structure (Kwak et al. 2010). It is clear that more subtle questions about network behavior and how it relates to focused research issues should guide analyses of social media networks in this context.

Other ways of slicing into crowd-enabled protests suggest that these involve networks of networks that are complex and extraordinarily dynamic. In a case such as the Occupy protests discussed in this chapter, there are many different Twitter accounts generating many hashtags, while other digital networks intersect with them, often with embedded links. Emerging analyses of Occupy suggest that content and action circulate in these networks in several ways, including flowing into the larger network from peripheral tails. In addition to the continuous dynamics that go into the overall network, there are surges of content and action that more contextualized analyses connect with specific contested situations and strategic outcomes (Agarwal et al. 2012). There may be large hubs, such as social networking platforms or, in the case of Occupy, city encampments, but the intersections among users of those platforms are also important in producing various organizational patterns in the crowd, such as surges of action, selective distribution of different types of information, and changes in the focus of attention or agendas for discussion or problem solving.

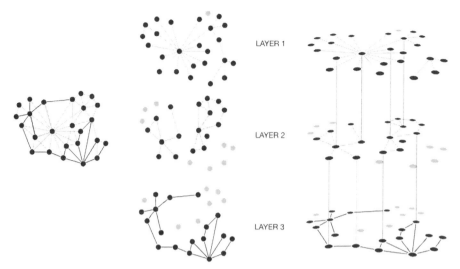

FIGURE 5.2. Network of networks organization model showing intersecting network threads stitching different networks together. Center view shows identifiably discrete networks. Right view illustrates how layers may be threaded with various networking connections. Left view represents a look through the layers. Used with the permission of Martin Krzywinski, University of British Columbia Cancer Research Center (www.hiveplot.com).

These shifting organizational patterns often depend on finer-grained concerted efforts by more strongly tied sub-networks within the crowd to do things such as develop and launch the "We Are the 99%" Tumblr, while others deploy stitching technologies – technologies, such as Twitter, that connect different networks across different platforms – to intersect with larger distribution hubs that may (or may not) refresh and refocus the broader crowd.

Reflecting these complex network paths, the power relations in terms of recognition in crowd-enabled networks such as Occupy are often dispersed and have a significantly dynamic quality. Highly dynamic crowd-enabled connective networks with their traffic control signals of Twitter hashtags, forwards/retweets, and links to other places become challenging to chart in power law terms, and the task becomes impossible when the multitude of surrounding technology-enabled network layers are brought into the picture. It also fails to capture the dynamic qualities of networks of networks that are such an important part of their power: the circulation of content and action between the layers in various directions (which widespread stitching technologies facilitate) and the surges of content and action across the network, which we describe in terms of a "pulsing" character.

Under such circumstances, we propose that a more accurate visualization of a crowd-enabled network is the multi-dimensional layered model shown in Figure 5.2. In this, we are indebted to Martin Krzywinski and colleagues

(Krzywinski et al. 2011), who have developed what they term a "hive plot" method for better visualizing and analyzing complex large-scale networks.[10]

The hive plot network mapping method may be used in the context of all kinds of large-scale networks, including gene regulation and Internet traffic (see Engle and Whalen 2012). However, the structure illustrated in Figure 5.2 is particularly helpful for our purposes because it highlights two salient characteristics of the crowd-enabled connective action networks. On the one hand, the figure suggests how the "whole" of the network is made up of discrete and only partially connected layers, making it more likely that power and recognition in terms of prestige or influence will be dispersed somewhat disjointedly throughout the network. On the other hand, the figure draws attention to the degree to which the various layers intersect: some nodes link to other layers and some do not link onward to anything at all. Such threaded transmission belts between layers suggest the potential for content to travel up, down, across, and back. There will, of course, be layering in most connective networks, including the organizationally enabled types; the differences here are that the layering and inter-layer connections are salient in the overall structure of the network and that the circulation between the layers is not limited to the "trickle-down" kind. A relevant focal point in this type of network is not just the dynamics of the communication traveling across and down networks (as it is in the more centralized networks) but also that circulating between layers in various directions.

In the case of U.S. Occupy protests focusing national media attention on the question of inequality in the United States, there are many more layers than just the three in Figure 5.2. Indeed, we know that beyond the networks around the platforms reported in Table 5.2 (see p. 182), the vast crowd-enabled Occupy network included dozens upon dozens of important layers, including those not tied to particular digital platforms. For the purpose of simplifying the visualization for now, however, we can assume that layer 1 in Figure 5.2 is the Tumblr microblog platform from which the "We Are the 99%" personal action frame became widely disseminated, and that layers 2 and 3 are a Twitter network and the network of Occupy city websites, respectively, where important traces of the 99% meme became displayed and further networked. The connection points between network layers may be where, for example, a Tumblr post gets picked up on Facebook or a city site gets linked to in a message on Twitter. The 99% meme spread through these and other layers and spilled into the streets in the form of posters and chants, and traveled through the mass media in thousands of references, which became linked back through the Occupy network layers, signaling that this message was working well for the movement. Protesters and publics could also, of course, see that the message was moving to larger audiences by simply reading the papers or observing how everyday conversations flowed when topics such as inequality

---

[10] We are very grateful to Martin Krzywinski for developing this figure and helping us think it through as applied to our large-scale crowd-enabled networks.

and economic justice were introduced in terms related to the idea of the 99%. Yet what connected the grand ecology of all these networks most systematically in Occupy – what stitched them together – was Twitter. As we will discuss later in the chapter, no other networking platform threaded the network layers together this consistently.

A dynamic interchange between larger networking hubs and smaller sub-networks in the crowd often leads to the appearance of networks of networks as "all tails." While the all-tails description is not always fully accurate, it does suggest that some network organizations cannot be modeled in conventional terms and instead require finer-grained analyses of interconnections and dynamics over time (Chadwick 2013). As we noted at the beginning of this section, it also indicates that networks of networks cannot be plotted in typical power law terms. While there are ways to generalize about crowd-enabled networks (such as finding their most common intersecting or threading networks), comparing dynamic and significantly layered networks with the more organization-centered networks shown in Figure 5.1 is a bit like comparing apples and oranges. This said, it is possible to go some way in parsing crowd-enabled networks to reveal some of their relational junctures and to suggest points of access for making sense of them. We suggest that examining power signatures, the degree of concentration or dispersal of recognition throughout the action network, offers one such dimension of comparison.

Drawing on these different conceptions of power signatures, we now turn to think about how to compare the political capabilities of two qualitatively different types of connective action: the organizationally enabled Robin Hood Tax campaign in the United Kingdom and the crowd-enabled Occupy protests in the United States. Both networks peaked in terms of visible activity levels and political impact at around the same time (2011), and both addressed broad questions of economic justice and the ill effects of financial speculation and concentration of wealth. Even though the two networks display very different power signatures, neither of which resembles the classic power law concentration, they have rather comparable political outcomes. We propose that, contrary to many expectations, connective networks with different power signatures, ranging from moderately concentrated to extremely dispersed, may in fact have similar abilities to shape political outcomes.

Power Signatures and Political Outcomes

The cases discussed in this chapter display two of the contrasting power signatures just outlined (i.e., moderate power concentration and dispersed power sharing). Both exemplify connective action through easily shared person-to-person content over social networks (although the engagement processes are differently arranged). What is notable is that the organizationally enabled network in which the Robin Hood Tax campaign was embedded in Britain has a greater concentration of inlinking within the large NGO hubs forming the "head" of the network. However, as indicated in Figure 5.1, the curve of the broad economic justice network in which the Robin Hood Tax campaign was embedded sloped rather gently, particularly in the curve beyond the stand-alone campaign organization website, which was the campaign site that most of the network linked to. This moderate power curve suggests that the co-sponsoring organizations tended to avoid trying to "own" the Robin Hood campaign and focused instead on sharing it with the aim of mobilizing publics and creating broader awareness among conventional media and elites. Meanwhile, the crowd-enabled Occupy networks in the United States tended to be more dispersed, with many loose ties that enabled a good deal of action to emanate from their "tails," leading one observer to describe them in terms of being "all tails" (Jarvis 2011). The network power signatures in these two cases suggest different conceptions about association and, put simply, how to get things done. Intriguingly, both have similar political capacity in terms of agenda strength.

Different Political Networks, Similar Outcomes

In the United Kingdom on Christmas Day, 2011, the archbishop of Canterbury delivered a sermon about the breakdown of trust in British society. He cited a range of symptoms: riots in the cities, rampant speculation in financial markets, and the breach of faith in bailing out financial institutions with little attention to the underlying causes of the financial crisis:

> The most pressing question we now face, we might well say, is who and where we are as a society. Bonds have been broken, trust abused and lost. Whether it is an urban rioter mindlessly burning down a small shop that serves his community, or a speculator turning his back on the question of who bears the ultimate cost for his acquisitive adventures in the virtual reality of today's financial world, the picture is of atoms spinning apart in the dark.

> And into that dark the Word of God has entered, in love and judgment, and has not been overcome; in the darkness the question sounds as clear as ever, to each of us and to our church and our society: "Britain, where are you?" Where are the words we can use to answer? (Archbishop of Canterbury 2011a)

A few weeks before this, the archbishop, Dr. Rowan Williams, had written an editorial in the *Financial Times* calling for a financial tax on speculative financial exchanges. He urged citizens and political leaders to join in more focused and effective global responses to social and economic injustices (Archbishop of Canterbury 2011b). Dr. Williams had long been a supporter of debt relief and other economic justice causes, but he was now joined by an unlikely list of supporters in the United Kingdom and beyond, including Pope Benedict, German Chancellor Merkel, (then) French President Sarkozy, and Bill Gates. That level of official support would soon get the issue on the political agendas of a number of nations and the European Union. In Britain and elsewhere, the tax had taken on the popular name of the "Robin Hood Tax," after the legendary bandit who robbed the rich to give to the poor.

In the United States at about the same time, President Obama gave a speech in Osowatomie, Kansas, presaging an emphasis on equity and fairness that would later characterize his 2012 State of the Union Address. A statement by Alan Krueger, chair of the President's Council of Economic Advisors, confirmed the impression that there had been a change of discourse on the economy. Noting that he had previously been quoted as preferring to use the economists' euphemism "dispersion" to refer to labor market inequities, Krueger now wrote: "But the rise in income dispersion – along so many dimensions – has gotten to be so high, that I now think that inequality is a more appropriate term" (Krueger 2012).

The general inattention among elites to 30 years of growing inequality in the United States and Britain seemed to be shifting. The rise of elite discourses on inequality suggested a fracture in the neo-liberal consensus that built the global economic regime – a regime that was undergoing a series of massive shocks. This shift in elite discourses could hardly be regarded as a bold move among leaders to awaken sleeping publics. To the contrary, leaders seemed to be responding to a deepening crisis that had triggered substantial pressure from below. In our cases, that pressure came from NGO advocacy networks that had been promoting a Robin Hood Tax for more than a decade in Britain, and the Occupy protests that swarmed public spaces in the United States (and elsewhere, as in the case of the *indignados* in Spain). Opinion polls showing broad changes in popular perceptions of inequality further softened the resistance of elites to raising the subject.[11]

This chapter documents and traces these shifts in elite discourses on inequality to the organizational characteristics and power signatures of two different types of activist networks: the Robin Hood Tax (RHT) and the Occupy movement.[12] Both cases can be contrasted with organization-brokered collective action patterns in terms of emphasis on personal action frames and the use of communication technologies as organizational processes that distribute power and (various degrees of) control outward toward publics and away from central organizations. The Robin Hood campaign was pushed onto the agenda by an organizationally enabled network in which NGOs shared a broad campaign while enabling highly personalized public engagement via

---

[11] For example, a Pew survey in the United States showed a nearly 20-point jump between 2009 and 2011 in the percentage of those who felt there were "strong" or "very strong" social conflicts between rich and poor in society. This jump occurred with remarkable uniformity across different demographic lines, from age and ethnicity to income level and party identification (Morin 2012).

[12] By focusing on the RHT in the United Kingdom, we do not mean to underplay the Occupy protests that also occurred there. The Occupy protests spread quickly to Britain and became an additional source of pressure on elites. Similarly, there was some activity surrounding the RHT in the United States. However, Occupy UK was not as prominent in promoting the RHT as was the broad NGO campaign network, and conversely, the RHT campaign in the United States was relatively minor compared with the more focused discourses surrounding the 99% theme.

interactive digital media. By contrast, the rise in "inequality" discourse among U.S. elites and media can be traced to the relatively crowd-enabled connective action found in the Occupy networks of networks.

Power in the Organizationally Enabled Robin Hood Tax Campaign

When the world financial crisis erupted in 2008, many economic justice advocacy organizations signaled that they wanted governments and financial institutions to take broader public interest and equity principles into account in working out solutions. In the United Kingdom, leading NGOs like Oxfam, Greenpeace, Friends of the Earth, and Tearfund (along with more than 100 others) appeared behind the scenes in networks such as the Put People First demonstrations surrounding the outbreak of the financial crisis and more long-standing campaigns such as the Robin Hood Tax campaign discussed in this chapter. One advantage of such organizational networks is that NGOs often have the resources and connections to take a long view of advancing different causes and related political agendas. Many of them shared similar assessments of the deepening financial crisis and a failing climate treaty, which had resulted in interrelated problems of downward economic pressures, worsening climate conditions, and soaring commodity prices that threatened all societies, particularly those in the global south.

Among the initiatives that this broad network attempted to bring to prominence was the campaign for a Robin Hood Tax on financial transactions. The idea of such a tax had been around for decades. Something like it was first proposed by the economist John Maynard Keynes during the Great Depression of the 1930s as a means of curbing speculation and market volatility, while channeling some speculative profits back into more productive economic activities at the discretion of governments. The idea reappeared when Nobel economics laureate James Tobin reformulated it as a means of discouraging or stabilizing currency speculation after the fall of the Bretton Woods monetary regime in 1971 (Patomäki 2012). The idea received little public exposure until the Asian financial crisis of the late 1990s, which prompted an editorial in *Le Monde Diplomatique* that proposed forming an association with the acronym ATTAC (Association for the Taxation of Financial Transactions for the Aid of Citizens). An organization by this name was subsequently formed and spread to a number of countries, making it an important early player in the organization of global justice protests and the World Social Forum (Attac 2012). Tobin, however, disavowed association with this version of the idea, which led activists to search for a better name.[13]

---

[13] Tobin stated in an interview: "I have absolutely nothing in common with those anti-globalization rebels.... Look, I am an economist, and like most economists, I support free trade. Furthermore, I am in favour of the International Monetary Fund, the World Bank, the World Trade Organization. They've hijacked my name" (Von Reiermann and Schiessl 2001; as translated from the German interview in *Der Spiegel* in Wikipedia and verified by the authors).

It took some time before the appropriation of Tobin's idea settled into the new frame of the Robin Hood Tax. An important move occurred when War on Want, the British NGO that had campaigned on the issue since the late 1990s, set up a Tobin Tax Network and released a set of proposals on the "Robin Hood Tax" in 2001. Other movement organizations joined in promoting the idea and pressuring elites to formalize it as policy. The movement around the Robin Hood Tax finally came into its own in the United Kingdom in 2010 with the formal launching of a campaign organization site, replete with videos featuring well-known actor Bill Nighy playing a blustering banker. The organization site was backed by a broad coalition of development and climate change NGOs, unions, and faith organizations. The initial list of supporters included more than 60 organizations; at the time of this writing the number of coalition members had grown to 115.

The website served as the campaign's most publicly accessible organization. It had its own face and its own brand, and a long list of affiliated supporters. Aside from presenting the coalition, the "Who Are We?" page offered a look at the scale of world engagement, enumerating other campaigns and supporters (politicians, "thinkers," and celebrities, and currently more than 260,000 Facebook friends). The site also contained a policy library that included reports on the coalition's own position as well as other reports on the issue and, in some cases, coalition organization statements about the campaign.[14]

Consistent with our observations about personalized engagement in organizationally enabled networks, the website featured dense personal action framing and an interesting array of interactive media. The "Get Involved" page invited individuals to enter their postal codes and add their personal stories to the dense geo-map of individual stories. Clicking on a single dot on the map opened clouds of tiny Robin Hood caps, each of which suggested a personal story. Among these statements were "I wrote my local paper about the Robin Hood Tax," "I asked my election candidates to support a Robin Hood Tax," "I asked the chancellor to introduce a Robin Hood Tax in the budget," and "I helped pay for billboards in the Westminster Tube station." The website also invited supporters to "start a conversation" with others in their vicinity to spread the word about RHT.

With its focus on both economic and environmental concerns, the Robin Hood Tax intersected the broader set of British economic justice / fair trade

---

[14] As, for example, expressed in this interview excerpt with Dame Barbara Stocking, CEO of Oxfam: "'Obama has said there has to be a system for bailing out the banks without the taxpayer simply paying. Clearly we'd agree with that, but we'd go further into ways to get money to fight climate change and poverty, given what the banks do in those areas has affected poor people so badly.' But is Oxfam campaigning on this in vain? There's a lot of scepticism about whether a Robin Hood tax will ever come about. 'Give it time, give it time,' the mother of two says with a smile. 'Given the debate is raging in so many countries, it suggests there is a real chance of pushing something like this through. There is this idea of people getting very rich from speculation while causing problems elsewhere in the world – there should be some payback for that'" (Sibun 2011).

and environment / climate change networks that we have followed throughout the book. After the initial drop-off in linking from the campaign coordinating site that most of the other sponsoring organizations linked to, the moderately centralized network power signature (shown in Figure 5.1) easily accommodated "branching" into other affiliated networks that drove traffic to the RHT campaign. In particular, the national fair trade network analyzed in Chapter 4 and also shown in Figure 5.1 shared 28 organizations with the core RHT campaign network, with a concentration of overlapping organizations toward the head of the networks. Fifteen of the same organizations appear in the top 35 of both. Five NGOs appear in the top 20 in all four of our UK networks (the fair trade network, the Robin Hood Tax campaign, the Wave, and Put People First networks, all shown in Figure 5.1). The overlapping members were Christian Aid, CAFOD, Oxfam, World Development Movement, and the Jubilee Debt Campaign.

This analysis suggests that the network in which the Robin Hood Tax campaign was embedded had a power signature that was centralized to the head of the network, and that each of those lead organizations were also members of other bounded but intersecting networks that also have similar moderately concentrated distribution properties. These capacities to coordinate, engage, and draw attention to issues, events, and campaigns clearly distinguishes organizationally enabled networks in terms of agenda strength, as measured in part by the degree to which issues and campaigns shared by these networks get into the mainstream media. Indeed, the ramped-up campaign with its engagement mechanisms driving public input targeted at various officials and institutions helped the RHT land squarely in elite circles and in the public media sphere. The idea moved from endorsements by the archbishop of Canterbury, as already noted, and the usual suspects, such as rock star Bono, through a growing circle of political and economic elites: the British prime minister in 2010, Gordon Brown, introduced it to a G20 meeting on the financial crisis; German Chancellor Angela Merkel joined (then) French President Nicolas Sarkozy in calling for such a tax in the European Union; support also came from Japan, Austria, Spain, Portugal, Finland, Belgium, and the Vatican; investors such as George Soros and Warren Buffet joined in, as did economists such as Paul Krugman and Joseph Stiglitz; and Bill Gates addressed the G20 at Cannes in 2011 and later spoke to the World Economic Forum in Davos in 2012 to promote the idea, along with other public-interest reforms of capitalism, in a report under his direction that was commissioned by Sarkozy.[15] By the time of this writing, fully 10 of the 27 EU member nations (including France, Germany, Italy,

---

[15] Elliott (2011). Estimates of the revenues that would accrue from such a tax range wildly from a conservative estimate by Gates of $9 billion a year if only Europe adopted the tax, to as much as $100 billion if the tax were adopted globally. "Gates Gives a Glimmer of Hope," November 3, 2011, Philanthrocapitalism blog, www.philanthrocapitalism.net/tag/robin-hood-tax/; also "Merkel Tells UK to Back a Robin Hood Tax," November 16, 2011, robinhoodtax.org/latest/merkel-tells-uk-back-robin-hood-tax (accessed December 26 2011) (cf. Robin Hood Tax.org, accessed September 5, 2012).

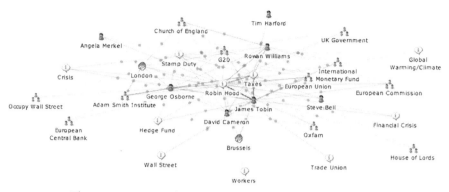

FIGURE 5.3. The semantic network in UK mainstream news media and blogs surrounding the Robin Hood Tax during December 2011. N = 185 news items, 24 blogs. *Source:* Silobreaker; used with permission.

and Spain) agreed to implement a tax on their banks and financial institutions (BBC 2012).

Figure 5.3 shows the semantic network surrounding the Robin Hood Tax during the month of December 2011. This network is based on a Silobreaker search of British news articles and blogs in online media. The links indicate articles containing the search term (Robin Hood Tax) and linked terms in close proximity (e.g., in the same paragraph) to each other in the same article. The chains of association involve terms connected with the more centrally linked terms arrayed by diminishing proximity to the central term. Thus, David Cameron, British prime minister at the time, appeared frequently in articles expressing concern that the RHT might drive financial transactions out of the United Kingdom, while articles containing Rowan Williams and the G20 tended to contain more positive endorsements of the tax. Other articles referenced Tobin as part of the history of the idea. More peripheral actors such as the Church of England were linked in turn through coverage of more central actors such as Archbishop Williams. What the map shows is that there was a lively debate among the British media on this policy idea that had emerged from protest networks. The map in Figure 5.3 is based on 185 news stories and 24 major blog posts appearing in December 2011, the month of the archbishop's Christmas sermon. It is interesting to note that this media debate located the United Kingdom within a larger policy community of the G20 and the European Union, where both Merkel and Sarkozy had urged Cameron's government to support the tax in order to make it harder for bankers to take their business to countries that did not support it.

This interesting case shows how moderately networked power in an organizationally enabled network using personal action framing and digital media to engage publics can saturate the public sphere with a position engaged by different institutional decision blocs. This is the sort of outcome many movements dream of: a focused debate in national and transnational public spheres on a policy challenge that would eventually become realized.

However, an obvious question is whether the RHT campaign was a special case of a perfect alignment of economic and political crisis and receptivity among elites to the popular idea of taxing bankers. The meeting of a focused campaign with a ripe political opportunity in the form of leaders trying to handle a crisis and quell popular discontent may have been what pushed RHT farther onto the policy process agenda than many other campaigns. For this reason, it is important to assess whether the organizationally enabled networks involved were able to move other campaigns into various positions along the public agenda spectrum as well. We addressed this by analyzing all campaigns in one of the companion networks of the RHT campaign network. As previously suggested, the RHT contained overlapping memberships with several related issue networks in the UK economic and climate justice spheres, including the fair trade network introduced in Chapter 4 and shown as one of the moderate power curves in Figure 5.1. The question explored in the next section is whether this steady-state fair trade issue network proved similarly capable of pushing other campaigns into the mass media sphere.

A Broader Assessment of Campaign Outcomes in Organizationally Enabled Networks

Recall from Chapter 4 that we crawled the UK fair trade network in April 2010, which, conveniently, was around the same time as the formal launch of the RHT as a stand-alone campaign co-sponsored by a large coalition. We crawled the core partners list of the Fairtrade Foundation (FTF) using a co-link method that entailed a search for all sites receiving links from two or more of our starting set of 15 "charity shareholders" of the FTF.[16] The crawler moved through thousands of linked sites in the process of producing a core network of 96 co-linked sites that were within one link from the innermost set of starting points.[17]

The resulting fair trade network was moderately centralized in terms of recognition. The power curve was a gently sloping one, as can be seen in Figure 5.1, reflecting, perhaps, the long associations among the lead organizations predating their collaboration in the formation of the FTF in the United Kingdom. The core issue network consisted of 94 organizations that received link recognition from at least two of the starting points. The distribution of power at the top of the network (as measured by which organizations received the most

---

[16] By including organizations that receive recognition from two or more starting points, the co-link method guards against more isolated relationships and arbitrary or casual linking, and often fails to return a network at all if relations are too loose or unstable among the organizations.

[17] We have tracked this network since 2006, and note that it is remarkably stable: most of the top organizations stay in place and also appear in other networks, such as the climate justice, development, and disaster relief networks, and they often deploy social and interactive media to engage publics with their causes.

links from others in the network) ranged from the FTF (with 31 inlinks) and continued through a gentle power curve that included CAFOD at 28, Oxfam at 27, Christian Aid at 25, the Trade Justice Movement at 25, the World Development Movement at 24 (all of these were members of the initial 2010 RHT coalition), the Jubilee Debt Campaign at 17, and so on until we came to the newly launched Robin Hood Tax campaign site, ranked 17th with links from 12 organizations in the core network.

As discussed earlier, "recognition" in this method of analysis is signaled by the extent to which one actor is linked to by multiple other organizations from the network. There may be several reasons that some nodes have more prestige than others; for example, they may have greater credibility on a particular issue (e.g., fair trade) that is of general interest to others, they may be a major sponsor of multiple campaigns (e.g., Oxfam), or they may serve as a general partner in other activities tying different networks together (e.g., the Fairtrade Foundation). This means that the method is especially suited for considering the relative prestige of nodes that interact with each other, and the highest prestige in this case points to organizations that are actively engaged in concerted work throughout this network.

Following the methods outlined in Chapter 4, we inventoried the core network to select for organizations that were focused primarily on economic justice issues (or, like Oxfam, that had a substantial focus on such issues) and that were chartered primarily in the United Kingdom. This filtering for issue focus did not appreciably affect the power curve of the network. In particular, the filtering did not screen out any of the top 11 sites in the original network, suggesting that the network had attained a fairly coherent power order over its years of activism. Just as the head of the network remained intact, it also retained a long tail that included more than half of the original (non-filtered) sites in the tail of the network (i.e., half of the issue-focused sites remained in the inlink distribution from the 30th position to the 93rd position in the original 94 inlink rankings from the unfiltered network). The power curve of the issue-focused fair trade network thus retained its moderate power signature.

Turning to the question of how this sort of network may orchestrate campaigns, we searched each organization site in the filtered network for the presence of all campaigns in the general area of economic justice, as described later. We next developed a number of measures of network power signature and public engagement strength, as well as an outcome measure defined as media coverage of the campaigns. *Our basic hypothesis is that the power concentration of campaign-sponsoring (i.e., explicitly supporting) organizations across a network will be associated with higher levels of news coverage for those campaigns.* We operationalize power concentration of sponsorship in two ways: the percentage of organizations in a network sponsoring each campaign found in the network and the positions of those sponsoring organizations in the network hierarchy of recognition (links) received from other members of the network. *We also hypothesize that the proportions and positions of campaign-sponsoring organizations will be associated with the levels of web traffic attracted by those organizations.* Web traffic here can be conceptualized as both an outcome variable (visible campaigns shared by multiple organizations drive people to their collective sites) and an intermediate step in public agenda building (public buzz about a campaign increases the likelihood of news coverage). Our measures for the variables in these hypotheses are outlined in the following sections.

Identifying Economic Justice Campaigns

This network-wide campaign inventory involved training two student researchers to search each website in the network for campaigns related broadly to economic justice causes such as fair trade, redistributive taxation, and solutions for poverty, hunger, unfair debt burdens, and other aspects of want. These campaigns could be focused on British society and/or transnational contexts. The research team systematically investigated content under sections of the website with labels such as "campaigns," "get involved," and "what you can do." They also used the search function of sites to identify pages with the term "campaign." Both coders searched every site, documented campaigns they deemed relevant, compared their results under the supervision of and in discussion with the authors, and reconciled discrepancies via this deliberative process.[18] The list of campaigns is found in Table 5.1.

Power Signature Measures for Campaign Networks

We worked with two network power signature variables for networked campaigns: (a) the percentage of organizations in the networks that co-sponsor a campaign; and (b) the location of those sponsoring organizations in the network power distribution as measured by the network inlink ranking of each campaign sponsor. In order to allow for positive correlations, we reversed the network inlink rankings so that the organization ranked first in receiving the

---

[18] Because the goal was to capture all the campaigns featured across rather compact networks, we opted for a process involving independent searches by assistants, followed by a comparison of results and reconciliation of the few remaining differences through deliberations with the authors. Since campaigns were typically identified as such by organizations sponsoring them, recognizing them was relatively unproblematic. However, the boundaries of different issue campaigns were important to establish given the number of multi-issue organizations such as Oxfam in our networks. The assistants were instructed to look for campaigns that defined the issue or political focus of our network crawls. In the case of the fair trade / economic development network these were the boundary instructions:

"For *fair trade*: look for campaigns that have to do with *fair trade, economic justice, trade justice, economic development policy* and related issues (not crisis relief, humanitarian aid, housing or health that are not clearly defined in the above terms). If you have a doubt about a topic or issue, ask us." (The authors were the final arbiters of the few remaining questions about whether a problematic finding fell into the category of an economic justice campaign.)

"For *climate change*: look for campaigns that have to do with *environmental issues* such as *climate change, global warming, carbon emissions, pollution, renewable energy, sustainability, biodiversity* and related issues (not disasters). If you have a doubt about a topic or issue, ask us."

TABLE 5.1. *Analysis of Network Power, Direct Public Engagement, and Press Coverage in UK Economic Justice Network Campaigns*

Campaign	% of Network Sites Featuring Campaign[a]	Total Inlink Rank of Sites Featuring Campaign[b]	Total Number of Unique Monthly Visits to Sites Featuring Campaign[c]	Number of News Articles[d]
Put People First	38	1208	629,297	87
Fairtrade Fortnight	33	929	593,687	782
Robin Hood Tax	33	1047	595,392	198
Global Campaign Against EPAs	22	579	508,025	0
Trade Justice Movement	22	637	461,743	119
Climate Debt Campaign	13	385	434,028	0
Right Corporate Wrongs	11	234	51,605	0
Lift the Gaza Blockade	9	246	454,114	5
Clean the Banks	9	278	16,541	0
Go Bananas, Fairtrade	7	270	479,964	50
The Big Lunch	4	118	19,225	206
Be a Trade Hero	4	181	67,543	0
Act on Poverty	4	184	63,340	13
Pedal Against Poverty	4	161	103,857	1
War on Want	4	142	390,956	0
Sip for South Africa	2	93	59,636	0
15 Years of Fairtrade	2	93	59,636	1
Give It Up for Lent	2	92	31,670	0
Don't Drop the Ball on Aid	2	91	390,956	0
Fair Deal	2	91	390,956	0
Green Gone Wrong	2	88	7,907	0

Note: Correlation between number of news items and percentage of network sites featuring campaign: $r = .58$ ($p < .01$, one-tailed). Correlation between number of news items and total inlink rank of sites featuring the campaign: $r = .55$ ($p < .01$, one-tailed). Correlation between total visits for sites featuring campaign and valid press hits for campaign: $r = .39$ ($p < .05$, one-tailed). Correlation between total visits for sites featuring campaign and percentage of sites featuring campaign: $r = .73$ ($p < .001$, one-tailed).

[a] $N = 45$.

[b] Inlink rank is based on reversing the rank number of each organization in the original fair trade network (1–94) and summing that rank position across all organizations sponsoring each campaign.

[c] Visits calculated as number of unique monthly visitors summed for all sites featuring a campaign, using May 2011 data from Experian Hitwise.

[d] News data were gathered for the life of each campaign dating back to 2000 from UK LexisNexis news searches.

most inlinks became number 94, and the organization ranked at 94 became 1, and so on.[19] As already noted, this did not change the distribution at the top of the network, where more of the power is concentrated. This inlink ranking for each organization was then summed across the number of organizations sponsoring or promoting each campaign, creating an inlink rank score for the group of sponsors for each campaign, noted in Table 5.1 as the total inlink rank of sponsoring sites.

Public Engagement Measures for Networked Organizations

The public engagement in this complex field of multiple organizations and multiple campaigns was assessed with a rough proxy measure of unique monthly visitors to websites of the organizations thanks to data provided to us by Experia Hitwise on UK web traffic for the month of May 2011. As previously noted, web traffic can be regarded as a rough indicator of mid-level public opinion transmission, one that increases grounds for media coverage. At the same time, web traffic may also be regarded as something of an outcome variable in itself (i.e., interest in organizations' campaigns may bring visitors to their sites), as many of the large organizations in these networks have hundreds of thousands of unique monthly visitors.[20]

Measuring Media Coverage Outcomes

To assess the outcome of the campaigns in terms of media coverage, we created a database of the news media coverage of the network campaigns. A team of two trained student researchers entered all of the campaign names into news searches of the LexisNexis database of UK news sources, specifying a date between 2000 and 2011. The broad time period allowed us to capture not only campaigns that were ongoing for many years, but ones that had come and gone during this period but remained as legacy models or memory traces on some sites. The challenge in gathering and validating the search results was that many campaign names were not perfectly matched in news articles (e.g., the Robin Hood Tax was sometimes referred to as the financial transaction tax), or terms from the campaign name popped up in irrelevant contexts (as one might imagine with Robin Hood). As they were now familiar with all of the campaigns after producing the network inventories, the research assistants eliminated news stories that were not about the campaigns and brought the

---

[19] As already explained, we left the original network rank positions the same after filtering the network for the 45 organizations with a clear issue focus on economic justice causes (vs. intersecting issues such as climate change and health care delivery). We decided to leave the distances among organizations as they were in their more natural multi-issue intersectional network rather than arbitrarily compress them.

[20] Similarly, the batteries of personalized public engagement mechanisms inventoried in Chapter 4 can also be considered in the background of this analysis as measures of the generally high mobilization capacity of this network.

few difficult decisions to the authors for resolution.[21] The campaigns that had different terms of reference in the news led us to additional searches using cognate campaign names for the same campaign. Through this process we assembled a reliable database of news coverage of the campaigns from our network inventory. If we admitted too much error into these data, the noise would work against our hypotheses. Indeed, the possible errors in setting up such a broad and complex study design all tend to work against our hypotheses, making the results shown in Table 5.1 rather robust. This said, we want to alert the reader to the various sources of noise in the data.

Caveats about the Data Set

An important caveat to be noted about the data set is that the time frames of the web traffic data (May 2011) and the network inlink rankings (2010–2011) are not matched perfectly to the campaign news coverage periods (2000–2011). Such matching would be imprecise at best, and in our case, some ongoing campaigns stretched back in time before we began mapping the networks and before the period for which we have web traffic data. However, given what we know about this network, it seems reasonable that our organization sponsorship data reflect stability over time in the coalition.[22] We know from following some of the campaigns for a number of years that organization sponsorship has been stable. For example, we have tracked the Fairtrade Fortnight campaign, which has been a featured campaign along this network, for more than six years and found many of the same core sponsors promoting the campaign even as the number of British towns that have joined as "fair trade towns" has grown over time (Bennett, Foot, and Xenos 2010).[23]

Perfectly matching all the periods for web traffic, network rankings of organizations supporting campaigns, and news coverage is not possible due to missing web traffic data. Rather, our aim here is to present a preliminary study testing a set of predicted associations to see whether they seem promising for future research. Any slippage among the periods of data for the different variables only biases the outcomes against our hypotheses, which means that findings supporting our hypotheses have overcome the sources of error in the study.

---

[21] We are particularly grateful for the research assistance of Anna Bohm and Bing Vong in this study and for the training, supervision, and data analysis work of Michael Barthel.

[22] The argument in favor of our somewhat rough measures is that this network (as noted earlier) is highly stable, both in terms of historical longevity of relationships among the lead coalition partners and in terms of the minimal change among their positions as we have charted the network in other research since 2006.

[23] This campaign involves annual local celebrations of fair trade living, with more recent additions of personal statements about "steps" people have taken to promote fair trade. In 2012 the Fairtrade Fortnight launched "Take a Step for Fair Trade," in which individuals could use a digital platform to share steps they have taken to promote fair trade (e.g., baking fair trade cupcakes, using fair trade coffee or tea at the office, holding a town arts and crafts fair featuring fair trade products). According to the site at the time of this writing, nearly 1 million steps were shared on a national website: step.fairtrade.org.uk.

Network Power, Public Engagement, and Press Coverage in Economic Justice Campaigns

The analysis confirmed both of our hypotheses: the power concentration of campaign sponsoring across a network was associated with higher levels of news coverage for the campaigns, and the proportions and positions of campaign-sponsoring organizations were associated with the organizations' web traffic levels. The data and associations on which these findings are based are shown in Table 5.1. The findings suggest that the Robin Hood Tax campaign was not an exception: campaigns shared along a network with a moderate network power configuration are indeed likely to make the news.

Campaign sponsorship was concentrated at the head of the fair trade network. We found 22 active campaigns among the 45 organizations, with each organization sponsoring, on average, 2.33 campaigns. The impact of organizations at the head of the network on the political campaign capacity of the network is reflected in the very strong correlation between the inlink ranking of organizations and the number of campaigns sponsored ($r = .46, p < .01$). Thus, organizations at the head of the network were far more likely to co-sponsor campaigns than were organizations in the tail (recall that we reverse-scored these rankings so that those most linked to are ranked 94, 93, 92, etc., and those least linked to are ranked 3, 2, 1). So although tails may lend important solidarity and mobilization when campaigns heat up or take to the streets, this is an initial indication that campaigns in organizationally enabled networks of this kind flow down from the top, instead of trickling up from the periphery.

Looking more closely at these data, we found that the top three campaigns each received sponsorship from more than 30 percent of the organizations in the network: the Put People First campaign had 38 percent sponsorship, while the aforementioned Fairtrade Fortnight and the newly launched stand-alone Robin Hood Tax campaign site tied for second place with 33 percent shares of co-sponsorship each. All had sponsorship concentrated toward the head of the network, as reflected in the high inlink ranking scores summed across the campaign sponsors.[24]

As noted, our primary outcome measure was press coverage. Following the procedure described earlier, we included findings from both large metropolitan and small town papers in order to capture coverage of campaigns such as Fairtrade Fortnight and the Big Lunch, which involved hundreds of local events scattered throughout the country. The results show a strong correlation between the summed inlink rankings of network campaign-sponsoring organizations and news coverage ($r = .55, p < .01$). This means that the more

---

[24] The interesting exception to the patterns reported here was the Big Lunch campaign, an effort to get neighbors together over lunch to battle isolation and recognize the importance of community. This campaign was on the boundary of our economic justice category and it was relatively new (2009). It was strongly branded and owned by the Eden Project, a charity that received support from the Big Lottery Fund and that listed more corporate partners than other charities did. Indeed, the Eden Project was not even a member of our economic justice network, and the campaign was supported by just two other members.

organizations in the network linked to each campaign co-sponsor, the more likely the campaign was to be reported in the news. We also looked at the percentage of organizations in the network sponsoring each campaign and found a strong correlation between this measure and campaigns making news ($r = .58$, $p < .01$). Thus, we found that more campaigns are sponsored by organizations at the head of the network; campaigns sponsored by more organizations tend to make the news; and campaigns sponsored by organizations more densely linked to by other organizations are also more likely to make the news. These findings suggest that a moderate network power configuration can result in a strong likelihood that campaigns shared along the network will make the news.

We also suggested that direct public engagement through web traffic may be regarded as both an outcome and an intermediary step in generating the buzz that helps news organizations find stories. In the preceding chapter we found that this issue network offered dense personalized engagement mechanisms. It is not surprising that web traffic to the top organization sites in the network numbered in the hundreds of thousands per month (a check of other months on Hitwise determined that our traffic data are typical). What is more interesting is that there is a strong correlation between the density (network percentage of) campaign-sponsoring organizations and the total visitors to the groups of organization sites sponsoring different campaigns. As shown in Table 5.1, the correlation between the number of site visitors per month and the percentage of sites in the network sponsoring common campaigns was a robust .73 ($p < .001$). When we looked at the correlation between the number of unique monthly visits to the campaign-sponsoring sites and the number of news stories generated on those campaigns, we found another strong relationship ($r = .39$, $p < .054$).

This volume of direct engagement with networked issues and campaigns, magnified by the secondary activation of personal social networks (along with conventional face-to-face organizing) can result in high-visibility public actions that receive positive news coverage. Thus, as noted in Chapter 2, the peaceful demonstration of 35,000 people in the streets of London during the height of the Put People First campaign made a good deal of news. And the news was highly favorable, as public officials such as the prime minister recognized the worthiness of the cause. In this way cascades of attention can be triggered across links in networked communication chains, creating a news framing flow from what Pfetsch and Adam (2011) term "challenger networks." The news from our analysis is that this framing flow, driven by the moderate power structure of challenger networks, can (though it certainly does not always) run counter to the more familiar top-down elite-driven source pattern of "cascading activation" in news framing described by Entman (2004).

However, we should note that since organizationally enabled networks are a hybrid type between conventional collective action and crowd-enabled connective action, they are also likely to employ some of the more familiar organizational resource mobilization strategies. One measure we were able to obtain (although we do not feel as confident about it as we do about the other measures reported that generate more robust data) was the number of press releases used by organizations for various campaigns based on items identified as press releases in LexisNexis searches. There was also a very strong correlation between this more conventional strategy and the occurrence of news reports on campaigns in our sample ($r = .75$, $p < .001$). Thus, both the more personal connective action and conventional organizational resource mobilization that we should expect from this hybrid network type come into play in giving campaigns and their related issues broader media attention.

Finally, we ran similar analyses on outcomes for campaigns in the UK environment network and found essentially the same patterns across the board with even higher correlations.[25] The German networks, however, were interestingly different. Since, as Chapter 4 showed, the German environment network, while displaying a moderate power signature, traded off public mobilization in favor of institutional attachments, we did not expect and did not find network inlink and campaign sponsorship densities as significant predictors of news coverage in this network. Also the German fair trade network departed from the British pattern in interesting ways. Recall from Chapter 4 that although the German fair trade network was higher on our measures of public engagement than its environment counterpart, it was significantly lower across the board than either of the UK national issue networks. The gaps with the UK networks were particularly large (30–40 percent lower presence of online engagement mechanisms) in the areas of interactive information sharing and both managed and co-produced online action. As a result, the network campaign sponsorship factors were not as significant in explaining German press coverage of campaigns as were more conventional organizational public relations tactics such as issuing press releases. What this suggests is that network power signatures and outcomes such as press coverage are contingent on high levels of online engagement capacity being integrated with networked campaigning, as reflected in the combined power and engagement signatures of the organizationally enabled UK networks.

Power in the Occupy Network of Networks

A very different story about the organization of power emerges when we look at the crowd-enabled Occupy protests in the United States. In this case, geographically separated local groupings organized protests, often around local issues as much as national ones. There were de facto leaders in and around the groupings (Gerbaudo 2012), but few conventional organizations in the mix. The Occupy protesters who lived in camps and took physical action used highly

---

[25] We screened environment / climate change campaigns on multi-issue organization sites with this instruction to the assistants: "For *climate change*: look for campaigns that have to do with environmental issues such as climate change, global warming, carbon emissions, pollution, renewable energy, sustainability, biodiversity and related issues (but not natural disasters or relief aid). If you have a doubt about a topic or issue, ask us."

ritualized face-to-face procedures to conduct local general assembly meetings, some of which (e.g., raising arms and wiggling fingers up or down to signal ongoing reactions to speakers) were modular forms of group process dating to earlier stages of the globalization movement. Those direct activists and circles of engaged but less physically committed supporters also employed a broad array of digital networking technologies to connect with dispersed local support networks, other Occupy groups, and broader attentive publics. These technologies, some of which are inventoried later, include SMS networks, email lists, Facebook, Livestream, YouTube, and Twitter. In this chapter we are interested in the larger Occupy network of networks, and in particular the crowd-enabled technology networks that were involved. It is important to emphasize that significant tensions often existed between the face-to-face activist networks in the camps and the digital crowds that swarmed, often in the millions, around them, and we return to these tensions in evaluating clashes among different models of networked organization in the concluding chapter. In this chapter, however, we focus on making sense of an emergent protest that grew rapidly and made a powerful impact on the political discourse of the United States.

The Occupy movement commenced in earnest when the Canadian culture jamming media organization Adbusters issued a call in its blog on July 13, 2011, for people to "Occupy Wall Street" on September 17, 2011.[26] The initiative was inspired by the Arab Spring uprisings and the *indignados* protests in Spain, as the Adbusters call to action noted, claiming that new large-scale protests were being organized less as movements than as swarms in which face-to-face and virtual organizational processes would merge.[27] In early August, two informal activist groups, including one inspired by the Adbusters idea, joined in a protest at the Wall Street sculpture of a charging bull. In the days that followed, a convergence of factors gave momentum to the emergent Occupy protests, including the efforts of groups in New York City to develop the form of the general assembly, statements in establishment media by prominent elites expressing concern about growing economic inequality and financial corruption in politics, and calls from the hacker collective Anonymous for its affiliates to lend support to the protests.[28] Finally, on September 17, this loose organizing resulted in some 1,000 protesters marching on Wall Street and setting up a camp in Zuccotti Park, effectively "occupying" the space to express their discontent. From these scattered nodes in a small emergent network, a thunderous protest network grew in a matter of weeks, aided by webs of communication technologies deployed by activists and supporters who seized the political opportunities surrounding a severe economic crisis.

---

[26] For a closer look at the early days of these protests, see Gitlin (2012); Gerbaudo (2012).

[27] The Adbusters blog post is at www.adbusters.org/blogs/adbusters-blog/occupywallstreet.html.

[28] For example, financier Warren Buffet published an op-ed in the *New York Times* with the title "Stop Coddling the Super Rich" (Buffet 2011). Anonymous called for setting up camp in a video that reflected many others that would travel through Occupy networks: www.adbusters .org/blogs/adbusters-blog/anonymous-joins-occupywallstreet.html.

Soon the city encampments had spread around the United States and the world, varying widely in location, focus, and style of participation.[29] The activists ranged from veteran protesters inspired by anarchist ideology to newcomers who were displaced by the economic crisis. Most embraced an ethos distancing themselves from conventional practices of leadership and movement organization. Many more were simply content to participate, often virtually, on the periphery (see Byrne 2012; Lang and Lang/Levitsky 2012; Occupy Wall Street Activists 2012). In addition to the spread of physical camps, assemblies, and protest actions, the flow of ideas and discourses created network bonds of different kinds, often in dense, fine-grained interpersonal ties established on- and offline.

The personal action frame that aided in stitching these networks together emerged early on from a long tail in the crowd. In late August, a person identified only as "Chris" (later with the help of Priscilla Grim, an information science student and online organizer) started the "We Are the 99%" Tumblr microblog, after a rallying call that had emerged in the incipient New York general assembly (Sharlet 2011). The Tumblr invited individuals to upload brief personal statements about their experiences of the economic situation and tag them with "occupywallst.org." As with much of the media that became central in the creation of Occupy networks, the Tumblr site was appropriated by users in ways not fully imagined by its creators. Indeed, Chris soon abandoned the idea that users would post a short sentence with a full photo, as most of the actual statements were long, highly personalized stories, often written in longhand and held in front of part or all of the writer's face in a desktop or cell phone photo (Weinstein 2011). "We Are the 99%" posts soon numbered in the thousands, and new posts were still appearing at the time of this writing, more than a year afterward. More important, the 99% meme quickly swirled through other media and technological networks, moving through Occupy groups, appearing on posters, on placards, in jokes and media mashups, and traveling through levels of networks into the mass media.

The connections among dispersed physical locations and broad general publics were not focused on a core network the way the Robin Hood Tax campaign and the other organizationally enabled networks were. We conceive of Occupy in terms visualized in Figure 5.2 as a multi-layered network of networks. Table 5.2 presents a rough overview of some of the key Occupy-related digital media platforms inventoried between September 2011 and September 2012.[30]

---

[29] The Occupy movement was dispersed and included disparate participants. However, it is important to note that the movement was also criticized for its lack of diversity (see, e.g., contributions to Lang and Lang/Levitsky 2012; Campbell 2011).

[30] We are grateful to Social Media Labs and for the research assistance of Sheetal Agarwal and Courtney Johnson, who supervised the undergraduate team that conducted this inventory: Sze Vanessa Yuan, Yuri Choi, Stafania Appia, Fabiola Jiminiz, Brian Eng, Laurie Sperry, and Natalia Shafa.

TABLE 5.2. *Occupy Network Platforms (September 2011–September 2012)*

Platform	Characteristics
City or group websites	251 stand-alone organization sites identified by locations
Tech development sites	Four primary U.S. resource sites linking to a network of 50 open-source developer sites and foundations[a]
Twitter	889 accounts documented by Occupy protesters themselves, with more than 11 million followers[b]
	More than 200 hashtags (and some 38 million tweets related to Occupy) collected by Social Media Lab between October 19, 2011, and March 10, 2012[c]
Facebook	More than 450 pages[d]
Livestream	244 feeds (179 U.S., 79 international)
Meetup	2,857 groups in 2,649 cities
Tumblr	30 accounts
Hubs intersecting platforms	71 U.S. hubs (regional, campaigns, identity)[e]
	Individual network hub claiming 2,900,000 connections[f]
Geo-location contact maps	1,487 world occupy locations linked by one or more of the above[g]

[a] Including a resource cluster wiki: wiki.occupy.net/wiki/Main_Page. Resource network mapped using Issue Crawler methods outlined in Chapters 2 and 4, starting from the four occupy technology sites.

[b] Source: theoccupyhub.com/.

[c] Twitter reported more than 100,000 total hashtags using occupy (twitter.com/#!/twittercomms/status/127483371059298304; accessed March 13, 2012). However, many of these were playing with the meme (#occupybritney, #occupychipotle, #occupymy____, etc.). We believe that the tags central to the organization of the crowd numbered in the hundreds.

[d] Ninety percent of these Facebook pages were active as measured by at least one daily update on average, through February 2012. The top 10 sites were updated every few minutes during high-activity periods in late 2011.

[e] interoccupy.net/hubs/.

[f] www.occupynetwork.com.

[g] directory.occupy.net.

As this overview suggests, by early 2012 the U.S. Occupy movement involved a thick mesh of communication networks. Some of these technologies and platforms were rather localized. One of these, Meetup, enabled people to find each other and meet (while checking out details on meetings in other places). Others, like Livestream, enabled reporting on events such as assembly meetings or police raids on camps to global audiences. Many of these technology platforms were thus involved in network layers that were differently organized and often distinct from each other, as pictured in Figure 5.2.

If the crowd-enabled Occupy network is a multi-tiered network with shifting layers as represented in Figure 5.2, then its power signature will be different than that of an organizationally enabled action network with a defined coalition backbone such as the Robin Hood Tax and the networked campaigns in our earlier discussion. We will show that there were heads and hubs in Occupy networks. However, as we argued earlier, the dense layering of distinct networks with limited overlap suggests that the relationships that build networked recognition of prestige and influence in the wider crowd-enabled network are granular, multi-tiered, and dispersed. Moreover, those relationships may shift as the network surges in undertaking various actions or suffering various external threats. As noted, not just dynamic circulation but also the pulsing surge of action and content in and through the network as a whole is an important element in the dispersed power signature.

Occupy differed from organizationally enabled action networks we have discussed, but it was also notably different from other kinds of political swarm actions such as the "smart mobs" discussed by Rheingold or "flashmobs," which converge on a location, perform an action, and disappear forever (Rheingold 2002; cf. Segerberg 2010). Occupy persisted for many months, and different actions, large and small, local and global made the protests an unavoidable part of public life. There were camps, marches, street theater, port shutdowns, and swarming demonstrations around various institutions and politicians, including President Obama.

What made it possible for this large-scale crowd-enabled network to sustain action over time? We note two features of Occupy that make it similar to other large-scale persistent protests that made notable impacts on their targets, such as the Icelandic uprising, Tahrir Square, and the *indignados*, as compared by Castells (2012). First, there were persistent personal action frames such as the 99% meme that enabled messages to flow across networks and offered easily shared scripting for endless personal and collective activities on- and offline. This was DIY politics at its best. Anyone could do it, and many did. Indeed, a strong ethos emerged from our ethnographic studies of the core activists: anyone could propose anything and do it with anyone who chose to join in.[31] This chaotic upwelling of ideas and proposals resulted in the endless meetings that Polletta (2002) associated with most movement politics, even if the assemblies were often so frustrating and tedious that attendance declined (Gitlin 2012).

Second, some layers of the network were structured in moderate power signature terms, indicating a flow of influence and recognition among smaller nodes that looked to larger ones for signals of various sorts. The network of the city encampments and bridging sites that were set up to provide resources and connect parts of the movement is one example. An important distinction here is that unlike the organizationally enabled networks we have analyzed, where the websites were often extensions of substantial NGOs and other brick and mortar organizations, the Occupy city and bridging (or umbrella) sites were more complete organizations in and of themselves, embodying the

---

[31] In these and other ethnographic observations we gratefully acknowledge the work of Sheetal Agarwal and a team of students under the joint supervision of Agarwal and Bennett who conducted interviews and attended assembly meetings in Seattle and talked with national and local Occupy technology developers.

often ephemeral and sporadically attended local assemblies. The importance of websites-as-organizations became particularly apparent after the police evictions of protestors from the Occupy city camps across the United States in the late fall of 2011, when scattered activists used city organization sites and Facebook groups to coordinate events and post news and share ideas about the future.

Interested in seeing if there was a coherent network of websites serving as organization hubs, we mapped the networks of Occupy city encampment websites (e.g., occupywallst.org, which was the primary New York City organizing site) and bridging sites (e.g., occupytogether.org, which was a global resource and coordination site spanning geographical locations and diverse actions) from November 2011 through June 2012. We found a moderate power signature in this network with a stable core of widely recognized sites at the top, including the "bridging" sites occupywallst.org and occupytogether.org and the city site nycga.org, the New York general assembly site that contained minutes of meetings and activities of the first Occupy assembly. Beyond this were city sites (Seattle, Portland, Oakland, Los Angeles, Chicago, Boston, Atlanta, and others) that moved up and down the inlink rankings as attention shifted across the network following protest actions and confrontations with the police. Other sites orbited on the periphery, including the original Adbusters and 99% microblog, specific campaign and action sites such as howtooccupy.org, and technology development and resource sites (e.g., occupy.net). This "city and bridges" network was the most stable over time of all the networks we tried to map, and much the same network was produced whether we started crawling from a few top sites (the New York websites and the bridging sites) or many city sites. Taken by itself, this network layer was not unlike the organizationally enabled networks discussed earlier.

Yet what is significant is how the network of "city and bridge" sites intersected with the many other less interconnected networks that gave the larger crowd its broad connectivity and dynamic capacity to shift focus and coordinate actions and in which there were independent patterns of recognition. When we allowed social media to enter the networks being crawled, we found that Twitter became the largest and most commonly dominant node, looming far larger in most of our network maps than the supporting battery of less linked-to media such as Facebook, Livestream, YouTube, and Tumblr. Stitching together this network of networks seemed to rely on these other media and on Twitter in particular.[32]

In a study involving one of the authors (Agarwal et al. 2012), samples of a vast Occupy Twitter archive of some 60 million tweets were coded for the kinds of links they contained. The coded links were tracked back into the big data set to see (a) what link resources (b) traveled along what pathways (c) with what frequencies and (d) with what frequencies of retweeting (e) at

---

[32] This pattern is also found by other researchers, including our partners at the University of Washington Social Media Lab (somelab.net/page/2/).

what points in time, (f) corresponding to what external and internal developments in the protests. Following from some of the ideas in Chapter 3, this analysis looked at the Occupy protest ecology using Twitter as an overarching integrative mechanism that linked to most of the dominant platforms and physical locations used by protesters and surrounding publics.

An important finding was not only that Twitter was the platform most linked to from the other network layers of Occupy, but that it was heavily used by people from all layers of networks. The messages in the sample included more or less official status reports from assemblies and city camps; communiqués from members of the hacker network Anonymous, which provided many high-quality and heavily viewed videos; and various resources (from news reports to offers of legal assistance) circulated in links embedded in tweets from tens of thousands of individual supporters, both physically involved and virtually engaged. There are tens of millions of Occupy-related tweets originating from tens of thousands of accounts and proliferating thousands more hashtags carrying messages and link resources across networks.[33] On most days the number of tweets was about 300,000 and on several occasions the number approached a million. During the period of peak activity from mid-October through December 2011, there were more than 20 million tweets (Agarwal et al. 2012).[34] A few hashtag streams, such as the consistently largest #ows stream, were mentioned disproportionately, numbering in the hundreds of thousands per day during important internal and external events. Those events ranged from marches and protests to clashes with police, evictions, and arrests. As we followed these Twitter streams over time, they merged and dissolved into thousands of streams of crowd-produced information that branched into each other via interconnections among people and artifacts (photos, other sites, videos, news articles, etc.) that link across various platforms in this network of networks.[35] Unlike some other kinds of hubs, Twitter relates dynamically to various parts of the action ecology, which is why it was the dominant connective tissue of the network system. Along with the presence of numerous physical occupations

---

[33] It is also worth noting that these intersections included outside networks engaging with the Occupy crowd in various ways. Two major political umbrella networks were consistently in the top 10 most mentioned hashtags throughout the peak period of Twitter Occupy activity in the fall of 2011. The #tcot (top conservatives on Twitter) stream collects other conservative twitterers, and the #p2 is an umbrella tag for progressives. Both streams engaged with Occupy throughout the protests, perhaps helping to carry themes from the protests into other media layers.

[34] These requests were initiated by members of the University of Washington Social Media lab who monitored emerging new Twitter accounts, hashtags, and key terms, and requested tweets containing them through the formal API (application programming interface) as specified by Twitter.

[35] Of course, not all content passes through these bridging hubs, as suggested by the uneven threading among players in Figure 5.2. An interesting study of Occupy-tagged YouTube clips on YouTube and Twitter by Kjerstin Thorson and colleagues (2013) found that the overlap between the clips on the two platforms was surprisingly small, indicating the broad range of circulation loops and the fact that disparate crowds were indeed involved.

of spaces, this dynamic connection across the often disjointed network layers also helps to explain how Occupy persisted as a larger crowd-enabled action network.

In terms of relations of recognition, the dense interlinking among the Occupy networks reflects influence in various directions, not just primarily downward and outward. It enabled circulation and coordination of action and information in flows moving up, down, and across networks that often included millions of people on a given day. During the peak activity period in the fall of 2011, of the first 16 million tweets analyzed, fully 5 million contained links to other sites.[36] Such connectivity can quickly link millions of tail dwellers into their own and others' networks. It is not just that action and ideas may flow from those network intersections of larger and smaller nodes in many different directions. The various features of each platform set in play by users also entail layers of networks with interestingly different structural properties. Agarwal et al. (2012) found that varying link patterns occurred at different network levels and at different periods in the life of the protests. For example, the overarching #ows stream contained substantially fewer links to personal artifacts (blogs, photos, websites) than the local hashtags, such as #occupyseattle. When the face-to-face protests began to fall apart in early 2012, the crowd experienced something of a diaspora, with tweets containing links to these individual artifacts also containing a far larger number of multiple hashtags, suggesting individual-level attempts to try to reconnect the larger networks. As the protest activity declined, links to Occupy city and bridging organization websites increased substantially, indicating that those left in the crowd were pointing to places where regrouping might occur.[37] At the same time, these intersections of networks with organizing resources corroborate findings by others that crowds may circulate content in different (and sometimes conflicting) ways in different parts of the network and different parts of the movement (Thorson et al. 2013; cf. Baym and Shah 2011).[38]

Given the combination of local autonomy and easy cross-network connectivity, many dispersed actions took place and many of these were replicated elsewhere. For example, the New York City and Washington, D.C., networks staged their own Robin Hood Tax marches in early November 2011, complete

---

[36] Personal communication from Shawn Walker, Social Media Lab.

[37] Recall that we found much the same pattern of "resource-seeking" behavior in the crowd in our analysis of the global climate change network in Chapter 3.

[38] Thorson et al. (2013) found that whereas Occupy-tagged YouTube videos were more likely to convey scenes from the encampments and related events and seemed in part to be posted as personal archives of the events, the clips that were embedded in Occupy-related tweets were more likely to show archived material such as a music video not originally about Occupy but repurposed for this context through the comment in the tweets. Similarly, even different streams in one medium may be quite distinct. As shown in Chapter 3, Twitter streams from different protest events show different patterns of organization, reflecting the kinds of actors involved, the nature of the event, and its context. In another example, snapshots of Twitter networks in Tea Party and Occupy protests rendered by Marc Smith show substantially different patterns of organization (Aldhous 2011).

with costumed protestors (some naked save for their Robin Hood caps). A month later other Occupy groups moved to shut down ports on the West Coast amid local and nationwide disagreements within unions and in the broader movement about whether these shutdowns should take place. The diversity of action often resulted in some outward confusion about what protesters stood for. For the first months, the press story on the Occupy protests typically included the question "What do they stand for?" or "What do they want?" Encouraged by the Adbusters image of a graceful dancer poised atop the charging Wall Street bull, Occupy protesters and sympathizers soon presented a plethora of interpretations of the question "What is our one demand?" They fashioned responses in blogs, tweets, and videos and on signs during protest events, which were circulated back through the crowd via links in tweets and other forms of communication. Many who were involved in this crowded conversation pointed out that there were so many problems that formulating a single demand was impossible. At the same time, these diverse demands were commonly promoted under the personal action frame of "We Are the 99%," which fueled the increasingly focused public discussions of inequality.[39]

Because of the sheer volume of activity, combined with the repetition of popular protest repertoires that traveled through the crowd, this network of networks had an impressive impact, particularly in shifting discourses on inequality in the mainstream media and among elites. Indeed, the most prominent subtext in media discussions about the protests, often framed by the 99% meme, was the story of *inequality*, which had grown to levels in the United States not seen since the run up to the Great Depression. The United States and Britain far outstripped inequality growth in other leading OECD democracies.

There may have been a long-suppressed interest among many journalists and left-leaning politicians in raising the visibility of this topic, but until Occupy came along, there were few news sources willing to speak out against the neoliberal consensus that growth and profits at the top were inarguably good for society. Thus, mainstream journalists had little on which to peg stories about inequality until Occupy and its refrain of the 99% became household expressions. We continuously monitored media content surrounding Occupy using the Silobreaker search and semantic networking tool, which enables real-time searching of online media, broken down roughly by type (e.g., news, blogs),

---

[39] Thus, a press release issued by Occupy DC ahead of its own Robin Hood march captured the diversity of issues the protesters sought to promote: "Wall Street's reckless trading of risky financial products like mortgage-backed securities, credit default swaps, and derivatives helped redistribute wealth to the rich and wreck the global economy. Despite receiving enormous publicly-funded bailouts, bankers have yet to pay for the damage they caused. Now we're being told there's no money for what the 99% needs to: create jobs, get healthcare to millions of Americans, support green energy efforts, ensure AIDS drugs for Africa, protect Social Security, and more. Creating a financial transaction tax, also known as a Robin Hood tax, would return funds from the financial sector to public coffers and discourage some of Wall Street's most dangerous activities." dcist.com/2011/10/Occupy_dc_to_march_for_robin_hood_t.php (accessed December 20, 2011).

language, nationality, and other boundary markers in the loosely bounded online media sphere. What we found was that Occupy was soon at the center of a mainstream media exploration of inequality that triggered an investigation of a variety of topics: the meaning of inequality for social mobility, class conflicts, the social sensibilities of the rich, and the impact of inequality on democracy and the American Dream. Yet for more than two months after the protests began, leading Democratic Party politicians, most notably President Obama and his administration sources, avoided the topic.

Polls showed that increasing segments of the public were following the Occupy protests in the news and, even more startling, that a majority of the public had become concerned about inequality. Although public opinion did not strongly approve of the protesters themselves, the public did embrace their most visible issue, and the media looped that issue back to the protests.[40] A Pew Research poll released in early December 2011 showed that the perception of conflicts between rich and poor in society had jumped ahead of the perception of other major social conflicts, including immigration, race, and generational differences. Those who perceived strong or very strong conflicts between rich and poor jumped from 47 to 66 percent of the population between 2009 and 2011 (Morin 2012). Researchers at the Center for American Progress (a think tank closely affiliated with the Democratic Party) began citing polls showing that 61 percent of Americans felt that the U.S. system unfairly favored the wealthy, compared with just 36 percent who regarded the system as generally fair (Teixeira 2012).

As these trends developed, politicians on the center left such as Barack Obama began easing into the inequality discourse. They were also pressed by strategic occupations of Democratic Party fund-raising sessions with wealthy elites and, in particular, a well-covered "occupation" of Obama himself when he went to Wall Street, hat in hand for a $35,000 a plate dinner. Under this cover of growing press coverage of inequality, shifting polls, and the "occupation" of Obama, the president moved from the periphery to the center of the national discussion of inequality.

In early December 2011, Obama delivered an important speech reminiscent of Teddy Roosevelt's speech in Osawatomie, Kansas, where Roosevelt famously addressed the inequities in U.S. society nearly a century before. The speech, along with a *60 Minutes* interview that week, offered a number of trial balloons testing themes for Obama's presidential campaign. Among these ideas was an elliptical reference to the grand "1% vs. 99%" meme of the Occupy protests: "I'm here in Kansas to reaffirm my deep conviction that we're greater

---

[40] Various polls showed that in the early weeks of the protests the public was fairly evenly divided among supporters, opponents, and those undecided and that the level of support slowly dipped in the coming months when the protests were marred by police actions and clashes, a fairly typical pattern for social protests that become chaotic. The overall support for the Occupy protesters was somewhat lower than that for the Tea Party, which contested issues related to the financial crisis from the right (Kleefeld 2011). All of this suggests that it is important to separate public opinion about protesters from public opinion about the issues they are raising.

together than we are on our own. I believe that this country succeeds when everyone gets a fair shot, when everyone does their fair share, when everyone plays by the same rules. These aren't Democratic values or Republican values. These aren't 1% values or 99% values. They're American values. And we have to reclaim them" (Washington Post 2011). This triggered a large volume of press coverage and commentary. Obama amplified the fairness and inequality themes, and added the idea of economic sustainability, in the 2012 State of the Union Address, titled "A Nation Built to Last." Many observers took that speech as a preview of his 2012 election stump speech.[41]

We conducted content and semantic network analyses of U.S. media online sites using Silobreaker. We tracked co-occurrences of the terms "inequality" and "occupy," along with other terms associated with them as those discourses rippled through other topics. We followed these semantic networks from before the first Occupy protests in September 2011 through February 2012. Even as late as November 2011, semantic network maps showed that the terms most closely associated with Occupy and inequality were "Adbusters," "taxes," and, at some remove, a conservative oppositional cluster that included "Tea Party," "Tea Party Movement," "Paul Ryan," and "Republican Party." By contrast, terms such as "Democratic Party," "unions," "White House," "Obama administration," and "Obama" did not even register their co-appearance in any substantial volume in the increasingly dense media discourses (thousands of news and blog posts per month) surrounding the central terms "occupy" and "inequality." In the early period of the protests (September 17 to mid-October 2011) the inequality story was closely attached (by journalists, bloggers, and political analysts) to the protests themselves. By November, inequality had taken on a life of its own and was being discussed as a social issue independently of the protests (although still undergirded by Occupy activities that received coverage). The first organizations to join the core inequality discourse circles were unions. Meanwhile, the protesters continued to put heat on the politicians: Obama and the Democratic Party were "occupied" as they courted big donors, including the Wall Street bankers they had just bailed out.

When Obama delivered his Kansas speech on December 6, he immediately moved into the center of the semantic "inequality" space, along with "Occupy Wall Street" (and variations on that term) and such associations as "Teddy Roosevelt," "Osawatomie," and "White House." For a few days Obama even displaced Occupy Wall Street from its nearly exclusive position as the actor at the center of the inequality discourse space in the media.[42] Figure 5.4 shows the U.S. media discourse space surrounding inequality for the month of December

---

[41] The tone of these speeches was dampened by a campaign strategy aimed at undecided middle voters, but Obama advocated tax increases on the wealthy and the importance of opportunity and fairness for the middle class as key 2012 campaign themes.

[42] Based on Silobreaker searches on November 20, 2011, and December 8, 2011, for co-occurrence of "inequality" and "occupy" and third term co-occurrences in all U.S. news and blogs online.

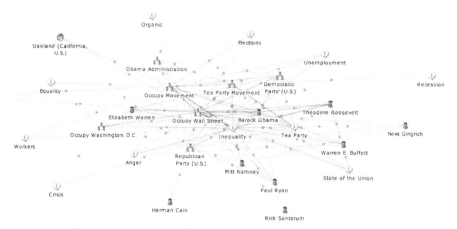

FIGURE 5.4. Sources associated with inequality discourse in U.S. media, December 2011. A total of 520 news items; 134 blogs and other sites. *Source:* Silobreaker; used with permission.

2011, with Obama sharing proximity with Occupy to mentions of inequality in news, commentary, and blogs.

By the time of the 2012 State of the Union Address, Obama co-occupied the inequality discourse space, even taking periodic ownership of the political discussion. Around the time of the January speech U.S. news reports and political commentary disproportionately associated Obama with the term "inequality." In a few short months inequality discourse was suddenly everywhere. And it spiked whenever Occupy protests popped up at elite gatherings (at least whenever police clashes did not dominate the stories). There were even reports of hand-wringing among elites at the Winter 2012 World Economic Forum in Davos, Switzerland, where Forum organizers offered Occupy protesters an ersatz headquarters outside the main conference venue. Some masters of the financial universe even fretted about the growth of inequality undermining popular faith in capitalism itself. Others worried that shrinking consumer income might stall the growth engine that powered sales, profits, and jobs. The icon of late modern capitalism, Bill Gates, delivered a speech at Davos titled "A New Approach to Capitalism in the 21st Century." And the CEO of the World Economic Forum, Klaus Schwab, issued this remarkable comment that the *New York Times* deemed fit for an Occupier:

Vast numbers of people in many countries seem tired and disillusioned. Even pillars of the establishment are shaken. Klaus Schwab, executive chairman of the World Economic Forum, whose annual gathering in Davos is financed largely by corporations, recently sounded as if he were ready to pitch a tent in Zuccotti Park, the hub of the Occupy Wall Street protests until it was cleared in November.

"Capitalism, in its current form, no longer fits the world around us," Mr. Schwab said in a statement last week. "We have failed to learn the lessons from the financial crisis of 2009." (Ewing 2012)

Whether or not capitalism would be substantially reformed to the satisfaction of the Occupy protesters, it is remarkable that they were able to change the economic conversation in such a short time, using such highly personalized network organizations.

The early Occupy movement presented various networks with "heads" and "hubs" such as found in and among specific city encampments and social media platforms. However, overall it was a crowd-enabled action network with a power signature characterized by multi-tiered yet interconnected networks in which recognition was dispersed and dynamic. The dispersed power signature in this network was quite unlike the moderate power signature of the organizationally enabled network in which the Robin Hood Tax campaign was embedded. Power operated differently in these two connective action network types. Yet both had similar – and, in these cases, impressive – outcomes.

Conclusion

Understanding different configurations (and ideas) about power in networks is important for understanding the impact of protests faced with different kinds of opportunities and challenges. In both of our cases, connective action networks of differing types pushed their issues onto the public and elite agendas, although it is important to caution that many aspects of activist agendas can get lost in such a translation (cf. Yanacopulos 2009; Mattoni et al. 2010). Our point is that networks with distinct power signatures can wield different kinds of power with some success. In our comparison cases, neither of the networks had the signatures of centralized brokered coalitions or tightly bounded social movement or other collective action networks. Yet both in their own ways contributed to the rapid rise of inequality-related issues on national agendas.

The case of the Robin Hood Tax campaign suggests that the power of organizationally enabled networks stems from the collection of organizations sharing power or influence broadly at the head of the network (with campaign-coordinating websites sometimes receiving a larger share of the links, as one would expect). This moderate power signature puts a twist on common assumptions about the proclivities of resource-rich organizations for centralizing recognition and influence. The strong organizations at the core of these organizationally enabled networks achieved a great deal not solely because they were resource rich, but also because they shared those resources with their networks. The case of the early Occupy movement, by contrast, suggests that the power of the crowd-enabled Occupy network does not stem exactly from heads or tails, but rather from the dynamic interconnections between multiple networks and layers stitched together through dynamic linking by crowd-enabled technologies such as Twitter.

Although the two kinds of network organization achieved similar outcomes in the short term, different network power signatures may have different political capacity strengths in a broader perspective. For example, it is seemingly easier for organizationally enabled networks to sustain focused efforts in the long term. The Robin Hood Tax was a decade-long campaign that finally reached the agendas of political and civic elites when world events cracked the neo-liberal consensus. By contrast, crowd-enabled networks may succeed not so much by staying on message and aiming at the same political targets over time, as by swarming different political targets until those targets begin to notice they have common adversaries that seem to be making similar points and will not go away. Such networks also have an adaptive capacity enabled by communication technologies that aggregate and filter huge volumes of individual inputs: these aggregation, filtering, and feeding properties allow crowd-enabled networks to recombine after the loss of key nodes. The Occupy networks demonstrated a remarkable capacity to regroup and stage occupations of other things (the Supreme Court, the U.S. Congress, President Obama, and even the year 2012) after cities displaced many of the encampments that seemed to be the key nodes in the early stages of the protests. Unlike conventional organizations and coalitions that may suffer setbacks and be difficult to rebuild, people in connective networks are relatively easy to reactivate and refocus on new causes or adding new issues to old ones. The capacity to rise up quickly in response to emerging opportunities is part of the power of crowd-enabled mobilization.

Even the press eventually got this idea about the regenerative power of dynamic networks. A Reuters story revealed a shift in press coverage from earlier concerns about "What is their demand?" and "What will happen when the encampments disperse?" to a story about diversity and flexibility as strengths: "Occupy 2012: Firmly Disorganized, Driven by Dreams" (Harrison and Nichols 2012). The story noted that the original notion of occupation from 2011 that revolved around the physical occupation of public space in the form of camps had broadened in 2012 to encompass new versions of occupation, including Occupy the Election, Occupy Cyberspace, Occupy Culture, and Occupy the Economy. Many of these anticipated occupations did not occur, for reasons we discuss in the next chapter. However, the emergent capacity of the crowd-enabled network made it possible for large-scale contention to arise in unanticipated settings and in response to rapidly developing opportunities.

Both types of connective networks may achieve impressive results (separately or together). However, they do not always do so. This highlights the critical importance of opportunities for the successful wielding of power (Tarrow 2011). In the cases discussed here, the growing attention to inequality on public and elite agendas was surely aided by the political opportunities afforded by the continuing financial crisis, which provided openings for challengers. High levels of joblessness and lost property values, combined with the lack of repentance of financial leaders, no doubt made it more difficult for politicians to ignore pressures from below.

Given that there are different kinds of power and network structures, it seems clear that they interact with different political opportunities in shaping political outcomes. In an analysis of civic organizations (NGOs, SMOs, and community groups) in two UK cities (Glasgow and Bristol), Mario Diani found that network centrality and density had uneven relationships to political access and recognition from power holders in the two cities (Diani forthcoming), whereas an earlier study had shown that network centrality had a strong effect on access to power in Milan (Diani 1995). He concluded that while different civic networks may build comparable internal coherence and resource concentration, the political context in which they operate affects how their power is wielded, accounting for differences in the quality of action and political successes achieved.

A key to variation in political outcomes lies in how the seemingly paradoxical mix of highly personalized and widely shared relationships becomes organized and how the resulting networks interact with contextual factors such as opportunities and the receptiveness of targets. This suggests that there is no clearly superior type of protest organization, although some may work better in some situations than in others. Yet, as we suggested earlier in the book, there may be ingrained conceptions about ideal organization and applications of power in movements operating below the surface of both scholarship and praxis in contentious politics. The next chapter considers what happens when such ideals conflict.

6

Conclusion

When Logics Collide

Recent years have witnessed large-scale protests in a multitude of national and transnational contexts, from long-running actions focused on economic justice and climate change politics to large-scale political uprisings in Iceland, the Middle East, Europe, and North America. Reactions to the sudden waves of protest that brought massive crowds into public squares, streets, and parks framed the discussion in stark and polarizing terms. Some observers implied that social media caused these political upheavals or that they erupted spontaneously; others insisted that technology was as good as irrelevant in these contexts. Some commentators concentrated on the lack of correspondence between the crowd protests and the type of contentious action based on conventional movements that has predominated in modern democracies; others overlooked the fact that many NGOs have altered their network structures to accommodate more inclusive and personally engaging media affordances. In all, many observers of these flexible, multi-issue networks seemed to miss or misconstrue several key factors, including the roles and organizational properties of digital media and the increasingly personalized nature of shared political action.

This book offers a framework for distinguishing the roles of digital media in different types of large-scale collective action. Our aim was to explore how digitally networked action works: how it is organized, what sustains it, and what political capacity it can have. The point was not to replace existing perspectives, but to show what their scope and boundaries are and to illuminate how different kinds of action networks have different signatures that characterize their engagement of publics, their organization, and their acquisition and utilization of political power.

Some of the confusion about how digital media operate in political mobilization stems from observers having a single view of what collective action is and how it is organized. One such view takes for granted the roles of collective action framing, resource mobilization, and strong leadership in collective action, as well as the need to bridge collective action frames and broker coalitions. Those who adopt this perspective tend to miscast large-scale mobilizations as having more conventional and less technology-enabled organization than may actually be the case and to equate different kinds of mobilizations that in fact entail very different levels of socialization, cultural reproduction, and commitment. Another view overestimates the centrality of technology and fails to see the conventional organizations and organizing in the mix. These perspectives can be particularly confusing when applied to the hybrid cases of organizationally enabled networks, which display a "now you see it, now you don't" quality with elements of both views in play. The value of our framework lies in its ability to help us understand the different logics of fundamentally different forms of mobilization – to understand why people join, how they engage, what keeps them involved, and what power looks like in different forms. We can also use our three ideal types of large-scale action networks to help sort out interesting questions about fissures, factions, stability, and outcomes.

This concluding chapter retraces central steps of the book via the themes outlined in the introduction that have worked as analytical touchstones throughout our discussion. We then point ahead to future questions for developing our understanding of contentious connective action. These are centered on challenges and problems that may develop in different kinds of connective networks. The cases analyzed throughout the book exemplify relatively successful protests and campaigns. We focused primarily on connective action that attained impressive degrees of coherence and political success in order to explore variations in how processes unfold, how individuals become engaged, and how power is wielded. In moving forward, it will be important to thoroughly explore networks that break down and fail, as well as to examine conflicts that may develop within them in ways that affect their dynamics. This chapter takes a first step in examining such problems by discussing the limits on organizational and political capacities of connective action. The larger questions have to do with how such networked organization may persist and transition, and what role different ideals and ideologies of action and organization may play in this context.

Connective Action in the Spectrum of Large-Scale Contention

We begin by reviewing the main points of the book. Four broad, yet interconnected topics underpin our analyses. Three were introduced in the introduction: (a) multiple logics of action, (b) the personalization of action, and (c) communication as organization. Here we weave in a fourth key theme that emerged in the course of our discussion: (d) power in different forms of networked organization. Initially we defined and addressed the themes separately. Now we examine them together to show how they account for different kinds of mobilization.

The first broad theme is that *multiple logics are at play in digitally networked action* and that these are analytically distinct and deserving of consideration on their own terms. The study of large-scale action has often focused on the

problem of collective action, the logic by which individuals are averse to joining in common, and possibly costly, action. Understanding the problem of
participation from this perspective typically leads to organizational solutions
that focus on the importance of leadership, resources, framing, and brokerage
among resource-rich organizations aiming to create incentives for individuals
to join in a common cause, take risks, and participate in the networking process
with others.

   Alongside this well-known model of action, which still accounts for a good
many cases of contentious action, we argued for adding a second – connective –
logic of action that yields an organizational dynamic based on more fine-
grained individual engagement using technologies to carry personal stories
and other content across networks. We further suggested that two ideal types
of large-scale action networks build on this second logic. The first involves
conventional organizations creating backbone networks that host the digital
engagement mechanisms for individuals to use in their own networking and
participation choices. The second relies on people in the crowd, some with
technology development skills, to create networks and platforms that take the
place of more formal organizations and enable layered networks to organize
activity. Both of these forms of mobilization rely significantly on face-to-face
participation, from attending meetings and rallies to incorporating social values
into everyday life and sharing them with friends and associates.

   Connective and collective action logics do not compete; rather, they complement one another and extend the range of analysis. The important point is that
theoretical frames developed for understanding historic collective action do
not satisfactorily illuminate the connective organization principles in a growing range of contemporary contentious politics, from the entirely online actions
discussed by Earl and Kimport (2011), to the hybrid organizations identified
by Chadwick (2013), to our own organizationally enabled and crowd-enabled
cases.

   Using one-size-fits-all models of collective action to analyze large-scale action
networks obscures more than it clarifies. In the context of digitally networked
action, such models yield largely descriptive accounts that fail to distinguish
between individual pathways to participation; fail to specify concepts such as
collective action frames, which quickly become circular and apply to all rallying symbols; and under-specify the roles of information and communication
technologies in the dynamics of large-scale action networks. Digital media can
reduce organizational costs of communication and coordination in both connective and collective action networks. In collective networks, however, they
tend mainly to enhance the action dynamics already in play as organizers use the
technology instrumentally to do pretty much what they were already doing. By
contrast, connective networks employ a different organizational logic to bring
people in and to help them stay involved. To an important degree, information and communication technologies become agents in connective networks,
automating and organizing the flow of information and providing various
degrees of latitude for peer-defined relationships.

The logic of connective action is rooted in self-motivated sharing and what Benkler (2006) termed "peer production." Such connective networks grow to the extent that people can engage in content themes that are amenable to personalization, appropriation, and collaboration through the sharing of ideas and multimedia content, as well as through access to technologies that enable such sharing. The rich and varied troves of individually produced content found in the cases analyzed throughout this book were not just the result of individuals hitting the send key with blog posts or images attached. The palpable sharing, linking, commenting, and celebration of individual creativity became the meshwork connecting often-disparate people to a set of common activities. Personal action frames that support this personalized sharing travel more easily across network barriers than more exclusive collective action frames that require more cultural production work to get people to adopt, or at least acknowledge, a collective identity. This means that digital media might well be found in all kinds of action networks but have differing roles in differing contexts. It also suggests that media in the context of organization logics make a difference in the way the discourse around the action is framed.

The importance of distinguishing different logics of action is thus also reflected in the analysis of *personalization in contentious political action*, which touches on the second theme of the book. As a starting point, we called attention to the trends of personalization in late modern democracies in which citizens are moving away from what they perceive to be imposed or rigid ideological ways of understanding issues and engagement. As we discussed in Chapter 2, such personalization processes pose challenges to modern conventional means of organizing political action, such as promoting memberships and branded identification with formal organizations and their causes (Bimber, Flanagin, and Stohl 2012). Personalized action pairs with access to personal information and communication technologies in different ways than does collectivized action. Personal action frames allow people to specify their own connection to an issue rather than adopt more demanding models regarding how to think and act. People can share their engagement and contributions in forms easily adopted by others as personal action frames that do not narrowly specify identity and that thus travel more easily beyond identity boundaries (e.g., group, ideology, geography, culture) across social networks. Technological networking mechanisms, and in particular digital and social media, enable sharing with distant others and may also offer multiple levels of entry into an action space. Connective action networks in this sense build on and scale up via personalization. For many, the issue of future commitment is also personalized, resulting in the "opt in/opt out" varieties of engagement that seem at odds with conventional forms of sustained commitment and collective identification. Indeed, the precipitous decline of the Occupy protests following police raids on the camps may be explained in part by the relatively thin commitments of the large number of followers who joined the festival atmosphere from their offices or desktops but who drifted away when the generative core of physical action was dispersed. There is more to this story, however, as we will see when we examine the organizational role of core encampment activists later in the chapter.

Whether we are looking at densely layered, crowd-enabled networks or organizationally enabled varieties with clearer structural backbones, we see the importance of thinking about *communication as central to organization itself*, which is the third key theme of the book. The question here is not how media reduce the costs of messaging followers or other stakeholders, as is often associated with how organizations use media in mobilizing collective action, but how action becomes significantly organized through digital media platforms that enable and activate political networks that play into or against one another.

Thinking about digital media in this way spotlights how the organizational qualities of communication can define differences between connective and collective networks. In connective action networks, the network itself, with all its component parts (including individuals, organizations, and technologies), carries relatively more of the organizational burden than is normally the case in organizationally brokered networks. In crowd-enabled action, information and communication technologies involve layers of unevenly connected platforms that make it possible for people to establish relationships, transmit information, and coordinate activities. In organizationally enabled networks, the connectivity is typically more evenly distributed, more technologically sophisticated (i.e., purpose built), and powered by the more recognized organizations at the head of the power signature. In either their crowd-enabled or organizationally enabled forms, connective networks can be understood as distinct kinds of network organizations in their own right.

Once we start to understand the organizational capacities of connective action, a closely related set of questions concerns how connective action networks fare in terms of achieving results, which entails *network organizational forms of power*. The studies presented in this book suggest that both types of connective action networks can result in focused action and not simply "noise." Under the right conditions, digitally networked action can mobilize publics, sustain or develop network organization, and have an impact on policy agendas.

The power signature of networks helps to explain the capacities of differently structured connective networks. Networks in which centered and deliberately networking organizations have more control play out differently than ones in which individuals and technology are more prominent. In organizationally enabled networks, power can be thought of as a function of the emergence of organizational linkages among coordinating websites (which can include campaign websites as stand-alone organizations in themselves) that enable personalized communication through social networking technologies. By contrast, the power of crowd-enabled networks lies more in the crossing of multiple networks with traffic driven by mixes of commercial platforms, custom-built sites, small individual sites, email and SMS chains, and the high degree of activity in the tails of these networks, where fine-grained linkages join intersecting networks that may in turn feed back into large distribution nodes that refresh and focus the crowd.

In our analysis of Put People First in Chapter 2 and the Robin Hood Tax in Chapter 5, we showed that organizationally enabled networks received noteworthy levels of positive media coverage and official recognition. The crowd-enabled networks of Occupy involved large numbers of people (if one includes the multitudes who gave online support) and was also able to influence the public agenda. But Occupy did not always attain similarly consistent markers of worthiness, unity, and commitment. Indeed, by our earlier definitions of personalized engagement in connective networks, one would expect commitment levels to vary widely and to vary among individuals over time. This suggests there could be reasons to expand the understanding of these elements in Tilly's (2006) well-known WUNC framework. For example, the measures of commitment may have to be modified to include ideas about how social networks and technology affordances may be successful in the *reactivation* of lost participants over time. Similarly, we might want to distinguish the perceived worthiness of the crowd (which was never embraced by a majority of bystander publics in the United States) from the popular embrace of ideas that come from the crowd (such as "We Are the 99%").

Moving forward, there may be reasons to consider the measures used to evaluate large-scale political action more generally. The discussions in this book stayed close to conventional markers for both contentious action and capacity: we considered cases that at some level relate to institutional politics and involve recognizable democratic public action, large street demonstrations, and the occupation of public spaces, and we focused primarily on conventional measures of political capacity in the areas of mobilization, agenda, and policy. To deepen the analysis, there are several other aspects to consider. These include the role of more incremental social and political change; how participants, networks, and repertoires become available for reactivation across time and opportunities; and how the repertoires of democratic public action may themselves change over time.

It is also important to continue to emphasize that, like conventional collective action, connective action is not sure to succeed (or to fail) on any given occasion (although just as with conventional collective action we should not be surprised if it often *does* fail). Judgments of the political capacity of large-scale action networks in specific instances vary depending on whether we focus on the short or the long term, and whether we look at institutional or broader societal change. But in all cases, political context, opportunities, and other actors play into the dynamics and the outcomes, and it follows that it is important to examine how digital and social media infuse specific ecologies of dissent.

This said, tensions in the forms of human and technological agency and organization are important subtexts in the analysis of connective action: the presence of and conflicts among networks infused with differing logics of action may play into the dynamics of an action network and how it develops in a given case. We have stressed how important it is to appreciate the analytical differences between connective and collective action in order to make progress in understanding different formations in contemporary contention, to identify and explain processes that models based on resource mobilization and collective identity cannot address. We also argued for the importance of appreciating that there are fundamental differences along the spectrum of connective action, and understanding the variations in different connective action types. Having come to this point, we now suggest that once we can see these broad outlines of different action types, it is also important to be sensitive to what can happen when logics collide.

When Logics Collide

Throughout this book, we have repeatedly pulled the logics and network types apart for the sake of analytical traction. But as we emphasized from the beginning, one might expect the ideal types of connective and collective action to appear in pockets, layers, and overlaps within the same protest space. In fact, when the different logics and types of action layer and combine within one and the same protest episode, they can be very effective. An example of this is the Wikipedia Internet piracy action described in Chapters 1 and 5, in which various actors following diverse logics – from Wikipedia, to Google, to Anonymous, to scattered individuals – came together to protest the U.S. Congress's consideration of Internet piracy legislation. Clean partitions in a protest space between different kinds of action networks can also be effective, as was illustrated in the case of the G20 London protests discussed in Chapter 2. In other cases, however, logics of action may come into clear conflict in ways that may lead to fragmentation, fizzling out, or failure to scale up. The following sections explore two important – and sometimes related – junctures at which logics may collide: (a) when action networks seek to transition as political conditions, opportunities, and goals change; and (b) when one and the same network harbors actors with fundamentally different ideals and ideologies of organization and action.

Organizational Conflicts in Political Transitions

We do not regard the three ideal types of connective and collective action in terms of an evolutionary logic in which crowd-enabled connective networks are the starting point and organizationally brokered collective action networks are the mature instantiation of large-scale organized dissent. Indeed, if there is any striking migration pattern evident among these types at present, it may be the responsiveness of conventional NGOs and SMOs to changing patterns of participation, resulting in more hybrid organizationally enabled networks. Within particular political contexts, there can be many ways in which action networks morph in response to internal processes or external changes in conditions. However, they do not always do so successfully.

Several of the action networks we have discussed showed a capacity, or at least a tendency, to adapt over time. The shifts we have traced mainly reveal connective networks reacting to changing conditions and opportunities while retaining a basic connective character. For example, some of the key players in the Tahrir Square uprisings have gone on to form technology-oriented NGOs and Facebook networks to organize youth activism, as has been the trajectory of Wael Ghonim, who launched the iconic Facebook page "We Are All Khaled Said," which commemorated the activist killed by police and spurred mobilization in his name.

This said, political conditions may become less conducive to connective action, and networks characterized by other organizational logics may find themselves better positioned as political opportunities shift. When this happens, such groupings may crowd connective networks out. This sort of disjointed transition occurred in the Egypt elections that followed Tahrir Square, leading some observers to ask, "What happened to the Arab Spring?" (Banco 2012). The Muslim Brotherhood seized the legacy of the uprisings in the later electoral phase and, in the process, may have reinforced the idea that the structures of conventional movements are superior. It is clear in this case that the efforts of the crowd to build an Arab Spring 2.0 or even 3.0 were not effective in the electoral arena. Nevertheless, this should not undermine recognition of the outcomes of the crowd-enabled action in its earlier phases: the sustained and digitally mediated protests toppled the Mubarak regime, led to popular elections, and created repertoires of action emulated in modular forms (Beissinger 2007) in other places, from Spain to Wall Street.

The dilemma faced by the *indignados* in Spain suggests a variation on a similar dilemma involving the capacity of crowd-enabled mobilizations to handle political transitions. Given the severe internal and external political constraints on any Spanish government organized during the dire financial crisis, few political opportunities were available to the *indignados*, whether or not they organized in more formal movement or party terms. Perhaps it is not surprising that the next phase witnessed an intensification of regional separatist activism, led by parties and old movement organizations, as occurred in Catalonia and the Basque Country. The role of those orchestrating these separatist actions was rather like that of the Muslim Brotherhood in that they were kept mostly offstage in the first act, only to steal the scene in the next. However, as in the Egyptian case, the short-term impact of the *indignados* should not be dismissed. They captured the attention of the public, the media, and leaders for sustained periods and raised the stakes of negotiations between successive governments, the European Union, creditors, and failing banks. In short, the achievements of Tahrir Square and the *indignados* are not minor. Nevertheless, these trajectories do suggest interesting questions about the relationship between opportunity structure and organizational form that deserve further analysis in the study of connective cases from a long-term perspective.

These transition patterns indicate that technologies and the organizational forms in which they may be embedded do not work independently of political opportunities and social context, a point emphasized by Tarrow (2011). However, it does seem to be the case that technological outlays and their interactions with the activists and organizations using them can affect the transformation potential of different kinds of networks at various stages of contention. The same technologies that enable the rapid rise of large-scale crowd-enabled networks may limit their capacity to transform and take on new roles. For example, Twitter may be a high-capacity stitching system across other networking platforms, but when political conditions change, action formations around those underlying platforms, from local websites to Facebook groups, may prove disjointed and incapable of sustaining mobilization. This does not mean that all crowd-enabled action is destined to dissolve (not that this is an inherently bad thing). However, it suggests that sustaining a crowd-enabled mobilization in the attempt to adapt to changing conditions and opportunities may among other things involve building and accepting robust platforms that can handle the work of reorganizing and repurposing scattered activists. This said, the prospect of concerted development of new technologies may reveal long-standing fissures in the crowd as actors split on questions of the proper organizational forms for succession.

Conflicting Network Organization within Mobilizations

Conflicts in action networks are not limited to differing visions of political strategy and ideology; they may also be grounded in differences over ideologies of organization and political action. The clash of different organizational ideals in different parts or different layers of a large-scale action network may impede a protest network's successful transition in adapting to new conditions and opportunities. What is more, it can have the consequence of fragmenting the network.

Working out differences among players can involve somewhat different issues in connective action networks than in what social movement scholars such as Gerhards and Rucht (1992) term "mesomobilization," the bridging of organizational differences among movement organizations within a protest arena. Organizations in the backbone of organizationally enabled networks may engage in some formal brokerage to deal with conflicts and differences among themselves. However, this often involves enabling the creation of easily personalized action frames rather than bridging existing ideological or other collective action frame differences. This process of "cutting the diamond" discussed in Chapter 4 may in fact result in looser network ties rather than stronger coalition relationships.

When we turn to the sorts of conflicts that may arise in crowd-enabled action, we find several scenarios. One involves crowds operating in the same mix with movement organizations and NGO networks, resulting in difficulties for organizers who are trying to manage campaigns or other actions. As Bennett (2003, 2005) has discussed, this can mean that formerly dominant conventional organizations, whether in brokered or more loosely enabling coalitions, may lose control of campaigns, as crowds join in unilaterally and continue the pressure even when lead organizations deem it time to stop. As a result, such organizations can lose effective negotiation standing and credibility with targets that expect pressure to be relieved if they comply with some demands. The long-standing campaigns against corporations over a host of economic justice and environmental issues often entail continued or sporadic attacks by activist networks (such as Anonymous hackers), culture jammers, and others, even after prominent NGOs may have let up their pressure in light of signs of cooperation from the target. In many policy areas related to corporate social responsibility, such as contests over standards for labor rights, environmental protection, or fair trade, one network may pursue higher or different norms even as another declares victory (Bennett 2003; Bennett and Lagos 2007).

Another scenario involves the mix of technology-inclined and technology-averse actors within the same larger network. This is a mix that can be found in action networks of all three ideal types, but in our cases it has emerged most saliently in the crowd-enabled type.[1] For example, for all of its technology buzz, Occupy remained at its core a staunchly face-to-face, democratic consensus-oriented process that attracted activists willing to make sacrifices, take risks, and take part in long face-to-face meetings. Amid all the noise and underneath the broad personal action frame of the 99%, Occupy continued to generate its action agenda largely through general assemblies with strict rules of participation, deliberation, and consensus. Activists held on to face-to-face meeting and decision-making requirements even after police disruptions and loss of public gathering places.

In a move that links organizational ideals with the challenges of transition, early observers questioned Occupy's sustainability and potential for political transition against the background of its demanding norms pertaining to co-present interactions such as camping and attending general assemblies (Taylor and Gessen 2011; Gitlin 2012). A number of activist scholars in the Taylor and Gessen anthology expressed optimism but also raised questions about whether the organizational preferences of many core activists would obstruct the long-term growth of a more popular movement. In a review of these essays, Hickel (2012: asked: "How did the biggest social movement in the US since the 1960s fail to parlay a moment of unprecedented political potential into substantive social change?" He traced the answer to the organizational ideal he identified at the core of the movement:

Occupy activists fell in love with their own horizontalism (the "prefiguration" of a new society, as they put it) and fetishized physical occupation as a revolutionary tactic. In the process, they ignored generations of accumulated wisdom about how to mobilize successful social movements. Even to the point of refusing to isolate and organize around specific demands. As a result, the nation – and most importantly, poor and working class

---

[1] Another kind of conflict situation could emerge when two action networks suddenly come together, as when NGOs deploy technologies to help provide public services in failed states (Livingston and Asmolov 2010).

Americans – lost faith in Occupy's ability to effect the change that people so desperately needed, and a moment of true revolutionary potential slipped through the fingers of history. (Hickel 2012)

As these early commentaries suggest, the Occupy movement of 2011–2012 offers an interesting case of a connective action network in which the challenges of transition and the challenges of conflicting ideals combined. In particular, this was a case in which the presence of strong and differing ideals of action within the network had important consequences for the development of the action as a whole. The following section examines this case more closely.

Organizational Ideals versus Purpose-Built Technologies in Occupy

As we dig deeper into contentious connective action, it will be necessary to consider more carefully the contribution of "core activists" to the political success of mobilizations that engage millions of participants at different levels through the use of digital media and social technologies. Aside from the obvious ways in which they are significant for the focus and development of a protest movement, core activists can also play a key role in the processes through which different logics of action – and ideologies of action – in different areas and layers of the protest space either combine or collide. In the case of Occupy, it is interesting to explore the influence that encamped activists had on the decision not to adopt a next-generation technological infrastructure that might have made for a different kind of political transition than the one seen to date.

The Occupy movement in the United States entailed an interesting and effective combination of physical occupation and participation by vast Occupy-oriented mediated publics. The local "prefigurative societies" were derided by Hickel (2012) for devoting inordinate time and focus to mundane activities related to running the camps, such as the procurement and preparation of food and establishing rules limiting the activity of drum circles (whose members claimed the right to drum into the night). Yet it is clear that the physical camps provided an important focus for the movement (Gerbaudo 2012) and attracted broad media and public attention. At the same time, during the height of the protests, many people on the periphery of the occupations made important mediated contributions to the movement and the organization of the crowd (Agarwal et al. 2012). The engagement of non-encampment occupiers could thus be considered an important factor in making the protests a *large-scale* public action. Part of the strength of (and the challenge for) the movement was the broad scope of participants and perspectives encompassed by the 99%. But the larger Occupy network also contained layers of actors who not only had diverse political questions and visions, but also had different ideals of political action and organization, some of which were related to the role of technology in the action.

Jeffrey Juris describes the presence of different action orientations among the activists in an ethnographic account of Occupy Boston (Juris 2012). From his standpoint as a participant-observer, Juris distinguished between a "logic of networking" (via horizontal, inclusive, open information-rich networks using media to organize on- and offline) and a "logic of aggregation" (using media to direct physical occupation and action). What is important about this observation is that he described much of the networking logic as being contributed by actors above the level of local assemblies and sustained by a mix of tech developers, activist mavens, and interested citizens who helped create and consume witness content, direct traffic, expand the network, and link otherwise isolated clumps of activists. Meanwhile, the logic of aggregation depended upon the activists in dispersed local occupations that continued to develop local cultures of their own.

We have formalized these networking layers as crowd-enabled connective action in our framework. The actions emanating from the camps and assemblies animated the protests and, as long as the crowd roared above them, created various networks of engagement and media attention. Yet when the crowd-enabled network faced physical disruption, as happened in the United States after the Occupy camps were disbanded during police raids in the late fall of 2011, a moment occurred in which the challenge of conflicting ideologies of action became intermingled with the multiple challenges of transition. In the case of Occupy, the challenge of transition became concretely embedded in issues related to networking and technology. One path to a new transitional form (perhaps still a crowd-enabled form) involved adopting more purpose-built tools to partly take the place of physical locations so that the crowd would still have hubs to connect. As we will see later, various sources of purpose-built technologies offered timely support to the disrupted protesters. At this point the question became whether actors at the focal point of the action were motivated enough to devolve some measure of their personal control and physical co-presence to more technology-enabled organization forms. In the wider perspective, examining this moment gives us the opportunity to consider what happens when underlying models of ideal action and organization clash with opportunities to encompass or shift to other organizational modes.

Activists who are otherwise highly committed to regrouping after setbacks, disruptions, or changes in opportunities may resist technology innovations as possible means of reorganizing themselves and reactivating peripheral supporters. This technology resistance among important actors in the Occupy network was observed by one of the authors (Bennett) and colleagues, who became involved in various projects with Occupy activists.[2] One of these projects

---

[2] Similar tendencies have been reported by others, as in a study of Occupy in the Netherlands by Mercea, Nixon, and Funk (forthcoming). The pattern is by no means unique to Occupy. Another case involved an attempt by different activists in the Pacific Northwest region of North America in 2006 to form a regional social forum. The organizing committee made a commitment to pursue personal-level network building and to include groups such as Native Americans, who did not rely on technologies in making tribal decisions or in establishing relationships with others. The result was that plans raced ahead of relationships, and the reluctance to switch to a weaker-tie technology network eventually led to the cancelation of the first planned gathering. No plans for future efforts had emerged at the time of this writing. See Center

included an ethnographic study of Seattle Occupy assemblies and participants, supplemented by a technology inventory of media platforms used in Seattle and other cities during 2011–2012. Led by Sheetal Agarwal and Lance Bennett, who supervised a team of undergraduate students at the University of Washington, the project provided an important ethnographic context for the technology development project discussed here.

The technology project that enabled us to study adoption decisions involving purpose-built online tools was undertaken in collaboration with computer scientists at the University of Washington. This project, dubbed Engage,[3] entailed working with community groups to develop purpose-built civic technologies aimed at improving the deliberation and agenda-setting capacities of online communities.[4] The Engage team developed several successful iterations of a crowdsourced voter guide with partnerships from CityClub of Seattle, a prominent civic organization, with support from the public libraries, and with traffic driven by endorsements from newspapers and other media, along with Facebook networks and Google search marketing. The voter guide resulted in a large volume of traffic, a large number of reasonable positions taken on ballot measures, a remarkably low level of flaming, and, equally surprisingly, a high level of engagement with opposing points of view. Analysis of the data indicated not only that otherwise disjointed publics were capable of civil political discourse, but that the results seemed richer and more engaging than the often confusing and less transparently sourced printed voter guides that arrive in the mail from state offices (Freelon et al. 2012).

A more general set of deployments was deemed possible as a result of the flexibility of the underlying platform, ConsiderIt, which could support (with minor modifications) a range of networked agenda-setting and decision-making processes (Kriplean et al. 2012). The team approached activists in both the Tea Party and Occupy protests about using the ConsiderIt platform to enhance or supplement face-to-face meetings and to share ideas and recommendations for actions with broader publics. Although the reactions were initially positive in both camps, we eventually ran aground with the Tea Party, as the national network had already begun to transition from a scattered, multi-issue network of networks to a more hierarchical insurgency within the Republican Party. According to Sheetal Agarwal, who attended two meetings and had discussions with activists, it seemed clear that after rather stunning electoral victories for the Tea Party in the 2010 congressional elections and the party's contribution to the defeat of the recall of Wisconsin Governor Scott Walker in 2012, the movement became focused on elections, and the interest

for Communication and Civic Engagement, "Which Way for the Northwest Social Forum?" ccce.com.washington.edu/projects/nwsf.html.

[3] engage.cs.washington.edu.

[4] The formal project was titled "Socio-computational Systems to Support Public Engagement and Deliberation," supported by National Science Foundation Grant 0966929 to Alan Borning and Lance Bennett, with Travis Kriplean as chief technology developer. www.nsf.gov/awardsearch/showAward.do?AwardNumber=0966929.

of its leaders in a broader-based public input and deliberation process had diminished.

Occupy initially seemed a more promising seedbed for examining the proposition that purpose-built technologies might aid the transition of a displaced or potentially reorganizing movement via technological augmentation. Our interest was not to push Occupy networks one way or another toward a particular technological solution, and we surely did not intend to become involved politically in their possible transition. Rather, we employed a value-sensitive design process (Friedman, Kahn, and Borning 2006; Borning et al. 2005). This was an iterative process in which the Engage team met in various groupings with Occupy technology developers both in Seattle and (via conferencing) around the country. The goal was to assess Occupy technology experts' views of their current media tools, both off the shelf (e.g., Twitter) and custom built (e.g., wiki.occupy.net/wiki/Main_Page) in order to understand how they viewed various technologies already in use in the protests and what new tools might be of interest during the transition away from physical camps. We could not build or assist in developing any tool they might request, as our grant was specifically aimed at deliberation technologies. Moreover, the skill levels (particularly in the national developer network) suggested that the technology experts were capable of doing most things on their own. The major aim was to explore where the activist-developers understood the protests to be heading and to get a sense of what technologies might serve as organizational hubs to connect displaced local networks. We made it clear that we were interested in exploring online deliberative patterns in the Occupy issue space and comparing them with voter deliberations from our voter guide deployments. We demonstrated the ConsiderIt platform and offered to help repurpose it for possible adoption, within the limits of our grant and the interests of the team.

Our initial discussions with groups of Seattle protesters revealed that the rank and file felt strongly committed to the face-to-face assemblies. Several expressed a strong personal identification with the community in the camps and felt that outsiders needed to demonstrate their commitment by attending meetings and taking action. Before the activists in the camps were evicted by the police, they were often not interested in adding a layer of technology to replace or augment face-to-face processes. They used technologies, but primarily to connect the core face-to-face community through email, SMS, and phone lists. Although participants in the protests generally expressed an interest in and support for social media, preliminary examination of a survey data set of some 5,000 Occupy participants suggests that those most likely to engage in high-cost action such as camping, confronting police, and participating in marches were the least likely to use such social media as Facebook and Twitter, which were the predominant technologies used by the crowd.[5]

---

[5] This survey was conducted between December 7, 2011, and January 7, 2012, using crowdsourced (i.e., not random, network-of-networks) methods. The Occupy Research Network collected

As one might expect, the tech developers constituted a different layer of the network in that they were concerned with broadening the participation base by designing and building technological engagement mechanisms. This interest in virtual hubs seemed to grow with the displacement of camps and assembly meeting places. Most of the developers expressed understandable concerns about surveillance and security, as well as the capacity of disruptive actors to intrude on open technology spaces. We found these challenges to be both interesting and solvable.

After numerous design meetings and site mockups, the interest of the Seattle developers we worked with appeared to be limited to building something on the order of an open-source "Kickstarter"[6] type of platform on which people could propose actions and find supporters. While we worked with this idea, our primary interest was in fostering online deliberation, decision making, and sustainable engagement, which were all potential extensions of ConsiderIt. Despite our ultimate inability to find a mutual technological meeting point, the Seattle developers were happy to connect us with a national developer network that was busy creating a set of tools to help Occupy document itself, list projects and organizations, and use technologies beyond the commercial varieties such as Twitter and Facebook.

We connected more successfully with the national network. Facilitated by Sheetal Agarwal and Travis Kriplean from our team, discussions went forward with a focus on using our platform to create an online version of a key face-to-face element of the Occupy meeting ritual: the Temp Check. The temperature check involves a series of hand signals displayed by those at the assembly to indicate reactions to what is being said. Upward wiggling of fingers (also known as "twinkling") indicates agreement, downward wiggling means disagreement, a flat hand means not sure, making the shape of a C is a call for clarification, a triangle indicates too much drift in the conversation, and so on.[7] ConsiderIt was retooled to enable propositions about actions or other items of business to be posted (either from face-to-face assemblies or, in another version, by any registered user) and then discussed by adding points in pro–con lists and dragging the points made by others into one's list to show areas of convergence and divergence in a discussion. Real-time summaries of positions being taken and the sense of the participants in the discussion were available, offering users an instant understanding of how they stood vis-à-vis others, what the overall distribution of sentiment was, how many were participating, and so on.

The development took place during the spring of 2012, and the launch was planned for a national gathering (#natgat) to be held in Philadelphia over the

---

5,074 surveys (see www.occupyresearch.net). For a description and access to the data, see www.occupyresearch.net/2012/03/23/preliminary-findings-occupy-research-demographic-and-political-participation-survey/.

[6] At the time, Kickstarter was a hot new technology for proposing projects and business ideas and attracting crowd-funding to support. www.kickstarter.com.

[7] See en.wikipedia.org/wiki/Occupy_movement_hand_signals.

Fourth of July holiday weekend. The platform was linked from the Occupy.net national technology wiki and was still linked as of this writing in 2012 (temp-check.occupy.net). However, despite the clear fragmentation of the national networks, the discussion about the new platform was unfocused and seemed to generate little interest from the small gathering.[8] The activists who were committed enough to travel to Philadelphia did not see the need for more accessible, technology-enabled hubs to reinvigorate their networks. In addition, another developer group had created another platform that was a bit more like Kickstarter, in that it enabled voting on ideas and proposals without the depth of deliberation that our team regarded as important to include in the design of a new hub. The emergence of a previously unheard of competitor platform was consistent with the dispersed networks of Occupy, as many parallel activities occurred throughout the protests, often without much coordination across (and sometimes within) city hubs. Consistent with the values in play at the July gathering, the competitor platform was not adopted either. Overall, this experience suggests that some highly committed activists were sufficiently averse to the use of technology in the core parts of the protests to shy away from technology-enabled means of continuing the movement in its large-scale public form. As we observed during the course of the activist technology development program, enough felt this way to inhibit the technology-enabled avenue of development.

Many factors may enter into the strong preferences of core activists for face-to-face organization in cases such as this. One element is surely skepticism about types of engagement that enable personalized action even on a large, crowd-enabled scale. The concern may be that personalized action undermines or replaces other, privileged ways of acting politically. Many fear that the hype around social media protests might lead people to underestimate what it takes to push through political change or that people who would otherwise take part in more high-cost action might become distracted by the fun of developing a personally expressive digital face. Others worry that personal action frames cannot lead to an effective understanding of collective problems or believe that the experience of co-present meetings is important to develop a participant's thinking about the issues and the common cause.[9] Still others do not see personalized action as a worthy form of political action, quite apart from the content of the politics.

For our purposes, the key question is: What do different sentiments about the ideal organization of contentious action revealed in these conflicts over the proper uses of technology mean for the development (and the potential for transition) of an action network in which connective action has been a

---

[8] An anonymous "citizen-journalist" blogging about the gathering said: "Approximately 200 people showed up, far less than the 1500 police were anticipating, indicating the moribund nature of Occupy" (Citizen Journalist 2012).

[9] This is ironic in that our efforts to deploy Temp Check were aimed at enabling crowds of individuals to arrive at deeper, common understandings of issues, ideas, and proposals.

prominent characteristic? Underlying media preferences associated with different styles of activism and ways of organizing may relate to different logics of action. As the case of Occupy suggests, activists in critical positions in local networks may reject the organizational capacities of digital technologies in favor of face-to-face assembly and organizational relationship building – even when the conditions for building a movement are changing.

What actually happened with Occupy is a challenging question. Did it fail to make the necessary transition because it could not sustain high levels of public outcry, or because it did not "occupy" the 2012 U.S. elections as many had hoped and projected it would? It is possible that its legacy is better understood in terms of the production of enduring discourses and action repertoires that infused popular culture and that continued to spawn small occupations in local settings. It is perhaps too early to tell. At this point, we can only observe that the city encampments constituted an important unifying focal point for the early Occupy movement, and their continued existence did demand concentrated organizational work of a particular kind. At the same time, the rejection of technology (and the related undervaluing of non-encampment action) in some cases may have constrained the capacity to sustain the scale of the action network and the blurring of the boundaries between encamped activists and the wider circle of public participants. The conflict of logics in different layers of the network may have contributed to the movement's decline as a large-scale public action network, even though seeds of Occupy and its iconic themes persisted in more localized forms.

The technology-centered disconnect described between developers who saw the value of new technology as a means of reactivating flagging networks and the activists who prioritized face-to-face ritual (and saw technologically enabled action as anathema) even as their numbers dwindled is not the typical ideological or collective framing dispute. Yet such biases among different models of organization may occur when activists who have different ideal-type models of action and organization co-exist in the same protest space. In other words, breakdowns in mobilization do not always have to do with clashes of political ideology, or organizational disputes over leadership, or organizational decision processes. Although such things can be important in explaining the dissolution of movements, other such developments may hinge on fundamental differences in the role of technologies and the perception of what technologies add to or subtract from the ideal composition and functioning of network organization.

Such tensions became starkly clear in Occupy after the size and noise of the crowd diminished, but they were in many ways evident throughout the Occupy era. They also reflect concerns that are more widely shared. Many scholars as well as activists express wariness of the kinds of personalization that open networks and technologies can engage. Often, this derives from larger empirical concerns about how communication processes that invite personalization relate to and even reproduce the atomization of society. It also touches on concerns about how ways of doing politics influence and develop alongside ideas about the content and goals of political action and the development of the imagined communities at the base of democratic life. Such questions deserve attention, but stretch beyond the scope of this book. For the present, we note their importance and their connection to how our models of action come into play and sometimes into conflict in actual practice.

Looking Ahead

This book represents only a start in the investigation of connective action networks and their political properties. Compared with the relatively rich pictures scholars have developed about organizationally brokered contentious collective action, our cases can only point the way toward better understandings of the organizational qualities and capacities of the looser connective action assemblages. Connective contentious action is worth further theoretical and analytical attention. We hope that the models and methods we have offered will become part of broader studies.

The key question in this work has been how digitally networked action works in an era of increasingly personalized political participation. In particular, we have asked how connective action is organized, what sustains it, and when it is politically effective. We have examined three ideal types of large-scale action networks based on differing logics of participation, involving differing constellations of personalization and media affordances, and presenting differing dynamics of network organization. One end of the action spectrum is occupied by familiar varieties of collective action that are dominated by strong organizational hubs that manage the framing of the action, share epistemic communities, provide leadership and resources, and try to broker political differences that have to be bridged in order for cohesive networks to grow. Beyond these types of action, we have filled in less well specified parts of the action spectrum by defining two complementary connective action types. In organizationally enabled networks, organizations seek loose network ties with coalition partners and seek to activate individual-level networks by deploying personalized communication mechanisms (action frames and social technologies) along those networks. In crowd-enabled networks, individuals and dispersed groups (often with websites serving as organizations) employ personal action frames that travel through layers of technology to build relationships and coordinate action.

The book has traced the organizational capacities and qualities of connective networks, concentrating in particular on the role of discursive and technological networking mechanisms. By making connections, sharing information, channeling resources, and coordinating action, people can help these network organizations grow, stabilize, direct resources, and adapt. Connective networks can thus be analyzed as flexible organizations with a measurable capacity for engagement and resource allocation, as well as a capacity to adapt to political conditions over time. We have also shown that crowd-enabled networks often include actors whose organizational ideals may not be those of the larger crowd. Some activists may see technology innovations as enabling weak or less committed forms of action or as threatening to distribute power and control too broadly. When such activists assume dominant positions on the ground, a small number of voices in the shrinking crowd may block the development and use of tools that could enable next-stage transitions that engage broader publics.

Beyond this, we do not attempt to explain all possible forms of connective action. While our models can be applied to diverse network mobilizations, we refrain from superficial attempts to categorize everything in the rich spectrum of contention around us. Thus, we remain silent on what these models would reveal about al-Qaeda, neo-Nazis, abortion rights networks, or many other areas of political activism. Some of these networks are far less transparent than the ones we studied and may not be open to serious analysis short of undercover investigation. Others would require more ethnographic study.

The book has also shed light on the substantive outcomes. We have looked at various ways of organizing power in contentious action in different forms, in different political arenas, and in national and transnational networks. Throughout our analyses of economic justice and climate change politics, we have seen an impressive amount and variety of action being undertaken, often with fairly thin resources. These efforts are not always successful in terms of wholesale policy change or in relation to the magnitude of the problems. This said, we can point to various successful outcomes of the mid-range variety, such as the growth of fair trade consumerism, the adoption of financial transaction taxes among many EU states, and the persistence of supermajorities nearly everywhere (with the notable exception of the United States) calling for national and international action on climate change issues. We also note the value of participation as a democratic good in itself (Pateman 1970), something that is often missing in the common refrains of spectators on the sidelines who proclaim, "But they didn't (stop the war / win the decisive climate change policy / change the global economy)." The persistence of large-scale action over time in so many areas is all the more remarkable given the uphill battles on so many fronts against the opposition of powerful and resource-rich opponents such as businesses, trade regimes, and public officials and states that have come to represent those interests (Smith and Wiest 2012).

Moreover, beyond the somewhat daunting challenge of "Did they change the world?" there are other ways of thinking about connective action outcomes that deserve further analysis. While we cannot embark on new investigations at this point in the book, we end by observing that one example of this relates to the everyday politics of contention. It is possible that intense bursts of action across loosely organized networks can operate as seedbeds for ideas and for the growth of future iterations of emergent action. Given the capacity to organize with few resources and across otherwise disjointed populations, connective networks are relatively easily reformed and repurposed, at least compared with more formal movements. The flexibility of this recombinant digitally networked action (a socio-cultural rDNA) derives from the broadly inclusive action frames that motivate participation and from the available technologies through which network relations develop. Rather than dismiss these features or lump them together with other forms of collective action, it is important to note their distinctive qualities.

The importance of ideas and how they are refigured and turned into memes that travel over networks into diverse discourse spaces should not be underestimated as inspiration for everyday personal engagement on a large scale. For example, Smith and Wiest (2012: 178) observe that many globalization activists are content with the ambiguities of broad and easy-to-embrace framing such as "Another World Is Possible," the overarching theme of the World Social Forum, in that it permits flexible refocusing and multi-level activism. They also note the importance of such flexibility in mounting everyday challenges to dominant value systems: "The modern world system is not simply a structure for organizing economic life, but rather the material relations that undergird the system and shape the structures of knowledge production, discourses, and systems of meaning or culture. Thus, the identities, models of organization, symbols, and practices we take for granted need to be contested because they are both products of the particular world system that produced them and essential to its continued operation" (Smith and Wiest 2012: 179). For many who choose to participate in personalized ways, a key aspect of their activism is how various deconstructions of the world system fit into the individual life world (Giddens 1991). The openness of personal framing and the sharing of stories and experiences via networking technologies enables what della Porta and colleagues have described as the emergence of "flexible identities and multiple belongings" in contentious politics (della Porta 2005; della Porta, Massimiliano, and Mosca 2006).

If we think of how ideas and action repertoires have been dispersed throughout society by networks such as the *indignados* in Spain or Occupy in the United States and elsewhere, it is not entirely accurate to say that those networks have died. While some transition scenarios were closed off at critical moments, as described earlier, other sub-networks and ideas have been planted far and wide. For example, a search of online U.S. media (local and national news, blogs, and point-of-view sites) at the time of this writing, nearly a year after the emergence of Occupy Wall Street, revealed 170 items for the three-month period from August 7 to November 7, 2012.[10] While there were understandably far fewer of these than the thousands of items circulating in the media sphere as Occupy broke onto the scene, the continuing media activity reveals interesting patterns in the wake of Occupy in the United States.

Some of the higher-level online media decried the failure of Occupy to "occupy" the 2012 election and claimed that, as a result, the movement had disappeared. As *Huffington Post* commentator Phillip Martin put it, the movement lost its opportunity to transition to an electoral force. He quoted social

[10] Source: Silobreaker, U.S. 90-day search conducted November 7, 2012.

movement historian Cyrus Veeser as saying, "The Occupy movement has completely disappeared from political discourse" (Martin 2012). While that bold claim may be true if one measures political success in terms of mobilizing power in the electoral arena and becoming part of the elite conversation, it does not hold for the many other levels of society in which Occupy and its associated action frames continued to circulate. Toward the end of his article, Martin acknowledged, almost as an afterthought, that Occupy offshoots were engaging in numerous "low visibility fights against foreclosures in New York, transportation inequality in Boston, education reform in Detroit, and against the off-shoring of jobs in the Bain owned company Sensata Technologies in Freeport, Illinois" (Martin 2012).

What seems at play in such dismissive accounts is an implicit expectation about what a successful transition looks like: namely that crowds need to turn into movements in order to have an impact. To devalue the dozens and perhaps hundreds of local branch networks that continued to thrive after Occupy peaked is to overlook the infusion of everyday life with ideas that continue to engage popular thinking about questions of justice, equality, and social values. As one protester in Portland, Oregon, said during a march to commemorate the first anniversary of the Occupy Portland encampment: "Just because we're not camped out anymore doesn't mean we're gone" (Heartquist 2012).

Fragmenting Occupy networks inserted themselves into issue arenas at local levels in diverse and sometimes unexpected ways. These included the local initiatives around Occupy Our Homes that was noted as a dismissive afterthought in the earlier *Huffington Post* appraisal, in which protesters resisted foreclosures on behalf of distressed homeowners in Atlanta, Washington, D.C., Los Angeles, Minneapolis, and elsewhere and enabled many to keep their houses.[11] They included the winner of a national Christian campus speech contest who spoke on the legacy of social justice in the Bible in a speech entitled "The Real Occupy Movement: Understanding Capitalism in a Christian Context" (Weaver-Stoesz 2012). They also included the relief operation Occupy Sandy, which involved veteran and newcomer Occupiers in the rapid response distribution of food and supplies in the New York area in the aftermath of Hurricane Sandy in November 2012 (Feuer 2012).

Looking for such seeds of Occupy a year after its inception, activist journalist Amy Goodman conducted a 100-city bus tour to investigate these and other local initiatives. Noting how far Occupy had spread, she wrote: "I think that any Madison Avenue advertising executive would be drooling right now if credited with the most effective slogan in history 'We Are the 99 Percent.' That was a message that was understood across the country. The word occupy occupied the language" (Eastman 2012). As the long-standing mantra of the earlier global justice movement would suggest, think globally and act locally seems alive, and its renewal takes many forms at the micro-level, from helping

---

[11] occupyourhomes.org (accessed November 8, 2012).

families stave off foreclosure, to giving humanitarian relief in crisis, to writing letters to the editor of local papers decrying cuts to human services. These emergent actions suggest how political renewal happens through personal discourses traveling over networks, providing reminders to larger publics and those in power that ordinary people still have voices in the public sphere.

Bibliography

Ackerman, Spencer. 2011. "Egypt's Top Social Media Activist Finds New Foes in Tahrir Square." *Wired*, July 18. www.wired.com/dangerroom/2011/07/egypt-social-media-activist/. Accessed April 3, 2012.

Aday, Sean, Henry Farrell, Marc Lynch, John Sides, John Kelly, and Ethan Zuckerman. 2010. *Blogs and Bullets: New Media in Contentious Politics*. Washington, DC: United States Institute of Peace.

Agarwal, Sheetal, W. Lance Bennett, Courtney Johnson, and Shawn Walker. 2012. "Networked Organization in Occupy Protests: A Multi-Methods Approach to Big Twitter Data." Paper presented at the Oxford Internet Institute "Big Data" Conference, Oxford, September 20–21.

Aldhous, Peter. 2011. "Occupy vs. Tea Party: What Their Twitter Networks Reveal." *New Scientist*, November 17.

Anderson, Chris. 2006. *The Long Tail: Why the Future of Business Is Selling Less of More*. New York: Hyperion Books.

Anduiza, Eva, Camilo Cristancho, and Jose M. Sabucedo. Forthcoming. "Mobilization through Online Social Networks: The Political Protest of the Indignados in Spain." *Information, Communication & Society*.

Arceneaux, Noah, and Amy Schmitz Weiss. 2010. "Seems Stupid Until You Try It: Press Coverage of Twitter, 2006–9." *New Media and Society* 20:1–18.

Archbishop of Canterbury. 2011a. "Archbishop's Christmas Sermon – 'Don't Build Lives on Selfishness and Fear,'" December 25. www.archbishopofcanterbury.org/articles.php/2292/. Accessed December 29, 2011.

Archbishop of Canterbury. 2011b. "Time for Us to Challenge the Idols of High Finance," November 1. www.archbishopofcanterbury.org/articles.php/2236/time-for-us-to-challenge-the-idols-of-high-finance. Accessed December 29, 2011.

Arquilla, John, and David Ronfeldt. 2000. *Swarming and the Future of Conflict*. Santa Monica, CA: RAND Corporation. www.rand.org/pubs/documented_briefings/DB311. Accessed June 25, 2012.

Ashcraft, Karen, Timothy Kuhn, and François Cooren. 2009. "Constitutional Amendments: 'Materializing' Organizational Communication." *Academy of Management Annals* 3(1):1–64.

Askanius, Tina, and Nils Gustafsson. 2010. "Mainstreaming the Alternative: The Changing Media Practices of Protest Movements." *Interface: A Journal for and about Social Movements* 2:23–41.

Askanius, Tina, and Julie Uldam. 2011. "Using Online Social Media for Radical Politics: Climate Change Activism on YouTube." *International Journal of Electronic Governance* 4:69–82.

Associated Press. 2010. "Neda Video Wins Polk Award: Iran Protest Death Video First Anonymous Winner of Journalism Prize." *Huffington Post*, April 17. www.huffingtonpost.com/2010/02/16/neda-video-wins-polk-award_n_463378.html. Accessed August 28, 2012.

ATTAC. 2012. "Overview." www.attac.org/en/overview. Accessed November 7, 2012.

Banco, Erin. 2012. "Islamist Mohamed Morsi Wins Egyptian Election: Inside Tahrir Square." *Daily Beast*, June 25. www.thedailybeast.com/articles/2012/06/25/islamist-mohamed-morsi-wins-egyptian-election-inside-tahrir-square.html. Accessed November 6, 2012.

Barabási, Albert-László. 2009. "Scale-Free Networks: A Decade and Beyond." *Science* 325:412–413.

Barabási, Albert-László, and Reka Albert. 1999. "Emergence of Scale in Random Networks." *Science* 286:509–512.

Barabási, Albert-László, and Eric Bonabeau. 2003. "Scale-Free Networks." *Scientific American* 288(5):50–9.

Barber, Benjamin. 1984. *Strong Democracy: Participatory Politics for a New Age.* Berkeley: University of California Press.

Barnard, David. 2008. "NGO Leadership Challenges: Creating a Space for Reflection." *NGO Pulse*, July 30. www.ngopulse.org/article/ngo-leadership-challenges-creating-space-reflection. Accessed December 20, 2011.

Barzilai-Nahon, Karine. 2009. "Gatekeeping: A Critical Review." *Annual Review of Information Science and Technology* 43:433–478.

Bauman, Zygmunt. 2000. *Liquid Modernity.* Cambridge: Polity Press.

Baym, Geoffrey, and Chirag Shaw. 2011. "Circulating Struggle: The Online Flow of Environmental Advocacy Clips from *The Daily Show* and *The Colbert Report*." *Information, Communication & Society* 14(7):1017–1038.

BBC. 2012. "Financial Transaction Tax for 10 EU States," October 23. www.bbc.co.uk/news/business-20041588. Accessed October 25, 2012.

Beck, Ulrich, and Elisabeth Beck-Gernsheim. 2002. *Individualization: Institutionalized Individualism and Its Social and Political Consequences.* London: Sage.

Beissinger, Mark R. 2007. "Structure and Example in Modular Political Phenomena: The Diffusion of Bulldozer/Rose/Orange/Tulip Revolutions." *Perspectives on Politics* 5(2):259–276.

Benford, Robert D., and David A. Snow. 2000. "Framing Processes and Social Movements: An Overview and an Assessment." *Annual Review of Sociology* 26:611–639.

Benkler, Yochai. 2006. *The Wealth of Networks: How Social Production Transforms Markets and Freedom.* New Haven, CT: Yale University Press.

Benkler, Yochai. 2011. "Networks of Power, Degrees of Freedom." *International Journal of Communication* 5:721–755.

Bennett, W. Lance. 1998. "The Uncivic Culture: Communication, Identity, and the Rise of Lifestyle Politics." *P.S.: Political Science and Politics* 31:41–61.

Bennett, W. Lance. 2003. "Communicating Global Activism: Strengths and Vulnerabilities of Networked Politics." *Information, Communication & Society* 6:143–168.

Bennett, W. Lance. 2005. "Social Movements beyond Borders: Organization, Communication, and Political Capacity in Two Eras of Transnational Activism." In *Transnational Protest and Global Activism*, edited by Donatella della Porta and Sidney Tarrow, 203–226. Boulder, CO: Rowman & Littlefield.

Bennett, W. Lance. 2012. "Grounding the European Public Sphere: Looking Beyond the Mass Media to Digitally Mediated Issue Publics." Free University, Berlin Working Paper No. 43 (August) from the Research Group "The Transformative Power of Europe." www.polsoz.fu-berlin.de/en/v/transformeurope/news/allgemeines/KFG_Working_Paper_No_43.html. Accessed September 27, 2012.

Bennett. W. Lance, Christian Breunig, and Terri Givens. 2008. "Communication and Political Mobilization: Digital Media Use and Protest Organization Among Anti-Iraq War Demonstrators in the U.S." *Political Communication* 25:269–289.

Bennett, W. Lance, Kirsten Foot, and Mike Xenos. 2011. "Narratives and Network Organization: A Comparison of Fair Trade Systems in Two Nations." *Journal of Communication* 61:219–245.

Bennett, W. Lance, Terri E. Givens, and Christian Breunig. 2010. "Crossing Political Divides: Communication, Political Identification, and Protest Organization." In *The World Says No to War: Demonstrations Against the War on Iraq*, edited by Stefaan Walgrave and Dieter Rucht, 215–238. Minneapolis: University of Minnesota Press.

Bennett, W. Lance, and Taso Lagos. 2007. "Logo Logic: The Ups and Downs of Branded Political Communication." *Annals of the American Academy of Political and Social Science* 611(1):193–206.

Bennett, W. Lance, Sabine Lang, and Alexandra Segerberg. 2011. "Digital Media and the Organization of Transnational Advocacy: Legitimacy and Public Engagement in National and EU Issue Networks." Paper presented at the annual meeting of the International Studies Association, Montreal, March 16–19.

Bennett, W. Lance, Sabine Lang, and Alexandra Segerberg. Forthcoming. "European Issue Publics Online." In *European Public Spheres: Bringing Politics Back In*, edited by Thomas Risse. Cambridge: Cambridge University Press.

Bennett, W. Lance, Sabine Lang, Alexandra Segerberg, and Henrike Knappe. 2011. "Public Engagement vs. Institutional Influence Strategies: Comparing Trade and Environmental Advocacy Networks at the National and EU Levels in Germany and the UK." Paper presented at the 6th European Consortium for Political Research. University of Iceland, Reykjavik, August 25–27.

Bennett, W. Lance, and Alexandra Segerberg. 2011. "Digital Media and the Personalization of Collective Action: Social Technology and the Organization of Protests Against the Global Economic Crisis. *Information, Communication & Society* 14:770–799.

Bennett, W. Lance, Chris Wells, and Deen Freelon. 2011. "Communicating Civic Engagement: Contrasting Models of Citizenship in the Youth Web Sphere." *Journal of Communication* 61(5):835–856.

Berglund, Frode, Sören Holmberg, Hermann Schmitt, and Jacques Thomassen. 2006. "Party Identification and Party Choice." In *The European Voter*, edited by Jacques Thomassen, 105–123. Oxford: Oxford University Press.

Bimber, Bruce. 2003. *Information and American Democracy: Technology in the Evolution of Political Power*. Cambridge: Cambridge University Press.

Bimber, Bruce, and Richard Davis. 2003. *Campaigning Online: The Internet in U.S. Elections*. New York: Oxford University Press.

Bimber, Bruce, Andrew Flanagin, and Cynthia Stohl. 2005. "Reconceptualizing Collective Action in the Contemporary Media Environment." *Communication Theory* 15:389–413.

Bimber, Bruce, Andrew Flanagin, and Cynthia Stohl. 2012. *Collective Action in Organizations: Interaction and Engagement in an Era of Technological Change*. New York: Cambridge University Press.

Blaschke, Steffen, Dennis Schoeneborn, and David Seidl. 2012. "Organizations as Networks of Communication Episodes: Turning the Network Perspective Inside Out." *Organization Studies* 33(7):879–906.

Bonabeau, Eric, Marco Dorigo, and Guy Theraulaz. 1999. *Swarm Intelligence: From Natural to Artificial Systems*. New York: Oxford University Press.

Borning, Alan, Batya Friedman, Janet Davis, and Peyina Lin. 2005. "Informing Public Deliberation: Value Sensitive Design of Indicators for a Large-Scale Urban Simulation." *Proceedings of ECSCW 2005 European Conference on Computer-Supported Cooperative Work*, 449–468. Paris. vsdesign.org/publications/pdf/Borning_et_al_2005_paper23.pdf.

boyd, danah, and Nicole Ellison. 2007. "Social Network Sites: Definition, History, and Scholarship." *Journal of Computer-Mediated Communication* 13:210–230.

boyd, danah, Scott Golder, and Gilad Lotan. 2010. "Tweet, Tweet, Retweet: Conversational Aspects of Retweeting on Twitter." HICSS-43. IEEE, Kauai, HI, January 6.

boyd, danah, and Jeffrey Heer. 2006. "Profiles as Conversation: Networked Identity Performance on Friendster." In *Proceedings of Thirty-Ninth Hawai'i International Conference on System Sciences*, 59–69. Los Alamitos, CA: IEEE Press.

Boynton, G. R. 2010. "COP15-Voice." Paper presented at "Internet, Politics, Policy 2010: An Impact Assessment," Oxford Internet Institute, Oxford, September 16–17.

Braman, Sandra. 2002. "Posthuman Law: Information Policy and the Machinic World." *First Monday*. December 2. firstmonday.org/htbin/cgiwrap/bin/ojs/index.php/fm/article/view/1011/932. Accessed August 9, 2011.

Braman, Sandra. 2006. *Change of State: Information, Policy, and Power*. Cambridge, MA: MIT Press.

Brand, Karl-Werner. 2010. "German Environmentalism: Still Feeding on Its Romantic, Anti-Modern Heritage?" *Nature and Culture* 5(2):209–226.

Brand, Karl-Werner, and Dieter Rink. 2007. "Institutionalisierung statt Mobilisierung? Dilemmata der deutschen Umweltbewegung." *Politische Vierteljahresschrift* 39(September):499–517.

Bruns, Axel. 2012. "How Long Is a Tweet? Mapping Dynamic Conversation Networks on Twitter Using Gawk and Gephi." *Information, Communication & Society* 15(9):1323–1351.

Bruns, Axel, and Jean Burgess. 2011. "The Use of Twitter Hashtags in the Formation of Ad Hoc Publics." Paper presented at the 6th General Conference of the European Consortium for Political Research, Reykjavik, August 25–27.

Buchanan, Mark. 2002. *Nexus: Small Worlds and the Groundbreaking Science of Networks*. New York: Norton.

Buffet, Warren. 2011. "Stop Coddling the Super Rich." *New York Times*, August 15. www.nytimes.com/2011/08/15/opinion/stop-coddling-the-super-rich.html. Accessed February 24, 2013.

Bunz, Mercedes. 2010. "Anonymous Video of Neda Agan-Soltan's Death Wins Polk Award." *Guardian*, February 16. www.guardian.co.uk/media/pda/2010/feb/16/george-polk-awards. Accessed July 21, 2011.

Byrne, Janet (ed.). 2012. *The Occupy Handbook*. Boston: Back Bay.

Calderaro, Andrea. 2011. "New Political Struggles in the Network Society: The Case of Free and Open Source Software (FOSS) Movement." Paper presented at the 6th General Conference of the European Consortium for Political Research, Reykjavik, August 25–27.

Cammaerts, Bart. 2006. "The eConvention on the Future of Europe: Assessing the Participation of Civil Society and the Use of ICTs in European Decision-Making Processes." *Journal for European Integration* 28:225–245.

Cammaerts, Bart. 2012. "Protest Logics and the Mediation Opportunity Structure." *European Journal of Communication* 27(2):117–134.

Campbell, Emahunn Raheem Ali. 2011. "A Critique of the Occupy Movement by a Black Occupier." *Black Scholar* 41(4):42–51.

Carrol, William K., and R. S. Ratner. 1996. "Master Framing and Cross-Movement Networking in Contemporary Social Movements." *Sociological Quarterly* 37:601–625.

Cascio, Jamais. 2009. "The Dark Side of Twittering a Revolution." *Fast Company*. June 17. www.fastcompany.com/blog/jamais-cascio/open-future/twittering-revolution. Accessed November 2, 2010.

Castells, Manuel. 1996. *The Information Age: Economy, Society and Culture*. Malden, MA: Blackwell.

Castells, Manuel. 2000. *The Rise of the Network Society*. 2d ed. Oxford: Blackwell.

Castells, Manuel. 2009. *Communication Power*. Oxford: Oxford University Press.

Castells, Manuel. 2012. *Networks of Outrage and Hope: Social Movements in the Internet Age*. Cambridge: Polity Press.

Catholic Agency for Overseas Development. 2009. "Put People First." www.cafod.org.uk/resources/videogalleries/put-people-first. Accessed October 7, 2010.

Cha, Meeyoung, Hamed Haddadi, Fabricio Benevenuto, and Krishna P. Gummadi. 2010. "Measuring User Influence in Twitter: The Million Follower Fallacy." Proceedings of the Fourth International AAAI Conference on Weblogs and Social Influence, Association for the Advancement of Artificial Intelligence. www.aaai.org/ocs/index.php/ICWSM/ICWSM10/paper/view/1538/1826. Accessed October 21, 2012.

Chadwick, Andrew. 2007. "Digital Network Repertoires and Organizational Hybridity." *Political Communication* 24:283–301.

Chadwick, Andrew. 2013. *The Hybrid Media System: Politics and Power*. Oxford: Oxford University Press.

Chesters, Graeme, and Ian Welsh. 2006. *Complexity and Social Movements: Multitudes at the Edge of Chaos*. London: Routledge.

Chong, Dennis. 1991. *Collective Action and the Civil Rights Movement*. Chicago: University of Chicago Press.

Citizen Journalist. 2012. "Occupy National Gathering Draws Small Numbers; March to NYC Already in Trouble," July 6. citizenjournalistdotorg.wordpress.com/2012/07/06/occupy-national-gathering-draws-small-numbers-march-to-nyc-already-in-trouble/. Accessed November 11, 2012.

Climate Action Network-International. 2009. "CAN-International." www.climatenetwork.org/. Accessed December 12, 2009.

Climate Justice Action. 2009. "Climate Justice Action," November 19, 2009. web. archive.org/web/20091119160954/www.climate-justice-action.org/.

Climate Justice Now! 2009. "Climate Justice Now!" December 5, 2009. Accessed via the Internet Archive, March 8, 2012. web.archive.org/web/20091205172041/www. climate-justice-now.org/. Accessed via the Internet Archive, March 9, 2012.

Conover, Michael D., Bruno Gonçalves, Alessandro Flammini, and Filippo Menczer. 2012. "Partisan Asymmetries in Online Political Activity." *EPJ Data Science* 1:2–19.

Cooren, François. 2000. *The Organizing Property of Communication.* Amsterdam: John Benjamins.

Cooren, François. 2004. "Textual Agency: How Texts Do Things in Organizational Settings." *Organization* 11:373–393.

Cooren, François, Timothy Kuhn, Joep Cornelissen, and Timothy Clark. 2011. "Communication, Organizing and Organization: An Overview and Introduction to the Special Issue." *Organization Studies* 32(9):1149–1170.

Cowhey, Peter, and Milton Mueller. 2009. "Delegation, Networks and Internet Governance." In *Networked Politics: Agency, Power, and Governance*, edited by Miles Kahler, 173–193. Ithaca, NY: Cornell University Press.

Crawford, Christopher G. 2012. "Disobeying Power Laws: Perils for Theory and Method." *Journal of Organizational Design* 1(2):75–81.

Daily Show. 2009. "Tea Partiers Advise G20 Protesters," October 1. www.thedaily show.com/watch/thu-october-1-2009/tea-partiers-advise-g20-protesters. Accessed April 4, 2011.

Dalton, Russell J., and Martin P. Wattenberg. 2002. *Parties Without Partisans: Political Change in Advanced Industrial Democracies.* Oxford: Oxford University Press.

Dassonneville, Ruth, Marc Hooghe, and Bram Vanhoutte. 2012. "The Decline of Party Identification in Germany, 1992–2009: An Age, Period and Cohort Analysis of a Two Decade Panel Study in Eastern and Western Germany." Paper presented at the 70th Annual Conference of the Midwest Political Science Association, Chicago, April 12–15.

Dawkins, Richard. 1989. *The Selfish Gene.* Oxford: Oxford University Press.

Dean, Jodi. 2010. *Blog Theory: Feedback and Capture in the Circuits of Drive.* Cambridge: Polity Press.

DeLanda, Manuel. 2006. *A New Philosophy of Society: Assemblage Theory and Social Complexity.* London: Continuum.

della Porta, Donatella. 1988. "Recruitment Processes in Clandestine Political Organizations: Italian Leftwing Terrorism." In *From Structure to Action*, edited by Bert Klandermans, Hanspeter Kriesi, and Sidney Tarrow, 155–169. New York: JAI Press.

della Porta, Donatella. 2005. "Multiple Belongings, Flexible Identities and the Construction of 'Another Politics': Between the European Social Forum and the Local Social Fora." In *Transnational Protest and Global Activism*, edited by Donatella della Porta and Sidney Tarrow, 175–202. Boulder, CO: Rowman & Littlefield.

della Porta, Donatella, and Mario Diani. 2006. *Social Movements: An Introduction.* 2d ed. Malden, MA: Blackwell.

della Porta, Donatella, Andretta Massimiliano, and Lorenzo Mosca. 2006. *Globalization from Below: Transnational Activists and Protest Networks.* Minneapolis: University of Minnesota Press.

della Porta, Donatella, and Lorenzo Mosca. 2007. "In Movimento: 'Contamination' in Action and the Italian Global Justice Movement." *Global Networks: A Journal of Transnational Affairs* 7:1–27.

della Porta, Donatella, and Lorenzo Mosca. 2009. "Searching the Net." *Information, Communication & Society* 12:771–792.

Diani, Mario. 1995. *Green Networks: A Structural Analysis of the Italian Environmental Movement*. Edinburgh: Edinburgh University Press.

Diani, Mario. 2000. "Social Movement Networks: Virtual and Real." *Information Communication and Society* 3(3):386–401.

Diani, Mario. 2003. "Networks and Social Movements: A Research Programme." In *Social Movements and Networks: Relational Approaches to Collective Action*, edited by Mario Diani and Doug McAdam, 299–319. Oxford: Oxford University Press.

Diani, Mario. 2004. "Networks and Participation." In *The Blackwell Companion to Social Movements*, edited by David Snow, Sarah Anne Soule, and Hanspeter Kriesi, 339–359. Malden, MA: Blackwell.

Diani, Mario. Forthcoming. *The Cement of Civil Society: Civic Networks in Localities*. Cambridge: Cambridge University Press.

Diani, Mario, and Doug McAdam. 2003. *Social Movements and Networks: Relational Approaches to Collective Action*. Oxford: Oxford University Press.

Donath, Judith. 2007. "Signals in Social Supernets." *Journal of Computer-Mediated Communication* 13:231–251.

Druckman, James, and Kjersten Nelson. 2003. "Framing and Deliberation: How Citizens' Conversations Limit Elite Influence." *American Journal of Political Science* 47:729–745.

Earl, Jennifer, and Katrina Kimport. 2011. *Digitally Enabled Social Change: Activism in the Internet Age*. Cambridge, MA: MIT Press.

Eastman, Janet. 2012. "'I'm Fascinated by Those Who Stand Up Against Power': Journalist Amy Goodman Brings Observations about the State of America to Ashland Visit." *Mail Tribune*, October 27. www.mailtribune.com/apps/pbcs.dll/article?AID=/20121027/NEWS/210270309/-1/rss01. Accessed November 8, 2012.

Eaves, Elisabeth. 2009. "Information Is Overrated: Twitter's Not Gonna Change the World." *Forbes*, June 19.

Elliott, Larry. 2011. "G20: Bill Gates Adds His Weight to Calls for Robin Hood Tax." *Guardian*, November 3. robinhoodtax.org/latest/merkel-tells-uk-back-robin-hood-tax. Accessed December 26, 2011.

Elmer, Greg. 2006. "The Vertical (Layered) Net." In *Critical Cyberculture Studies: New Directions*, edited by David Silver and Adrienne Massaanari, 159–167. New York: New York University Press.

Engle, Sophie, and Sean Whalen. 2012. "Visualizing Distributed Memory Computation with Hive Plots." In *Proceedings of the Ninth International Symposium on Visualization for Cyber Security*, 56–63. New York: Association for Computing Machinery.

Entman, Robert M. 2004. *Projections of Power: Framing News, Public Opinion, and U.S. Foreign Policy*. Chicago: University of Chicago Press.

Esfandiari, Golnaz. 2010. "Misreading Tehran: The Twitter Devolution." *Foreign Policy*, June 7.

European Commission. 2000. "The Commission and Non-Governmental Organizations: Building a Stronger Partnership." Brussels.

Ewing, Jack. 2012. "Across the World, Leaders Brace for Discontent and Upheaval." *New York Times*, January 25. travel.nytimes.com/2012/01/26/world/europe/across-the-world-leaders-brace-for-discontent-and-upheaval.html?_r=0. Accessed February 27, 2013.

Fenton, Natalie, and Veronica Barassi. 2011. "Alternative Media and Social Networking Sites: The Politics of Individuation and Political Participation." *Communication
Review,* 14:179–196.

Feuer, Alan. 2012. "Occupy Sandy: A Movement Moves to Relief." *New York
Times,* November 9. www.nytimes.com/2012/11/11/nyregion/where-fema-fell-short-
occupy-sandy-was-there.html?pagewanted=all&_r=1&. Accessed March 2, 2013.

Fisher, Ali. 2010. "Bullets with Butterfly Wings: Tweets, Protest Networks, and the
Iranian Election." In *Media, Power, and Politics in the Digital Age: The 2009 Pres-
idential Election Uprising in Iran,* edited by Yahya Kamalipour, 105–118. Lanham,
MD: Rowman & Littlefield.

Fisher, Dana. 2010. "COP-15 in Copenhagen: How the Merging of Movements Left
Civil Society Out in the Cold." *Global Environmental Politics* 10:11–17.

Flanagin, Andrew J., Cynthia Stohl, and Bruce Bimber. 2006. "Modeling the Structure
of Collective Action." *Communication Monographs* 73:29–54.

Foot, Kirsten A., and Steven M. Schneider. 2006. *Web Campaigning.* Cambridge, MA:
MIT Press.

Freelon, Deen G., Travis Kriplean, Jonathan Morgan, W. Lance Bennett, and Alan
Borning. 2012. "Facilitating Diverse Political Engagement with the Living Voters
Guide." *Journal of Information Technology & Politics* 9(3):279–297.

Friedman, Batya, Peter H. Kahn, and Alan Borning. 2006. "Value Sensitive Design and
Information Systems." In *Human–Computer Interaction in Management Information
Systems: Foundations,* edited by P. Zhang and D. Galletta, 348–372. Armonk, NY:
Sharpe. vsdesign.org/publications/pdf/non-scan-vsd-and-information-systems.pdf.

Gamson, William. 2004. "Bystanders, Public Opinion, and the Media." In *The Blackwell Companion to Social Movements,* edited by David Snow, Sarah Anne Soule, and
Hanspeter Kriesi, 242–261. Malden, MA: Blackwell.

Gavin, Neil, and Tom Marshall. 2011. "Climate Change and International Protest
at Copenhagen: Reflections on British Television and the Web." In *Transnational
Protests and the Media,* edited by Simon Cottle and Libby Lester, 197–212. New
York: Peter Lang.

Gerbaudo, Paolo. 2012. *Tweets and the Streets: Social Media and Contemporary
Activism.* London: Pluto Press.

Gerhards, Jürgen, and Dieter Rucht. 1992. "Mesomobilization: Organizing and Framing in Two Protest Campaigns in West Germany." *American Journal of Sociology*
98:555–596.

Giddens, A. 1991. *Modernity and Self Identity: Self and Society in the Late Modern
Age.* Stanford, CA: Stanford University Press.

Giddens, Anthony. 1998. *The Third Way: The Renewal of Social Democracy.* Cambridge: Polity Press.

Gillan, Kevin, Jenny Pickerill, and Frank Webster. 2008. *Anti-War Activism: New
Media and Protest in the Information Age.* Basingstoke: Palgrave Macmillan.

Gillham, Patrick F., and Gary T. Marx. 2000. "Complexity and Irony in Policing and
Protesting: The World Trade Organization in Seattle." *Social Justice* 27(2):212–236.

Gitlin, Todd, 1980. *The Whole World Is Watching: Mass Media in the Making and the
Unmaking of the New Left.* Berkeley: University of California Press.

Gitlin, Todd. 2012. *Occupy Nation: The Roots, the Spirit, and the Promise of Occupy
Wall Street.* New York: HarperCollins.

Gladwell, Malcolm. 2010. "Small Change: Why the Revolution Will Not Be Tweeted."
New Yorker, October 4.

González-Bailón, Sandra, Javier Borge Holthoefer, Alejandro Rivero, and Yamir Moreno. 2011. "The Dynamics of Protest Recruitment Through an Online Network." *Scientific Reports* 1:197, December 15. DOI: 10.1038/srep00197. www.ncbi.nlm.nih .gov/pmc/articles/PMC3240992/pdf/srep00197.pdf. Accessed December 29, 2011.

Gould, Roger V. 1991. "Multiple Networks and Mobilization in the Paris Commune, 1871." *American Sociological Review* 56:716–729.

Gould, Roger V. 1993. "Collective Action and Network Structure." *American Sociological Review* 58:182–196.

Granovetter, Mark. 1973. "The Strength of Weak Ties." *American Journal of Sociology* 78:1360–1380.

Greenhouse, Steven, and Graham Bowley. 2011. "Tiny Tax on Financial Trades Gains Advocates." *New York Times*, December 6. www.nytimes.com/2011/12/07/ business/global/micro-tax-on-financial-trades-gains-advocates.html?_r=1&hp=& pagewanted=all. Accessed December 29, 2011.

G20 Meltdown. 2009. www.g-20meltdown.org/. Accessed April 1, 2009.

Habermas, Jürgen. 1989 [1962]. *The Structural Transformation of the Public Sphere: An Inquiry into a Category of Bourgeois Society*, translated by Thomas Burger with the assistance of Frederick Lawrence. Cambridge, MA: MIT Press.

Habermas, Jürgen. 1998. *The Inclusion of the Other: Studies in Political Theory*, edited by Ciaran Cronin and Pablo De Greiff. Cambridge, MA: MIT Press.

Hadden, Jennifer. 2012. "Divided Advocacy Networks: Conflict and Competition in Global Climate Change Politics." Paper presented at International Studies Association San Diego Convention, San Diego, CA, April 1–4.

Hall, Mike. 2011. "Harken/DeFazio Robin Hood Tax Would Generate $350 Billion." AFL-CIO Blog, November 8. blog.aflcio.org/2011/11/08/harkindefazio-robin-hood-tax-would-generate-350-billion/. Accessed April 4, 2012.

Hands, Joss. 2011. @ *Is for Activism: Dissent, Resistance and Rebellion in a Digital Culture*. London: Pluto Press.

Harrison, Laird, and Michelle Nichols. 2012. "Occupy 2012: Firmly Disorganized, Driven by Dreams." Reuters. www.reuters.com/article/2012/01/09/us-usa-occupy-idUSTRE80807P20120109. Accessed November 10, 2012.

Heaney, Michael, and Fabio Rojas. 2006. "The Place of Framing: Multiple Audiences and Antiwar Protests Near Fort Bragg." *Qualitative Sociology* 29:485–505.

Heartquist, Erica. 2012. "Occupy Portland Marks One Year Anniversary." KGW.com, October 6. Accessed November 8, 2012. http://www.kgw.com/news/local/Occupy-Portland-protesters–172985021.html. Accessed November 8, 2012.

Herwig, Jane, Max Kossatz, and Viola Mark. 2010. "#unibrennt mit internet. Beobachtungen zu einer sich ändernden Protestqualität." In *Uni Brennt. Grundsätzliches, Kritisches, Atmosphärisches*, edited by S. Heissenberger, V. Mark, S. Schramm, P. Sniesko, and R. Süss, 210–221. Vienna: Turia + Kant.

Hickel, Jason. 2012. "How Occupy Activists Fell in Love with Their Own Radical Horizontalism and Fetishized Physical Occupation." *LSE Review of Books*, July 28. blogs.lse.ac.uk/lsereviewofbooks/2012/07/28/book-review-occupy-scenes-from-occupied-america/. Accessed November 5, 2012.

Honeycutt, Courtenay, and Susan Herring. 2009. "Beyond Microblogging: Conversation and Collaboration via Twitter." *Proceedings of the 42nd Hawai'i International Conference on System Sciences*. Los Alamitos, CA: IEEE Press.

Howard, Philip N., and Muzammil M. Hussain. 2011. "The Role of Digital Media." *Journal of Democracy* 22:35–48.

Huberman, Bernardo, Daniel Romero, and Fang Wu. 2009. "Social Networks That Matter: Twitter Under the Microscope." *First Monday* 14:1–9.

Hunt, Scott, Benford, Robert D., and Snow, David A. 1994. "Identity Fields: Framing Processes and the Social Construction of Movement Identities." In *New Social Movements: From Ideology to Identity*, edited by Enrique Laraña, Hank Johnston, and Joseph R. Gusfield, 185–208. Philadelphia: Temple University Press.

Indymedia London. 2009. "Pics from Today's 'Put People First' March." london .indymedia.org/articles/913. Accessed October 7, 2010.

Inglehart, Ronald. 1997. *Modernization and Post-Modernization: Cultural, Economic and Political Change in 43 Societies*. Princeton, NJ: Princeton University Press.

Jarvis, Jeff. 2011. "#OccupyWallStreet & the Failure of Institutions." *Buzzmachine*, October 3. www.buzzmachine.com/2011/10/03/Occupywallstreet-the-failure-of-insti tutions/. Accessed March 7, 2012.

Jasper, James M. 1997. *The Art of Moral Protest: Culture, Biography, and Creativity in Social Movements*. Chicago: University of Chicago Press.

Jenkins, Henry. 2006. *Convergence Culture: Where Old and New Media Collide*. New York: New York University Press.

Jewitt, Rob. 2009. The Trouble with Twittering: Integrating Social Media into Mainstream News. *International Journal of Media and Cultural Politics* 5:231–238.

Joachim, Jutta. 2007. *Agenda Setting, the UN, and NGOs: Gender Violence and Reproductive Rights*. Washington, DC: Georgetown University Press.

Juris, Jeffrey S. 2008. *Networking Futures: The Movements Against Corporate Globalization*. Durham, NC: Duke University Press.

Juris, Jeffrey S. 2012. "Reflections on #occupyeverywhere: Social Media, Public Space, and Emerging Logics of Aggregation." *American Ethnologist* 39(2):259–279.

Kahler, Miles. 2009. "Networked Politics: Agency, Power, and Governance." In *Networked Politics: Agency, Power, and Governance*, edited by Miles Kahler, 1–20. Ithaca, NY: Cornell University Press.

Kavada, Anastasia. 2009. "Engagement, Bonding and Identity across Multiple Platforms: Avaaz on Facebook, YouTube and MySpace." Paper presented at the ECPR General Conference, Potsdam, September 10–12.

Kavada, Anastasia. 2010. "Activism Transforms Digital: The Social Movement Perspective." In *Digital Activism Decoded: The New Mechanics of Change*, edited by Mary Joyce, 101–118. New York and Amsterdam: International Debate Education Association.

Kavanaugh, Andrea, Debbie Denise Reese, John M. Carroll, and Mary Beth Rosson. 2005. "Weak Ties in Networked Communities." *Information Society* 21: 119–131.

Keck, Margaret E., and Kathryn Sikkink. 1998. *Activists Beyond Borders: Advocacy Networks in International Politics*. Ithaca, NY: Cornell University Press.

Kleefeld, Eric. 2011. "Poll: Public Turning Against Occupy Wall Street." *Talking Points Memo*, November 16. tpmdc.talkingpointsmemo.com/2011/11/poll-public-opinion-turning-against-occupy-wall-street.php. Accessed October 29, 2012.

Kleis Nielsen, Rasmus. 2011. "Mundane Internet Tools, Mobilizing Practices, and the Coproduction of Citizenship in Political Campaigns." *New Media & Society* 13:755–771.

Klimaforum. 2009. www.old09klimaforum.org. Accessed March 8, 2012.

Kriplean, Travis, Jonathan Morgan, Deen Freelon, Alan Borning, and Lance Bennett. 2012. "Supporting Reflective Public Thought with ConsiderIt." In *Proceedings of the*

ACM 2012 Conference on Computer Supported Cooperative Work, 265–274. New York: Association for Computing Machinery.

Krueger, Alan B. 2012. "The Rise and Consequences of Inequality in the United States," January 12. www.whitehouse.gov/sites/default/files/krueger_cap_speech_final_remarks.pdf. Accessed January 18, 2012.

Krzywinski, Martin, Inanc Birol, Steven J. M. Jones, and Marco A. Marra. 2011. "Hive Plots – Rational Approach to Visualizing Networks." *Briefings in Bioinformatics 2011*. DOI: 10.1093/bib/bbr069.

Kwak, Haewoon, Changhyun Lee, Hosung Park, and Sue Moon. 2010. "Which Is Twitter, a Social Network or a New Media?" Paper presented at the World Wide Web Conference, Raleigh, North Carolina, April 26–30. product.ubion.co.kr/upload20120220142222731/ccres00056/db/_2250_1/embedded/2010-www-twitter.pdf.

Labor Union Report. 2011. "#Occupy Setup: Dems Introduce 'Steal from the Rich, Give to the Poor' Tax Act." *RedState*, November 4. www.redstate.com/laborunionreport/2011/11/04/occupysetup-dems-introduce-steal-from-the-rich-give-to-the-poor-tax-act/. Accessed December 30, 2011.

Lang, Amy Schrager, and Lang/Levitsky, Daniel (eds.). 2012. *Dreaming in Public: Building the Occupy Movement*. Oxford: New Internationalist.

Lang, Sabine. 2009. "Assessing Advocacy: Transnational Women's Networks and Gender Mainstreaming in the European Union." *Social Politics* 16:327–357.

Lang, Sabine. 2013. *NGOs, Civil Society, and the Public Sphere*. New York: Cambridge University Press.

Langlois, Ganaele, Greg Elmer, Fenwick McKelvey, and Zachary Devereaux. 2009. "Networked Publics: The Double Articulation of Code and Politics on Facebook." *Canadian Journal of Communication* 34:415–434.

Latour, Bruno. 2005. *Reassembling the Social: An Introduction to Actor-Network-Theory*. Oxford: Oxford University Press.

Lee, Dave. 2012. "SOPA and PIPA Protests Not Over, Says Wikipedia." BBC, January 19. www.bbc.co.uk/news/technology-16628143. Accessed January 22, 2012.

Lessig, Lawrence. 2006. *Code 2.0*. New York: Basic Books.

Lievrouw, Leah A. 2011. *Alternative and Activist New Media*. Cambridge: Polity Press.

Lindgren, Simon, and Ragnar Lundström. 2011. "Pirate Culture and Hacktivist Mobilization: The Cultural and Social Protocols of #WikiLeaks on Twitter." *New Media & Society* 13:999–1018.

Link TV. 2011. "Tahrir Square's Popular Slogans." *Link TV*, February 10. www.linktv.org/video/6364/tahrir-squares-popular-slogans. Accessed July 21, 2011.

Livingston, Steven, and Gregory Asmolov. 2010. "Networks and the Future of Foreign Affairs Reporting." *Journalism Studies* 11:745–760.

Lupia, Arthur, and Gisela Sin. 2003. "Which Public Goods Are Endangered? How Evolving Communication Technologies Affect 'the Logic of Collective Action.'" *Public Choice* 117:315–331.

Markham, William T. 2008. *Environmental Organizations in Modern Germany: Hardy Survivors in the Twentieth Century and Beyond*. New York: Berghahn Books.

Marsh, David, and R. A. W. Rhodes (eds.). 1992. *Policy Networks in British Government*. Oxford: Oxford University Press.

Martin, Phillip. 2012. "Occupy's Missed Opportunity to Impact Election 2012." *Huffington Post*, November 6. www.huffingtonpost.com/phillip-martin/occupys-missed-opportunit_b_2083095.html?utm_hp_ref=politics. Accessed November 8, 2012.

Mattoni, Alice. 2012. *Media Practices and Protest Politics: How Precarious Workers Mobilise*. Aldershot: Ashgate.

Mattoni, Alice, Andrejs Berdnikovs, Michela Ardizzoni, and Laurence Cox. 2010. "Voices of Dissent: Activists' Engagements in the Creation of Alternative, Autonomous, Radical and Independent Media." *Interface: A Journal for and about Social Movements* 2(2):1–22.

McAdam, Doug. 1986. "Recruitment to High Risk Activism: The Case of Freedom Summer." *American Journal of Sociology* 92:64–90.

McAdam, Doug. 1988a. "Micromobilisation Contexts and the Recruitment to Activism." In *From Structure to Action: Comparing Social Movement Research across Cultures*, edited by Bert Klandermans, Hanspeter Kriesi, and Sidney G. Tarrow, 125–154. Greenwich, CT: JAI Press.

McAdam, Doug. 1988b. *Freedom Summer*. New York: Oxford University Press.

McAdam, Doug, John D. McCarthy, and Mayer N. Zald. 1996. "Introduction: Opportunities, Mobilizing Structures, and Framing Processes – Toward a Synthetic, Comparative Perspective on Social Movements." In *Comparative Perspectives on Social Movements: Political Opportunities, Mobilizing Structures, and Cultural Framings*, edited by Doug McAdam, John D. McCarthy, and Mayer N. Zald, 1–40. New York: Cambridge University Press.

McAdam, Doug, and Ronelle Paulsen. 1993. "Specifying the Relationship between Social Ties and Activism." *American Journal of Sociology* 99:640–667.

McAdam, Doug, Sidney G. Tarrow, and Charles Tilly. 2001. *Dynamics of Contention*. New York: Cambridge University Press.

McCarthy, John D., and Mayer N. Zald. 1973. *The Trend of Social Movements in America: Professionalization and Resource Mobilization*. Morristown, NJ: General Learning Press.

McCarthy, John D., and Mayer N. Zald. 1977. "Resource Mobilization and Social Movements: A Partial Theory." *American Journal of Sociology* 82:1212–1241.

McDonald, Kevin. 2002. "From Solidarity to Fluidarity: Social Movements Beyond 'Collective Identity' – The Case of Globalization Conflicts." *Social Movement Studies* 1(2):109–128.

Mercea, Dan, Paul Nixon, and Andreas Funk. Forthcoming. "Unaffiliated Socialization and Social Media Recruitment: Reflections from Occupy the Netherlands." In *Views from the Cloud: Politics, Citizens and the Internet in Comparative Perspective*, edited by Paul Nixon, Rajash Rawal, and Dan Mercea. London: Routledge.

Melucci, Alberto 1985. "The Symbolic Challenge of Contemporary Movements." *Social Research* 52:789–816.

Melucci, Alberto. 1989. *Nomads of the Present: Social Movements and Individual Needs in Contemporary Society*. London: Radius.

Melucci, Alberto. 1996. *Challenging Codes: Collective Action in the Information Age*. Cambridge: Cambridge University Press.

Micheletti, Michele. 2003. *Political Virtue and Shopping*. New York: Palgrave.

Milgram, Stanley. 1967. "The Small World Problem." *Psychology Today* 1:60–67.

Mische, Ann. 2003. "Cross-Talk in Movements: Reconstructing the Culture-Network Link." In *Social Movements and Networks: Relational Approaches to Collective Action*, edited by Mario Diani and Doug McAdam, 258–280. New York: Oxford University Press.

Mische, Ann. 2008. *Partisan Publics: Communication and Contention Across Brazilian Youth Activist Networks*. Princeton, NJ: Princeton University Press.

Monge, Peter, and Janet Fulk. 1999. "Communication Technology for Global Network Organizations." In *Shaping Organization Form: Communication, Connection, and Community*, edited by Gerardine Desanctis and Janet Fulk, 71–100. Thousand Oaks, CA: Sage.

Monge, Peter R., and Noshir Contractor. 2003. *Theories of Communication Networks*. New York: Oxford University Press.

Morin, Richard. 2012. "Rising Share of Americans See Conflict Between Rich and Poor." Pew Research Center, January 11. www.pewsocialtrends.org/2012/01/11/rising-share-of-americans-see-conflict-between-rich-and-poor/. Accessed January 18, 2012.

Morozov, Evgeny. 2009a."Moldova's Twitter Revolution." *Foreign Policy*, April 7. neteffect.foreignpolicy.com/posts/2009/04/07/moldovas_twitter_revolution. Accessed November 1, 2010.

Morozov, Evgeny. 2009b. "Iran: Downside to the "Twitter Revolution." *Dissent*, Fall.

Morozov, Evgeny. 2011. *The Net Delusion: How Not to Liberate the World*. London: Allen Lane.

Mueller, Milton L. 2010. *Networks and States: The Global Politics of Internet Governance*. Cambridge, MA: MIT Press.

Neff, Gina, and David Stark. 2003. "Permanently Beta: Responsive Organization in the Internet Era." In *The Internet and American Life*, edited by Philip Howard and Steve Jones, 173–188. Thousand Oaks, CA: Sage.

Nelson, Jane. 2007. "The Operation of Non-Governmental Organizations (NGOs) in a World of Corporate and Other Codes of Conduct." Corporate Social Responsibility Working Paper No. 34 (March). Kennedy School of Government, Harvard University. www.hks.harvard.edu/m-rcbg/CSRI/publications/workingpaper_34_nelson.pdf.

Occupy Wall Street Activists. 2012. *Occupy Wall Street Revolution Handbook: The Unauthorized Collector's Edition*. Fix Bay Inc.

Olson, Mancur. 1965. *The Logic of Collective Action: Public Goods and the Theory of Groups*. Cambridge, MA: Harvard University Press.

Ostrom, Elinor. 1990. *Governing the Commons: The Evolution of Institutions for Collective Action*. Cambridge: Cambridge University Press.

Palfrey, John, Bruce Etling, and Robert Farris. 2009. "Reading Twitter in Tehran? Why the Real Revolution Is on the Streets – and Offline." *Washington Post*, June 21.

Parikka, Jussi. 2010. "Malcolm Gladwell and the (End) for Something That Never Started?" *Network Politics*, March 10. www.networkpolitics.org/blogs/jussiparikka/03/october/2010/malcolm-gladwell-and-end-something-never-started-network-politics. Accessed Oct 20 2010.

Paris Declaration (2009). www.indymedia.ie/article/90666. Accessed May 10, 2010.

Pateman, Carole. 1970. *Participation and Democratic Theory*. Cambridge: Cambridge University Press.

Patomäki, Heikki. 2012. "Tobin Tax." In *Wiley-Blackwell Encyclopedia of Globalization*, Volume 4, edited by George Ritzer. Chichester: Wiley-Blackwell. DOI: 10.1002/9780470670590.wbeog560.

Peretti, Jonah. 2002. "Culture Jamming, Memes, Social Networks, and the Emerging Media Ecology: The 'Nike Sweatshop Email' as Object to Think With." Center for Communication and Civic Engagement. depts.washington.edu/ccce/polcommcampaigns/peretti.html. Accessed July 7, 2011.

Pfetsch, Barbara, and Silke Adam. 2011. "Media Agenda Building in Online and Offline Media: Comparing Issues and Countries." Paper presented at the 6th Annual

Conference of the European Consortium of Political Research, University of Iceland, Reykjavik, August 25–27.

Pleyers, Geoffrey. 2010. *Alter-Globalization: Becoming Actors in the Global Age.* Cambridge: Polity Press.

Polletta, Francesca. 1998. "'It Was Like a Fever ...' Narrative and Identity in Social Protest." *Social Problems* 45:137–159.

Polletta, Francesca. 2002. *Freedom Is an Endless Meeting: Democracy in American Social Movements.* Chicago: University of Chicago Press.

Powell, Walter. 1990. "Neither Market nor Hierarchy: Network Forms of Organization." In *Research in Organizational Behavior*, Volume 12, edited by B. Staw and L. L. Cummings, 295–336. Greenwich, CT: JAI Press.

Putnam, Linda, and Anne Nicotera (eds.). 2009. *Building Theories of Organization: The Constitutive Role of Communication.* New York: Routledge.

Putnam, Robert. 2000. *Bowling Alone: The Collapse and Revival of American Community.* New York: Simon & Schuster.

Put People First. 2009. www.putpeoplefirst.org.uk/. Accessed March 28.

Reitan, Ruth. 2010. "Coordinated Power in Contemporary Leftist Activism." In *Power and Transnational Activism*, edited by Thomas Olesen, 51–71. London: Routledge.

Rheingold, Howard. 2002. *Smart Mobs: The Next Social Revolution.* Cambridge, MA: Perseus.

Risse, Thomas. 2010. *A Community of Europeans? Transnational Identities and Public Spheres.* Ithaca, NY: Cornell University Press.

Robinson, Andrew, and Simon Tormey. 2005. "Horizontals, Verticals and the Conflicting Logics of Transformative Politics." In *Confronting Globalization*, edited by Patrick Hayden and Chamsey el-Ojeili, 208–226. Palgrave: London.

Rogers, Richard. 2004. *Information Politics on the Web.* Cambridge, MA: MIT Press.

Roose, Jochen. 2003. "Umweltorganisationen zwischen Mitgliedschaftslogik und Einflusslogik in der europäischen Politik" [Environmental organizations between membership logic and influence logic in European policy]. In *Bürgerschaft, Öffentlichkeit und Demokratie in Europa*, edited by Ansgar Klein, 141–158. Opladen: Leske + Budrich.

Rootes, Christopher. 2012. "New Issues, New Forms of Action? Climate Change and Environmental Activism in Britain." In *New Participatory Dimensions in Civil Society: Professionalization and Individualized Collective Action*, edited by Jan W. van Deth and William Maloney, 46–68. London: ecpr/Routledge.

Rootes, Christopher, and Clare Saunders. 2007. "Demonstrations of Democracy: The Make Poverty History and Stop Climate Chaos Marches." Paper presented at the European Consortium for Political Research Conference, Helsinki, May 7–12. kar.kent.ac.uk/14955/1/Rootes.pdf.

Routledge, Paul, and Andrew Cumbers. 2009. *Global Justice Networks: Geographies of Transnational Solidarity.* Manchester: Manchester University Press.

rtve. 2011. "Más de Seis Millones de Españoles Han Participado en el Movimiento 15M," August 6. www.rtve.es/noticias/20110806/mas-seis-millones-espanoles-han-participado-movimiento-15m/452598.shtml. Accessed September 8, 2012.

Rucht, Dieter, and Jochen Roose 2003. "Germany." In *Environmental Protest in Western Europe*, edited by Christopher Rootes, 80–108. Oxford: Oxford University Press.

Salamon, Lester M. 1994. "The Rise of the Nonprofit Sector." *Foreign Affairs*, July/August. www.foreignaffairs.com/articles/50105/lester-m-salamon/the-rise-of-the-non profit-sector. Accessed December 20, 2011.

Schwartz, Mattathias. 2011. "Pre-Occupied: The Origins and Future of Occupy Wall Street," *New Yorker*, November 28.

Scott, James C. 1985. *Weapons of the Weak: Everyday Forms of Peasant Resistance.* New Haven, CT: Yale University Press.

Segerberg, Alexandra. 2010. "Swarming: Imagining Creative Political Participation." In *Creative Participation: Responsibility-Taking in the Political World*, edited by Michele Micheletti and Andrew McFarland, 34–49. Boulder, CO: Paradigm.

Segerberg, Alexandra, and W. Lance Bennett. 2011. "Social Media and the Organization of Collective Action: Using Twitter to Explore the Ecologies of Two Climate Change Protests." *Communication Review* 14:197–215.

Sharlet, Jeff. 2011. "Inside Occupy Wall Street." *Rolling Stone*, November 10. www.rollingstone.com/politics/news/occupy-wall-street-welcome-to-the-occupation-20111110. Accessed October 29, 2012.

Shifman, Limor. Forthcoming. "Memes in a Digital World: Reconciling with a Conceptual Troublemaker." *Journal of Computer Mediated Communication*.

Shirky, Clay. 2003. "Power Laws, Weblogs, and Inequality." *Clay Shirky's Writings About the Internet*, February 10. www.shirky.com/writings/powerlaw_weblog.html. Accessed January 21, 2012.

Shirky, Clay. 2011. "The Political Power of Social Media: Technology, the Public Sphere, and Political Change." *Foreign Affairs*, January/February. www.foreignaffairs.com/articles/67038/clay-shirky/the-political-power-of-social-media. Accessed February 22, 2013.

Sibun, Jonathan. 2011. "Oxfam's Dame Barbara Stocking: Challenges to Being Humankind in a Hungry World." *Telegraph*, December 20. www.telegraph.co.uk/finance/financetopics/profiles/8026205/Oxfams-Dame-Barbara-Stocking-Challenges-to-being-humankind-in-a-hungry-world.html. Accessed December 20, 2011.

Sikkink, Kathryn. 2009. "The Power of Networks in International Politics." In *Networked Politics: Agency, Power, and Governance*, edited by Miles Kahler, 228–247. Ithaca, NY: Cornell University Press.

60 *Minutes*. 2011. "Extra: Revolution 2.0," February 14. www.cbsnews.com/video/watch/?id=7349173n. Accessed August 5, 2011.

Small, Tamara. 2011. "What the Hashtag? A Content Analysis of Canadian Politics on Twitter." *Information, Communication & Society* 14:872–895.

Smith, Jackie, and Dawn Wiest. 2012. *Social Movements in the World-System: The Politics of Crisis and Transformation.* New York: Russell Sage.

Snow, David A., and Robert D. Benford. 1988. "Ideology, Frame Resonance, and Participant Mobilization." *International Social Movement Research* 1:197–217.

Snow David A., and Robert D. Benford. 1992. "Master Frames and Cycles of Protest." In *Frontiers in Social Movement Theory*, edited by Aldon D. Morris and Carol Mueller, 133–155. New Haven, CT: Yale University Press.

Snow David A., Burke Rochford, Jr., Steven K. Worden, and Robert D. Benford. 1986. "Frame Alignment Processes, Micromobilization, and Movement Participation." *American Sociological Review* 51:464–481.

Snow, David A., Louis A. Zurcher, and Sheldon Ekland-Olson. 1980. "Social Networks and Social Movements: A Microstructural Approach to Differential Recruitment." *American Sociological Review* 45:787–801.

St. John, Graham. 2012. "Protestival: Global Days of Action and Carnivalized Politics of the Present." *Social Movement Studies: Journal of Social, Cultural and Political Protest* 7:167–190.

Starbird, Kate, Grace Muzny, and Leysia Palen. 2012. "Learning from the Crowd: Collaborative Filtering Techniques for Identifying on-the-Ground Twitterers During Mass Disruptions." *Proceedings of the 9th Annual Conference on Information Systems for Crisis Response and Management (ISCRAM 2012)*, April, Vancouver.

Stein, Laura. 2009. "Social Movement Web Use in Theory and Practice: A Content Analysis of US Movement Websites." *New Media & Society* 11:749–771.

Stop Climate Chaos. 2009a. "The Wave." www.stopclimatechaos.org/the-wave. Accessed July 9, 2011.

Stop Climate Chaos Coalition. 2009b. "Twitterstorm." www.stopclimatechaos.org/twitterstorm/. Accessed November 15, 2010.

Stumpf, Michael P. H., and Mason A. Porter. 2012. "Critical Truths About Power Laws." *Science* 335(6069):665–666.

Sullivan, Andrew. 2009. "The Revolution Will Be Twittered." *Atlantic*, June 13.

Tarrow, Sidney. 2001. "Contentious Politics in a Composite Polity." In *Contentious Europeans: Protest and Politics in an Emerging Polity*, edited by Doug Imig and Sidney Tarrow, 233–252. Lanham, MD: Rowman & Littlefield.

Tarrow, Sidney. 2011. *Power in Movement: Social Movements in Contentious Politics.* 3d ed. New York: Cambridge University Press.

Taylor, Astra, and Keith Gessen (eds.). 2011. *Occupy! Scenes from an Occupied America.* London: Verso.

Taylor, James, and Elizabeth Van Every. 2000. *The Emergent Organization: Communication as Its Site and Surface.* Mahwah, NJ: Erlbaum.

Teixeira, Ruy. 2012. "Public Opinion Snapshot: Americans Believe Our Economic System Favors the Wealthy." Center for American Progress, January 23. www.americanprogress.org/issues/public-opinion/news/2012/01/23/10918/public-opinion-snapshot-americans-believe-our-economic-system-favors-the-wealthy/. Accessed October 29, 2012.

Theocharis, Yannis. 2012. "The Wealth of (Occupation) Networks? Communication Patterns and Information Distribution in a Twitter Protest Network." *Journal of Information Technology & Politics*; www.tandfonline.com/doi/abs/10.1080/19331681.2012.701106. Accessed June 29, 2012.

Thorson, Kjerstin, Kevin Driscoll, Brian Ekdale, Stephanie Edgerly, Liana Gamber Thompson, Andrew Schrock, Lana Swartz, Emily Vraga, and Chris Wells. 2013. "YouTube, Twitter and the Occupy Movement: Connecting Content and Circulation Practices." *Information, Communication & Society.* DOI: 10.1080/1369118X.2012.756051.

Tilly, Charles. 1978. *From Mobilization to Revolution.* Reading, MA: Addison-Wesley.

Tilly, Charles. 2004. *Social Movements, 1768–2004.* Boulder, CO: Paradigm.

Tilly, Charles. 2006. "WUNC." In *Crowds*, edited by Jeffrey T. Schnapp and Matthew Tiews, 289–306. Stanford, CA: Stanford University Press.

Tilly, Charles, and Sidney Tarrow. 2007. *Contentious Politics.* Boulder, CO: Paradigm.

Touraine, Alain. 2000. *Can We Live Together? Equality and Difference*, translated by David Macey. Stanford, CA: Stanford University Press.

Turner, Fred. 2006. *From Counterculture to Cyberculture: Stewart Brand, the Whole Earth Network, and the Rise of Digital Utopianism.* Chicago: University of Chicago Press.

Twirus UK. 2009. "Twitter Trending Topics in Any Language." uk.twirus.com. Accessed December 5, 2009.

Van Deth, Jan. 2012. "New Modes of Participation and Norms of Citizenship." In *New Participatory Dimensions in Civil Society: Professionalization and Individualized Collective Action*, edited by Jan W. van Deth and William Maloney, 115–38. London: Routledge.

van Dyke, Nella, and Holly McCammon (eds). 2010. *Strategic Alliances: Coalition Building and Social Movements.* Minneapolis: University of Minnesota Press.

Vicari, Stefania. 2012. "Twitter and Public Reasoning around Social Contention: The Case of #15ott in Italy." In *From Social to Political: New Forms of Mobilization and Democratization*, edited by Benjamin Tejerina and Ignacia Perugorría, 281–296. Bilbao: Servicio Editorial de la Universidad del Pais Vasco. hdl.handle.net/2381/10265.

Vinocur, Nick, and Noah Barkin. 2009. "G20 Marches Begin Week of Protests in Europe." Reuters, March 28. www.reuters.com/article/2009/03/28/us-g20-britain-march-idUSTRE52R0TP20090328. Accessed July 9, 2011.

Von Reiermann, Christian, and Michaela Schiessl. 2001. "Die missbrauchen meinen Namen." *Der Spiegel* 36 (September 3). www.spiegel.de/spiegel/print/d-20017795.html. Accessed March 9, 2012.

Wahlström, Mattias, Magnus Wennerhag, and Christopher Rootes. Forthcoming. "Framing 'The Climate Issue': Patterns of Participation and Prognostic Frames among Climate Summit Protesters." *Global Environmental Politics.*

Walgrave, Stefaan, W. Lance Bennett, Jeroen Van Laer, and Christian Breunig. 2011. "Multiple Engagements and Network Bridging in Contentious Politics: Digital Media Use of Protest Participants." *Communication* 16(3):325–349.

Ward, Mark. 2009. "Twitter on the Front Line." BBC, April 2. news.bbc.co.uk/2/hi/technology/7979378.stm. Accessed February 22, 2013.

Washington Post. 2011. "Full Text of President Obama's Economic Speech in Osawatomie Kansas," December 6. www.washingtonpost.com/politics/president-obamas-economic-speech-in-osawatomie-kans/2011/12/06/gIQAVhe6ZO_story.html. Accessed November 10, 2012.

Watts, Duncan J. 2003. *Six Degrees: The Science of a Connected Age.* New York: Norton.

Watts, Duncan J., and Steven H. Strogatz. 1998. "Collective Dynamics of 'Small World' Networks." *Nature* 393:440–442.

Weaver-Stoesz, Marlys. 2012. "Goshen College Student Wins Speech Contest." *Elkhart Truth*, October 30. www.etruth.com/article/20121030/NEWS01/710309985. Accessed November 8, 2012.

Weinstein, Adam. 2011. "'We Are the 99%' Creators Revealed." *Mother Jones*, October 7. www.motherjones.com/politics/2011/10/we-are-the-99-percent-creators. Accessed October 29, 2012.

Weller, Ben. 2010. "G20 Protests in Seoul." *Demotix*, November 11, 2010. www.demotix.com/photo/504262/g20-protests-seoul. Accessed July 9, 2011.

What the Hashtag?! 2010. "Now Trending." Accessed October 27, 2010; searched for #cop15, #cop16. Wthashtag.com.

Wikipedia. 2009. "2009 G20 London Summit Protests." en.wikipedia.org/wiki/2009_
    G-20_London_summit_protests. Accessed July 26, 2009.
Yanacopulos, Helen. 2009. "Cutting the Diamond: Networking Economic Justice." In
    Networked Politics: Agency, Power, and Governance, edited by Miles Kahler, 67–78.
    Ithaca, NY: Cornell University Press.
Youmans, William Lafi, and Jillian C. York. 2012. "Social Media and the Activist
    Toolkit: User Agreements, Corporate Interests, and the Information Infrastructure of
    Modern Social Movements." *Journal of Communication* 62:315–329.

Index

actor-network theory, 42–43
Adbusters, 7, 180
affordances, 9, 68
agenda strength, 61–62, 74–75
  G20 Meltdown and, 74–75
  Put People First (PPF) and, 74–75
Anderson, Chris, 154
Arab Spring, 41–42

Battle of Seattle, 4, 29–30
Benkler, Yochai, 34
bit.ly, 91
branding, organizational hybridity and, 51

clicktivism, 14, 40, 53, 114
Climate Action Network-International (CAN), 99
Climate Camp encampment, 63, 70, 99
climate change, protests about, 98–101. *See also* environment, globalization and
Climate Justice Action (CJA), 99
Climate Justice Now! (CJN), 99
Coldplay (rock band), 11
co-link analysis, 61–62, 77–82, 131–36. *See also* hyperlink analysis
collective action, 3
  definition of, 31–33
  logic of, 27–28, 196
collective action frames, 6, 39–40
  analysis of, 32–33
collective action networks
  as contentious action network type, 11, 12–13, 46*f*
  digital media in, 33, 41–42
  organizational processes and, 31

  organizationally brokered, 12–13, 46
  sustainable and effective, 33
  typology of, 45–46
communication
  in contentious action, 8–10
  organization and, 198
  as organization, 8–9, 10, 198
  personalized, 16
communication technologies. *See* information and communication technologies
connective action, 2–3, 5, 16, 31
  crowd-enabled, 13, 46–48
  definition of, 33–36
  global crises and, 4–5
  logic of, 10, 28, 33–36
  organizationally enabled, 13, 48
connective action networks, 9–10, 14, 16, 32, 36, 42, 52–53, 61–62, 99, 114, 148–56. *See also* crowd-enabled networks; organizationally enabled networks
  adaptation, 45, 49
  conflicts and, 17
  digital mechanisms in, 9, 43, 45, 67–72, 89–90, 136–37
  digital media in, 41–42
  key questions about, 15
  layers of technologies in, 41–42
  in London and Copenhagen, 101
  networking mechanisms in, 43–44
  personal action frames and, 36–38, 41–42
  political capacity and, 3, 17, 53, 58, 61, 87, 121, 156
  political context and, 116–17, 121–22, 144–45
  power and, 17, 36

235

connective action networks (*cont.*)
  scaling up of, 16, 36, 57
  sustainability and, 16, 17, 53, 57, 59, 114
  typology of, 45–46
ConsiderIt platform, 206, 208
contentious action networks
  digital media in, 40–42
  layering and overlap of, 48
  typology of, 10–14, 45–46
contentious politics
  analytical fallacies about, 93
  ideal organization of, 209–10
  models of action in, 10–14
  personalization in, 5–8, 55–57, 197
  role of communication in, 8–10, 31–33
  surge of interest in networks and, 44
COP15. *See* UN Climate Conference,
  Copenhagen, 2009 (COP15)
core activists, 204. *See* protest organizers
crowd-enabled connective action, 13, 46–48,
  198
crowd-enabled network organizations, 12, 89
crowd-enabled networks, 46–48, 87, 89–90.
  See also connective action networks
  as contentious action network type, 12, 13,
  46*f*, 46–48
  personal action frames in, 38
  power signatures in, 160–64
  role of conventional organizations in, 45
cutting the diamond, 125–26, 156, 202. *See
  also* organizationally enabled networks
  fair trade and, 126

December 12, 2009, climate change protests,
  100. *See also* 12dec09
  digital media in, 100–1
Democracia real YA!, 20–21
digital mechanisms, 43–44
  as actants, 43, 87–88
  on different platforms, 43, 90
  as networking mechanisms, 43
  in Twitter, 90–91
  on websites, 67–72
digital media, 1, 4, 7, 16. *See also* information
  and communication technologies
  confusion about, 194–95
  dynamics of action and, 28
  measuring use of, 67–68, 127–29
  in networks characterized by connective vs.
  collective logic, 41–42
  value of networking via, 30
digital media and contentious politics. *See*
  social media and contentious action

digital networking mechanisms, 90. *See also*
  networking mechanisms; Twitter
digital networks, as DNA of personalized
  politics, 57–59
digital technologies, collective action and,
  56–57
digitally enabled action networks
  differences in organizational patterns of, 22
  organizational patterns of, 22
  as political organizations, 42–45, 89–90
digitally networked action (DNA), 5, 114, 194
  absence of superiority among types, 14
  future of, 214–15
  logic of connective action at core of, 44
  multiple logics and, 195–96
  superiority of one type to another, 14
DIY (Do It Yourself) politics, 6
DNA. *See* digitally networked action (DNA)

economic justice, 3
economic justice campaigns
  fair trade advocacy and, 125
  identifying, 173
  network power in, 177–79
  organizationally enabled networks and, 173
  press coverage in, 177–79
  public engagement in, 177–79
effectiveness, connection action and, 52–53, 57
80–20 principle, 153
electoral politics, 23–24
engagement signatures, 119, 141
engagement strength, 60–61, 62, 73–74
environment issue networks, 129–30, 144–45
environment, globalization and, 2, 4–5. *See
  also* climate change

fair trade advocacy, 125
Fair Trade Labeling Organization (FLO), 125
fair trade networks, 124–26, 171–72
15M mobilization, 20–21
financial transactions tax. *See* Robin Hood
  Tax campaign
free-rider problem, 31–32, 34
Friends of the Earth, 19

G20 London Summit protests, 49, 62–64
G20 Meltdown, 40, 63–64
  action framing by, 64–67
  agenda strength of, 74–75
  as case of organizationally brokered action,
  57–59
  communication to individuals in
  mobilization process, 64

engagement strength of, 73–74
network stability of, 82–84
network strength of, 77–82
technology interfaces, 67–72
gatekeeping, Twitter protest space, 105–8
gatekeeping organizations, 129
Gladwell, Malcolm, 93
global crises, connective action and, 4–5
Global Justice Movement, 5, 44
global justice protests, 4
globalization, non-governmental organizations and, 118–19

hashtag#COP15, 101. *See also* December 12, 2009, climate change protests
changing dynamics in, 108
links in crosscutting mechanisms, 102–5
hashtags (#), Twitter, 90–91, 101, 105–8
as crosscutting networking mechanisms, 96
as digital mechanisms, 90–91
dynamics in, 97
gatekeeping in, 96–97, 105
thewave, 105–8
hive plot network mapping method, 162–63
hub-and-spoke network, 134–35
hyperlink analysis, 77–78. *See also* co-link analysis
co-link analysis in, 61–62, 77–82, 132–36
interactor analysis in, 134–35
issue-centered vs. solidarity networks, 84, 132–34
network power analysis and, 157
reading network maps in, 77–82, 132–34
hyperlinks, 91, 103–5
as indicators of recognition, influence, and prestige in, 61–62, 75, 157
mapping of, 9

Icelandic banking crisis (2009–2011), 12
individualization, contentious action and, 1, 24, 55–56
Indymedia, 30
inequality, rise in, 5
information and communication technologies. *See also* digital media
dynamics of connective action and, 44
organizational communication and, 11, 136–37
inlink distributions, 157–58, 172
interpersonal networks, 35–36
issue advocacy organizations, 114, 122–23
Issue Crawler, 78, 132–34

issue frames, 6
issue networks
issue-centered vs. solidarity networks, 84, 132–34
mapping, 77–82, 132–34
measuring, 127–29
sampling, 129–31

Juris, Jeffrey, 204–5

Keynes, John Maynard, 167
Kickstarter platform, 208, 209
Die Klima Allianz, 130, 131
Klimaforum09, 99

Latour, Bruno, 42–43
lifestyle politics, 56
links. *See* hyperlinks
logic of aggregation, 204–5
logic of collective action, 27–28. *See also* collective action
defining, 31–33
logic of connective action 10, 196–97. *See also* connective action
defining, 33–36
DNA at core of, 44
public action and, 36
los indignados (Spain), 2, 4, 12, 20–21, 38, 41–42, 155, 201
levels of communication with outside publics and, 21–22
levels of WUNC and, 21–22

media coverage, measuring, 75, 175–76
Meltdown. *See* G20 Meltdown
memes, 37–38
mesomobilization, 202
Milgram, Stanley, 153–54
Morozov, Evgeny, 92, 93
Muslim Brotherhood, 49, 201

network maps, 132, 134
drawing, 131–36
network of networks, 70–71, 160–61
analyzing power in, 161–64
configurations of dense, 160–61
Occupy protests as case of, 161–62
network organization, 16–17, 89–92, 144–45
network power. *See also* power
contested conceptions of, 150–52
in economic justice campaigns, 177–79
in organizationally enabled networks, 165–73

network power signatures, 152–53. *See also* power signatures
  measures for campaign networks, 173–75
  varieties of, 153–56
network routines, 9
network stability, Put People First (PPF) and, 82–84
network strength, 61–62, 77–82
networking, value of, via digital media, 30
networking mechanisms, 37–38. *See also* digital mechanisms; digital networking mechanisms
  in connective action networks, 43–44
  discursive and technological forms of, 9, 43
  organizational role of, 9, 43, 90, 101
networks
  advocacy, 120–21
  conflicts and dysfunctions in, 124–26
  crowd-enabled connective action of, 89–90
  examining forms of, 9
  issue, 84, 119, 127–31, 132–34
  organizationally enabled, 89
  power and, 148–56
  power signatures of, 157, 198–99
  solidarity, 61–62, 77–82, 132–34
non-governmental organizations (NGOs), 2
  engagement of publics and, 119
  globalization and, 118–19
  growth of, 117–18
  political dilemma of, 122–23
  public digital communication of, 115
  websites of, 115

Occupy protests (U.S.), 2, 4, 12, 41–42, 203–4
  activists and, 204–6
  beginnings of, 180–81
  as case of crowd-enabled action, 161–62
  evaluating, 210
  meeting rituals, 208
  as network of networks, 161–62
  power signature of, 189–91
Olson, Mancur, 31–32, 34
Oracle of Bacon, The, 153–54
organizational conflicts, 200–2
organizational hybridity, branding and, 51
organizational logics
  collective, 27–29
  connective, 27–29
  overlap and class of, 18
organizationally brokered action networks, 87
  digital media in, 33
  G20 Meltdown as case of, 63
  power signatures in, 158–60

organizationally brokered collective action, 13, 46
organizationally brokered networks, power signatures in, 158–60
organizationally brokered organizations, 11
organizationally enabled connection action, 13, 48, 116
  Put People First protest as case of, 63
  Robin Hood Tax campaign as, 165–73
  the Wave protest as case of, 97–98
organizationally enabled network organization, 11
organizationally enabled networks, 46f, 48, 87, 89, 116, 198. *See also* connective action networks
  assessing campaign outcomes in, 171–73
  as contentious action network type, 11, 13
  cutting the diamond and, 124, 125–26, 156, 158
  economic justice campaigns and, 173
  environment issue networks as case of, 114, 129–30
  media coverage and, 199
  methods of engaging publics by, 126–27
  power signatures in, 157–58
  press coverage and, 75
  public engagement and, 127–29
  role of conventional organizations in, 45
organizationally enabled public engagement, fundamental questions for, 122
Oxfam, 11, 19

Pareto, Alfredo, 153
peer production, 34, 196–97
personal action frames, 6, 24
  in connective action, 36–40
  in crowd-enabled networks, 38, 46–48
  in organizationally enabled networks, 48, 124
  social media networks and, 36–40
  spreading of, 39
personalization
  digitally mediated engagement and, 8–10, 14
  digitally meditated politics, origins of, 22–24
  organizational political communication and, 57, 59
  organizing political action and, 197–98
personalized communication
  dilemmas of, 59–62
  elements of, 36–37
  organizational communication and, 59–62, 64

as political form, 42
Put People First (PPF) and, 72–73
personalized politics, 6
challenges for protest organizers, 57
digital networks as DNA of, 57–59
origins of, 24
phenomenon of, 5–6
political action and, 2, 55–57
political capacity, connective action and, 58,
61, 156
political conditions, connective action and,
116–17, 121–22, 144–45
political transitions, organizational conflicts
in, 200–2
power, 149. *See also* network power; power
signatures
connective action and, 17
in Occupy protests, 189–91
in Robin Hood Tax campaign, 165–73
power law, 153–54
power signatures, 17, 152–53, 198–99. *See
also* network power signatures
dispersed, 160
in crowd-enabled networks, 160–64
in organizationally brokered networks,
158–60
moderate, 157
organizationally enabled networks in,
157–58
political outcomes and, 164–65
steep, 158
varieties of, 158–60
PPF. *See* Put People First (PPF)
precarity, 55–56
professionalization dilemma, 144
protest ecologies, Twitter and changing
dynamics in, 110–11
protest organizers,
challenges for, 57, 59–60
views about communication technology,
58–59
public engagement
digitally mediated, 144–45
in economic justice campaigns, 177–79
measuring, 136–37, 175
organizationally enabled networks and,
119–20, 126–27, 129
publics, methods organizationally enabled
networks engage, 126–27
Put People First (PPF), 11–12, 19–20,
199
action framing by, 64–67
agenda strength of, 64–67, 74–75

as case of organizationally enabled action,
63
communication to individuals in
mobilization process, 64
emergent groups in, 50
engagement strength of, 73–74
levels of WUNC and, 19–20
March 28 London mobilization, 63
network stability of, 82–84
network strength of, 77–82
as personal action frame, 37–38
personalized communication and, 72–73
technology interfaces, 67–72

resource mobilization theory (RMT), 31–32
Robin Hood Tax campaign, 3, 17, 164–65,
173, 199
as case of organizationally enabled action,
167–71
Rogers, Richard, 78

Save the Children, 19
SCCC. *See* Stop Climate Chaos Coalition
(SCCC)
Seattle Occupy, 205–6
Shirky, Clay, 154
Six Degrees of Kevin Bacon, The, 153–54
slacktivism, 14, 93
small-world phenomenon, 153
social media and contentious action, analytical
fallacy about, 93
social media networks, personal action frames,
36–40
socially mediated networks, 35
solidarity networks, 61–62, 77–82, 132–34
star network, 134–35
stitching technologies, 162
Stop Climate Chaos Coalition (SCCC), 83,
97–98, 130
personalizing public communication and,
105–6
sustainability, connective action and, 16, 17,
53, 57, 59, 114

Tahrir Square protests (Egypt), 12, 201
Tea Party, 4, 206–7
Tilly, Charles, 19–20, 59, 121, 199
tinyurl, 91
Tobin, James, 167–68
Transfair USA, 125–26
transition, 18
Tumblr, 7, 163, 181
Tunisian uprising, 12

12Dec09, 100
Twitter, 8–9, 87–88, 90–92
  as agent in and window on protest space,
    90–91
  changing dynamics in protest ecologies and,
    110–11
  COP 15 protests and, 101
  as crosscutting networking mechanism,
    102–5
  Occupy protests and, 184–86
  protest space, gatekeeping in, 105–8
  role of, in mobilizations, 41
  as stitching technology, 162
Twitter revolutions, 92–93
Twitter streams, 155
  analysis of, 95–97
  capacity to shift organizational functions
    and, 110–11

UN Climate Conference, Copenhagen, 2009
  (COP15), 49, 88–89

connective action surrounding, 97–101
crowd-enabled connective action and,
  100
organizationally enabled action and,
  97–98
URL hyperlinks (links), 91

Walker, Scott, 206–7
Watts, Duncan, 153–54
Wave, the, 98, 105–8, 130
Wealth of Networks, The (Benkler), 34
website analysis, 67–72, 136–37
Whiteband, 70–71
Williams, Rowan (archbishop of Canterbury),
  165, 170
World Vision, 19
WUNC (Worthiness, Unity, Numbers,
  Commitment), 19–20, 21–22, 49, 121,
  199

Yanacopulos, Helen, 123–24

Titles in the Series (*continued from page iii*)

Doug McAdam and Hilary Boudet, *Putting Social Movements in Their Place: Explaining Opposition to Energy Projects in the United States, 2000–2005*

Doug McAdam, Sidney Tarrow, and Charles Tilly, *Dynamics of Contention*

Holly J. McCammon, *The U.S. Women's Jury Movements and Strategic Adaptation: A More Just Verdict*

Sharon Nepstad, *War Resistance and the Plowshares Movement*

Kevin J. O'Brien and Lianjiang Li, *Rightful Resistance in Rural China*

Silvia Pedraza, *Political Disaffection in Cuba's Revolution and Exodus*

Eduardo Silva, *Challenging Neoliberalism in Latin America*

Sarah Soule, *Contention and Corporate Social Responsibility*

Yang Su, *Collective Killings in Rural China during the Cultural Revolution*

Sidney Tarrow, *The New Transnational Activism*

Ralph Thaxton, Jr., *Catastrophe and Contention in Rural China: Mao's Great Leap Forward Famine and the Origins of Righteous Resistance in Da Fo Village*

Charles Tilly, *Contention and Democracy in Europe, 1650–2000*

Charles Tilly, *Contentious Performances*

Charles Tilly, *The Politics of Collective Violence*

Marisa von Bülow, *Building Transnational Networks: Civil Society and the Politics of Trade in the Americas*

Lesley J. Wood, *Direct Action, Deliberation, and Diffusion: Collective Action after the WTO Protests in Seattle*

Stuart A. Wright, *Patriots, Politics, and the Oklahoma City Bombing*

Deborah Yashar, *Contesting Citizenship in Latin America: The Rise of Indigenous Movements and the Postliberal Challenge*

Andrew Yeo, *Activists, Alliances, and Anti–U.S. Base Protests*

24895679R00151

Printed in Great Britain
by Amazon